The INCREDIBLE SIXTIES

OTHER BOOKS BY JULES ARCHER

African Firebrand: Kenyatta of Kenya
Angry Abolitionist: William Lloyd Garrison
Battlefield President: Dwight D. Eisenhower
China in the Twentieth Century
Chou En-lai
Colossus of Europe: Metternich
Congo
The Dictators
Epidemic!
The Executive "Success"
The Extremists: Gadflies of American Society
Famous Young Rebels
Fighting Journalist: Horace Greeley
From Whales to Dinosaurs
Front-Line General: Douglas MacArthur
Hawks, Doves, and the Eagle
Ho Chi Minh: The Legend of Hanoi
Hunger on Planet Earth
Indian Foe, Indian Friend
Jungle Fighters: A G.I. War Correspondent's Experiences in the New Guinea Campaign
Laws That Changed America
Legacy of the Desert
Man of Steel: Joseph Stalin
Mao Tse-tung: A Biography
Mexico and the United States
1968: Year of Crisis
The Philippines' Fight for Freedom
The Plot to Seize the White House
Police State
Red Rebel: Tito of Yugoslavia
Resistance
Revolution in Our Time
Riot! A History of Mob Action in the United States
The Russians and the Americans
Strikes, Bombs, and Bullets: Big Bill Haywood and the I.W.W.
Superspies
Thorn in Our Flesh: Castro's Cuba
They Made a Revolution: 1776
Treason in America: Disloyalty Versus Dissent
Trotsky: World Revolutionary
Twentieth-Century Caesar: Benito Mussolini
Uneasy Friendship: France and the United States
The Unpopular Ones
Washington vs. Main Street
Watergate: America in Crisis
Who's Running Your Life?
Winners and Losers: How Elections Work in America
World Citizen: Woodrow Wilson
You and the Law
You Can't Do That to Me!

The INCREDIBLE SIXTIES

THE STORMY YEARS THAT CHANGED AMERICA

Jules Archer

Harcourt Brace Jovanovich, Publishers

San Diego   New York   London

Photo credits: Phillip Galgiani, 78 (bottom); Ken Regan, 95 (top); Lyn Hemmerdinger, 137; NASA, 159, 160; Jeffrey Nightbyrd, 178 (bottom); all others, AP/Wide World Photos

Library of Congress Cataloging-in-Publication Data
Archer, Jules.
    The incredible sixties.
    Bibliography: p.
    Includes index.
    Summary: A comprehensive look at the 1960s, which had the Vietnam War, a sexual revolution, a feminist revolution, the Kennedy era, scientific advancements, exploding ghettos, freedom riders, and other important changes in music, art, literature, science, politics, and civil rights.
    1. United States—Civilization—1945–
2. United States—Social conditions—1960–
3. United States—Popular culture—History—20th century. [1. United States—Civilization—1945–
2. United States—Social conditions—1960–
3. United States—Popular culture—History—20th century] I. Title.
E169.12.A7 1986   973.922   85-16421
ISBN 0-15-238298-4

Designed by G. B. D. Smith
Printed in the United States of America

    D E

CONTENTS

Contents

INTRODUCTION

Philip Trounstine, an editorial writer for the San Jose *Mercury News*, states that conservatism on campus is becoming a national trend, because college students are "less aware of history." He explains that this is a result of two factors. First, the history courses in most high schools don't cover the twentieth century, and second, the events in recent history which have most affected this year's elections occurred before today's young voters were born. "This election, for the first time, involved voters born after the assassination of John F. Kennedy. The only presidents they have known have been Jimmy Carter and Ronald Reagan."

UCSC [University of California, Santa Cruz] Politics Lecturer Rein Staal agrees that ignorance of history is widespread among college students today. He recently asked his class who Benjamin Disraeli, the great British prime minister and statesman, was. No one was able to respond. On Watergate, a more recent subject, he found that only a few people could explain the break-in, the cover-up, and the political action that ensued.

Another writer, Haynes Johnson of the Washington *Post*, believes that this generation of college students is becoming more conservative as a result of embracing the ideals of materialism. "There is no social commitment. It is as if the '60s never happened." He also agrees that the newest voters are unaware of history, and consequently have "no framework to judge current political debates." As a result, he says that if "Ronald Reagan states that he represents the political positions of Franklin D. Roosevelt, Harry S. Truman, and John F. Kennedy, students have no reason to disbelieve him."

—Bob Bielen,
City On a Hill,
November 8, 1984
(official newspaper of the University of California, Santa Cruz)

This lack of knowledge, historical background, and perspective of most high school and college students of the eighties is the reason for this book. It is the hope of the author that, after reading it, young Americans will in future elections be able to cast informed ballots that will be in their own best interests, whether they be for liberal or conservative candidates.

The reader is entitled to know my own background and perspective, in order to evaluate my views.

I was a teenager during the turbulent Depression years of the early thirties. I witnessed angry demonstrations against widespread unemployment, hunger, and bank foreclosures of homes, farms, and small businesses. Some corporations deputized ex-convicts to beat up and even shoot workers on picket lines. I joined the Congress of Industrial Organizations (CIO) to help organize underpaid white-collar office workers.

The thirties were also a time of great international danger. An Imperialist Japan had joined Nazi Germany and Fascist Italy in military aggression to conquer the world. Young Americans like myself were aware that we might soon be called upon to put on uniforms to defend our democracy. To work for a boycott of the Fascist powers, I joined the American League Against War and Fascism.

The stormy thirties were exciting years for idealistic youth. We had the vision of a better world we hoped to bring about by crusading for jobs for all; for honest trade unions to prevent the mistreatment of labor; for aid to poor farmers and sharecroppers; for government assistance to the hungry, homeless, and handicapped; and for stopping the war aims of the Rome-Berlin-Tokyo axis by cutting off their military supplies.

But like the youth of every decade, we of the thirties generation also had our lighter moments. If we carried picket signs for our impassioned causes, we also found time to swing and jitterbug to the jukebox records of Benny Goodman, Tommy Dorsey, and Guy Lombardo. The thirties delighted us with such memorable songs as "Stardust," "Stormy Weather," "The Very Thought of You," "Thanks for the Memories," and "Did You Ever See a Dream Walking?"

The attack on Pearl Harbor in 1941 found me already in uniform. I subsequently spent four years in Australia, the jungles of New Guinea, and the Philippines, serving both as a master sergeant in the Air Corps and as a war correspondent.

World War II changed the political climate in America. Our war ally, the Soviet Union, was subsequently viewed as our rival and enemy. The rest of the forties found the nation alarmed by the specter of Communist espionage. A newly elected conservative Congress passed punitive anti-Communist laws that were used to harass liberals and trade-union leaders. During the fifties many Americans hesitated to criticize any government action for fear of being labeled Communist or "un-American."

But the sixties swung the pendulum back to the dynamic challenges of the thirties. Once again, stormy years brought upheavals in America's life-styles, societal relations, foreign policy, politics, laws, and attitudes toward government.

My own experience in the thirties led me to empathize with idealistic youth of the sixties who protested and demonstrated against government policies and social credos that they perceived as unjust. With them I opposed the Vietnam War. While I myself had willingly fought overseas for four years in what I believed to be a just and necessary war of defense, I did not want my three draft-age sons to die in a war I viewed as unjust, unnecessary, and unwise.

The five years between 1963 and 1968 may have been the stormiest in American history, except for the years of the Revolutionary and Civil Wars. Over two million Americans took to the streets in antiwar demonstrations that resulted in over nine thousand casualties, two hundred deaths, and seventy thousand arrests. Over a million people marched in civil rights demonstrations, apart from those who took part in anti-Vietnam protests, and another two hundred thousand participated in urban riots.

Dissent was in the air. Other challenges to the status quo were mounted by an aroused consumer movement, as well as by Americans alarmed by industry's pollution of the environment. Liberals and left-wingers also protested the government's cold war tactics, warning that they could heat up to nuclear war.

Toward the end of the decade, Richard M. Nixon sought the presidency by appealing to the "silent majority"—millions of mostly older Americans upset by rejection of their values by the young. Puzzled by the rebelliousness of students they had sent to the best universities, many parents were indignant at being confronted by alternate life-styles and opposing ideas. Nixon promised to impose "law and order" on the generation that had spurned respect for authority, duty, and patriotism.

In many respects, the sixties were a decade of experimentation with new ways to live one's life that influenced all aspects of the American scene. Young middle-class rebels, disillusioned with the life-styles of their parents, rejected traditional values such as the use of competition to win personal gain. Many opted instead for cooperating to build a more loving society.

Questioning the sexual codes of their elders, they developed their own moral values. They opposed bulldozers that destroyed woods to clear the land for new shopping centers. Calling their decade the "age of Aquarius," they acclaimed spiritual values on earth as more important than the exploration of space.

America had never seemed so polarized. With Nixon's election, America entered a new conservative period marked by violations of civil liberties that drove the generations, as well as blacks and whites, even further apart.

Some social scientists have suggested that waves of liberalism and conservatism occur in our nation at thirty-year intervals—thus, the conservative twenties, fifties, and eighties; and the liberal thirties and sixties.

If that analysis is valid, this record of the sixties may forecast what our society will be like in the nineties.

And if we fail to learn from the mistakes of our past, we may well be doomed to repeat them.

Jules Archer
Santa Cruz, California

The
INCREDIBLE
SIXTIES

1

KENT STATE—THE TRAGEDY THAT SHOOK THE NATION

*I*t is a beautiful spring morning in 1970. Monday, May 4, is a day that twenty thousand students at Ohio's Kent State University will remember in horror and sorrow for the rest of their lives.

When the 10:45 classes end, several thousand students pour out across the rolling campus. Some six hundred gather for a peaceful demonstration against the unpopular war in Vietnam. They protest President Nixon's violation of his promise to end the war, instead widening it by ordering American troops to invade neighboring Cambodia, a neutral nation.

Antiwar turbulence in Kent has days before led Governor James A. Rhodes to rush the Ohio National Guard to the town, then onto the campus. In full military regalia they now march up Blanket Hill toward the peace rally. The students watch their advance in dismay, stunned that military force has invaded their campus.

They listen incredulously as campus police officer Harold E. Rice shouts through a bullhorn: "Attention! This assembly is unlawful! This is an order—disperse immediately!"

Indignant at what they see as a denial of their First Amendment right to assemble peaceably, many students boo and shout catcalls.

At 11:55, Guard commander General Robert H. Canterbury orders his troops, "Prepare to move out and disperse this mob."

The guardsmen lock and load their rifles with high-velocity, large caliber bullets that can tear clean through a body. Armed also with tear gas canisters, they don gas masks and fix bayonets to their rifles.

"General," a shocked faculty member protests to Canterbury, "you must not march against the students!"

"These students are going to have to find out," the general replies grimly, "what law and order is all about."

At noon the troops press forward with bayonets outthrust as they fire tear gas at the students. Gasping, choking, and weeping, the students scatter, reviling the guardsmen: "Toy soldiers! Murderers! Weekend warriors! Fascists!"

A few infuriated students express their frustration by hurling rocks and stones, but they are too far away from the troops for their missiles to have any serious effect.

Many students forced to flee are not even demonstrators, but simply onlookers or passersby on their way across campus to the next class. One is Sandra Scheuer, who earlier warned a friend not to get involved in the antiwar demonstration. Another is Bill Schroeder, so far from being an antiwar activist that he's the outstanding sophomore in the Kent State Reserve Officers' Training Corps (ROTC).

Yet these two are fated to share the destiny of two other students who are demonstrating—beautiful Allison Krause, an honors student planning a career helping emotionally disturbed children, and Jeffrey Miller, described by his friends as "ready to help you any time you needed him."

At 12:05 General Canterbury orders his men to continue advancing downhill against the retreating students and clear the campus. The guardsmen pause when they reach the football practice field. The students closest to them now are in a parking lot more than thirty yards away. Allison Krause is among indignant students who shout angry insults at their pursuers.

The guardsmen respond by using grenade launchers to fire more tear gas. A few students hurl some canisters back, while others fling stones. But few missiles reach the guardsmen, who are ordered to kneel and aim their rifles at the students. They hold their fire when a second order is given to retreat up the hill and regroup with other Guard units on campus.

Students follow them, shouting taunts. At first the guardsmen ignore them, continuing to march back up the hill.

Suddenly the men of Troop G pause and wheel around, rifles upraised. At 12:24 one of them, possibly an officer, fires his weapon. This is immediately followed by a staccato sound like a series of giant firecrackers exploding. At least ten guardsmen fire fifty-five rifle bursts, five pistol shots, and a shotgun blast at students over a hundred yards away in the parking lot.

When echoes of the fusillade fade away, thirteen bodies are sprawled on the ground. Nine students are wounded. Four are dead—Allison Krause, Bill Schroeder, Sandra Scheuer, and Jeffrey Miller. Of the thirteen who were shot, only two have been hit frontally. Seven have bullets in their sides and four in their backs, proving they were not advancing but fleeing.

One young guardsman is horrified by the spectacle. Falling to the ground and tossing hysterically, he cries out, "I just shot two teenagers!" The other guardsmen march off up the hill, leaving the dead and wounded behind.

"I saw the kids fall," art major Lucia Perry, 18, subsequently relates, "and I looked out at the crowd and there were people carrying, you know, people with blood all over them down the hill, and I just couldn't believe it. I've never seen people so mad and so horrified."

What events of the sixties had led up to the incredible murder of four American students on an American college campus by American troops?

Throughout most of the sixties, the United States had waged an undeclared war against the small Southeast Asian country of North Vietnam. Year after year, as more and more American youths were drafted to fight, casualties mounted alarmingly. A growing antiwar movement demanded that the conflict be brought to an end. "The gradual shift of Vietnam sentiment from hawk to dove, first in the Senate and then more grudgingly in the House, was heavily influenced by constituent mail," noted *The New York Times* correspondent Warren Weaver, Jr.

But Presidents Lyndon B. Johnson and then Richard M. Nixon persisted in seeking a military victory.

On April 20, 1970, President Nixon assured the nation that he was doing everything possible to bring the war in Vietnam to a negotiated end. But ten days later he went on TV to reveal that he had ordered American forces to invade neutral Cambodia to clean out enemy hideouts. He had not done so during the first five years of his term, he explained, "because we did not wish to violate the territory of a neutral nation." This assertion was branded untrue by foreign correspondents, who revealed that Nixon had authorized no less than 3,875 secret air strikes against Cambodia during the previous fourteen months.

The president's revelation that he was escalating the war instead of ending it sparked a rash of civil disorders greater than any the nation had experienced in this century.

Thirty-seven college and university presidents signed a letter to Nixon demanding that he take immediate steps to end the war. Campuses all over America erupted in huge demonstrations, some accompanied by bombings and other violence to "bring the war home" to the Nixon administration. Many demonstrations were led by Students for a Democratic Society (SDS).

Nixon reacted bitterly in a speech to civilian employees at the Pentagon. "You see these bums, you know," he told them, "blowing up the campuses today [who] are the luckiest people in the world, going to the greatest universities, and here they are . . . storming around this issue."

Vice President Spiro Agnew lashed out at antiwar demonstrators as the equivalent of Nazi storm troopers or Ku Klux Klansmen, urging the public to "act accordingly" in dealing with them.

On Saturday, May 2, antimilitary fervor ran high on the Kent State campus. That evening a crowd of some two thousand student demonstrators were exhorted to attack the campus's empty ROTC building and set it aflame. When local firemen tried to quench the fire, students cut their hoses.

General Canterbury arrived in Kent with about three thousand National Guardsmen. He was accompanied by General Sylvester Del Corso, the Guard adjutant, who ordered, "Shoot any rioter who cuts a fire hose!" But the ROTC building burned to the ground.

Students cheered. "I was glad it burned," junior Rita Rubin said later. "I'm against the war in Vietnam. I'm against anyone getting military training on a college campus. We've been trying to end ROTC for a year, and burning down the building was a reasonable answer to an administration that doesn't listen to its students."

But the student body was shocked when the guardsmen moved onto the campus in armored personnel carriers, army trucks, and jeeps, arrayed in full battle gear.

Twenty-three members of the faculty issued an indignant protest: "The appearance of armed troops on the campus of Kent State University is an appalling sight. . . . The president of the United States commits an illegal act of war and refers to his opposition as 'bums.' That students and faculty and, indeed, all thinking people reject his position is not only rational but patriotic. True, burning a building at Kent State University is no joke; we reject such tactics. Yet the burning of an ROTC building is no accident.

National Guardsmen throw tear gas at demonstrating students on the campus of Kent State University. Students were protesting President Nixon's invasion of Cambodia. This invasion triggered more college protests than any other incident in U.S. history. One and a half million students and over a thousand campuses were involved.

Blood flows from the body of a student killed at Kent State University on May 4, 1970. Four students died during a confrontation between antiwar demonstrators and National Guardsmen.

We deplore this violence but we feel it must be viewed in the larger context of the daily burning of buildings and people by our government in Vietnam, Laos, and now, Cambodia."

On Sunday, May 3, Governor Rhodes arrived in Kent by helicopter. At a news conference broadcast to the guardsmen as well as to all Ohioans, he attacked "dissident groups and their allies." He vowed, "We're going to use every weapon of the law-enforcement agencies of Ohio to drive them out of Kent. . . . They're the worst type of people that we harbor in America."

Robert I. White, the university's president, later suggested that the governor's threats were politically motivated. Polls showed him likely to lose his bid for the Republican senatorial nomination that was only "two days away from a primary that would end his political career." Rhodes, said White, was "desperately riding a last-minute law and order campaign train."

At 7:10 P.M., some seven hundred students gathered on campus to protest both the war and the guardsmen's presence on their campus. A Guard officer ordered them to disperse. When they refused, guardsmen hurled tear gas at them. Reeling and choking, they fled. Some two hundred surged into town, where they continued their defiance by sitting down in the street. Guardsmen stabbed seven students with bayonets; two had to be hospitalized.

One was a girl who had taken no part in the demonstration. She later testified, "I saw their faces. There was hate; and it was coming towards me in the form of swinging rifle butts and bayonets. They were yelling, 'Get back, get back!' Get back to where, I do not know. . . . There was nowhere to go—we were encircled by guardsmen. *There was no provocation.* . . . I was bayoneted in the lower abdomen and in the right leg."

The guardsmen drove the students back to the campus, pursuing them with tear gas. The propellers of a helicopter overhead swept the fumes into dormitories. When gasping students fled the buildings, guardsmen chased them back in. That night fifty-one students were arrested for violating a curfew that many had not heard about.

Those were the turbulent events that had led up to the murder of four Kent State students the following day.

———

The FBI sent agents to investigate the killings. The guardsmen insisted that they had fired their weapons only because their lives had been endangered by the demonstrating students.

General Canterbury declared that a "charging mob" had come within four or five yards of the Guard just before the shooting. But pictures taken by news photographers at the moment the Guard fired showed that only three students were anywhere near the Guard, the closest over twenty-three yards away. The nearest of those killed, Jeffrey Miller, had been over eighty-five yards distant from the Guard when he was shot.

One guardsman admitted to a reporter from the Knight newspaper chain, "The guys have been saying that we got to get together and stick to the same story—that it was either our lives or them, a matter of survival."

The FBI reported, "Six guardsmen, including two sergeants and Captain Srp of Troop G, stated pointedly that the lives of the members of the Guard were not in danger and that it was not a shooting situation. . . . We have reason to believe that the claim by the National Guard that their lives were endangered by the students was fabricated subsequent to the events."

Even Vice President Spiro Agnew, who had urged repressing antiwar demonstrators, stated, "It's not premeditated, but it's a murder and certainly can't be condoned."

Nevertheless, President Nixon held the students responsible. "This should remind us all once again," he said, "that when dissent turns to violence, it invites tragedy." Despite having witnessed the event on TV newscasts, sixty percent of the public condoned the shooting, according to a *Newsweek* poll.

A shock wave swept across the nation's campuses. Ten days after the Kent State deaths, two more demonstrating students were killed at Jackson State College in Mississippi by police and highway patrolmen.

Over 450 colleges and universities shut down in protest over these murders, the first sustained national strike in the history of American higher education. Some infuriated students set fire to ROTC campus buildings, while others inflicted damage on military property at their universities. In that turbulent year, over 7,200 students were arrested during antiwar demonstrations.

Resistance surfaced even within the Nixon administration itself. Health,

Education, and Welfare (HEW) Secretary Robert Finch charged that Agnew's fiery speeches against college students had contributed to "heating up the climate in which the Kent State students were killed."

In a letter made public, Secretary of the Interior Walter J. Hickel reminded the president that the British Empire had made a mistake in 1775 by refusing to listen to the violent protest of young men in its American colonies. "The outcome is history," he wrote. "My point is, if we read history, it clearly shows that youth in its protest must be heard."

"America was in anguish last week," Max Frankel wrote in *The New York Times*, "her population divided, her campuses closed, her capital shaken, her government confused, her president perplexed."

Former HEW Secretary John Gardner declared, "The nation disintegrates. I use the phrase soberly."

Hoping to calm the rising storm of opposition, President Nixon appointed a commission, headed by former Pennsylvania Governor William Scranton, to investigate the Kent State shootings and causes of campus unrest.

The Scranton Commission found that the shootings had been "unnecessary, unwarranted, and inexcusable," especially since the demonstration had been a "peaceful assembly" that the guardsmen had had no right to order dispersed.

The commission took a strong stand against violence, whether committed by students or agents of the law: "Students who bomb and burn are criminals. Police and National Guardsmen who needlessly shoot or assault students are criminals. All who applaud these criminal acts share in the evil." The commission went on to deplore the tragic effects of persisting in the Vietnam War: "The crisis on American campuses has no parallel in the history of the nation. This crisis has roots in divisions of American society as deep as any since the Civil War . . . [and] reflects and increases a more profound crisis in the nation as a whole."

Taking a poll of students, the commission revealed that seventy-five percent, most of them previously political moderates, now professed themselves disenchanted with the American system and felt it needed basic changes. They blamed the Nixon administration for widening the war, sabotaging civil rights, and responding to protest only with violence against demonstrators.

Despite the outrage of the dead students' parents, an Ohio grand jury refused to indict any of the guardsmen for the Kent State murders. Ohio's Senator Stephen M. Young called the grand jury's decision "a fraud and a fakery."

How had the state of affairs in the United States of America deteriorated to the point that the nation appeared to be coming apart at the seams? Why were millions of angry young people alienated from a baffled older generation?

The killings at Kent State were the culmination of all the dramatic events that had occurred during the decade leading up to it—the incredible sixties, the stormy years that changed America.

2

THE CAMELOT YEARS— THE KENNEDY ERA

*T*hey were a fairy-tale couple. He was the youngest, handsomest man ever elected to the presidency. She was the youngest, prettiest, most elegant First Lady in modern times. When the stylish young couple made a presidential tour of Europe, she dazzled the French press, which gave her the lion's share of attention. At a diplomatic luncheon, President John Kennedy introduced himself dryly as "the man who accompanied Jacqueline Kennedy to Paris."

The Kennedy style was exemplified on a frosty winter morning when demonstrators picketed the White House with signs demanding, "Ban the Bomb!" Instead of ignoring them, President Kennedy had coffee sent out to the freezing picketers. Later he invited one of the demonstrators, a nuclear scientist, to a White House dinner attended by many distinguished intellectuals.

"Never before has there been so much brilliance assembled under the roof of the White House," Kennedy told his guests with a smile, "since Thomas Jefferson dined here alone."

The nation had grown somewhat bored and restless under two Republican terms of the bland, conservative Dwight D. Eisenhower administration, and in 1960 voters elected, by a narrow margin, a Democratic candidate who promised to "get America moving again"—forty-three-year-old Massachusetts Senator John Fitzgerald Kennedy.

Kennedy's personality had a superstar quality missing in his Republican opponent—Vice President Richard M. Nixon. This difference was highlighted in a series of televised debates between the two candidates. Kennedy came across to viewers as youthful, charming, charismatic, sexy, earnest, witty, cool, but dynamic. The Nixon whom Americans saw on TV seemed awkward, ill at ease, pugnacious, humorless, and insincere, although listeners on radio thought Nixon had won the debate.

The election process, cartoonist-writer Jules Feiffer observed wryly, had "become much more of a Mr. America contest than a contest having to do with the quality of the individual."

The idea of electing a young president was immensely appealing to young Americans. Because of the baby boom following the return home of GI's after World War II, by 1960 over half the population was under thirty. Young people had begun to wield enormous influence over trends in dress, grooming, music, dancing, life-style—and elections. Young people felt that Kennedy was fired by the same high ideals of peace and social justice that inspired them.

Apart from his attractive personality, Kennedy appealed to the young as a romantic figure. As commander of an ill-fated PT boat in the Pacific, he had saved the lives of several of his men. In addition to being a war hero, he had married beautiful, fashionable Jacqueline Bouvier. The glamorous Kennedys were the American version of a royal family, the most stylish, admired couple in Washington's social circles.

Cultured and intelligent, they caused author John Steinbeck to exult when they took up residence in the White House: "What a joy that literacy is no longer . . . evidence of treason."

Intellectuals were delighted with a president whose book, *Profiles in Courage*, had won a Pulitzer Prize, and who invited 155 writers, artists, and scientists to his inauguration. Sports-loving Americans were impressed with a president who loved to hike and play touch football on the White House lawn.

Making way for the new president-elect, outgoing President Eisenhower startled his conservative adherents with his farewell address. He warned the nation against business lobbies greedy for government munitions contracts and fat profits.

"We must guard against the acquisition of unwarranted influence . . . by the military-industrial complex," he cautioned. "The potential for the disastrous rise of misplaced power exists and will persist. We must never let the weight of this combination endanger our liberties or democratic processes."

Inaugurated on January 20, 1961, Kennedy declared, "The torch has been passed to a new generation of Americans." Pledging his administration to preserving human rights and liberty at home and abroad, he promised also to ease world tensions by resuming arms-reduction talks with the Soviet Union. "Let us never negotiate out of fear," he said, "but let us never fear to negotiate."

He called the challenges facing his administration a "New Frontier," which he proposed to explore boldly, promising to seek "a grand and global alliance to combat tyranny, poverty, disease, and war." American youth thrilled when he cried, "To those people in the huts and villages of half the globe struggling to break the bonds of mass misery, we pledge our best efforts to help themselves for whatever period is required—not because the Communists may be doing it, not because we seek their votes, but because it is right. If a free society cannot help the many who are poor, it cannot save the few who are rich." Calling for idealistic sacrifices by Americans, he demanded, "Ask not what your country can do for you; ask what you can do for your country!"

Tens of thousands of enthusiastic young Americans rallied to Kennedy's crusade. Some flocked into the domestic struggle for black civil rights, especially in the South. Others volunteered for a new Peace Corps created by Kennedy's executive order on March 1. They went abroad to underdeveloped Third World countries to help the poor build schools, hospitals, roads, and health services and improve their living standards.

"It will not be easy," Kennedy warned. "None of the men and women will be paid a salary. They will live at the same level as the citizens of the country which they are sent to, doing the same work, eating the same food, speaking the same language. . . . I am hopeful that this will be a source of satisfaction to Americans and a contribution to world peace."

Working in forty-six countries, the Peace Corps brightened the image of America in the Third World, where the United States was often viewed, in Senator William Fulbright's phrase, as an "arrogant power" that supported unpopular dictatorships. Significantly, when diplomat Averill Harriman visited a village in India that had neither electricity nor plumbing, he found Kennedy's picture pasted prominently on a wall.

Kennedy also organized the Alliance for Progress, a cooperative program to help Latin American countries develop economically. Side by side with the Peace Corps, it helped convince America's Spanish-speaking neighbors to the south that the U.S. was sincerely concerned about poverty in Latin America.

Kennedy was also passionate about poverty at home. After visiting the tar-paper shacks of West Virginia miners, he urged that the government take responsibility for the poor in economically depressed areas. Congress passed his plan for aiding them. He also persuaded Congress to raise the minimum wage.

American college youth trusted a young president who surrounded himself with advisers who were Harvard intellectuals, rather than corporation lawyers or businessmen.

"The past eight years had been Eisenhower and Nixon and the Silent Generation of the '50s," observed Richard Celeste, a Peace Corps official. "You got put to sleep. And then here was a kind of human magnet who attracted people who wanted to make a difference. . . . I saw him as a tough, ambitious, attractive politician who . . . was going to *shape* history."

Gloria Steinem called the Kennedy years the only time she and others her age felt connected to the government. "Since then," she wrote later, "I have never felt the government belonged to me."

Black civil rights worker John Lewis, chairman of the Student Nonviolent Coordinating Committee (SNCC) in 1961, admired Kennedy as a staunch champion of black demonstrators who sought to integrate restaurants and other public places.

"Probably for the first time in modern American history," he declared, "we felt, 'Well, we have a friend in the White House'. . . . When someone asked him about the civil rights sit-ins . . . he said, 'By sitting down, these young people are standing up for the very best in the American tradition.' "

The popular Kennedy style gave him the aura of a TV celebrity. Long-

On January 20, 1961, Chief Justice Earl Warren administers the presidential oath of office to John F. Kennedy in Washington. A war hero and a graduate of Harvard University, Kennedy came from a wealthy Irish-American family, and he had won the Pulitzer Prize in 1957 for his book *Profiles in Courage*.

Widow Jacqueline walks with her brother-in-law Robert after the assassination of U.S. President John F. Kennedy.

haired youths felt a sense of identity with his abundant coiffure. Older liberal Americans welcomed the new atmosphere in the White House as a breath of fresh air.

Kennedy's dashing image led many political cartoonists to visualize him as a modern-day King Arthur, with his wife in the role of Lady Guinevere. Kennedy's aide for fourteen years, Lawrence O'Brien, observed, "I believe the Camelot image came about because of the glamour of the man."

"I believe President Kennedy will be regarded for many years as the Pericles of a golden age," his aide Fred Dutton mused after Kennedy's death. "He wasn't Pericles and the age wasn't golden, but that doesn't matter—it's caught hold."

Foreign correspondent Larry Newman declared, "Whatever he had, it was real and it was magic. . . . I thoroughly loved John Kennedy because he brought his country together in a way I hadn't seen in my time."

Washington columnist Joseph Alsop wryly considered the Camelot image of the Kennedy era "a third-rate cliché," but nevertheless he acknowledged, "It was a marvelously cheerful time, and you could have hope— a lot of hope—for the future."

In most respects, Kennedy's foreign policy decisions and his domestic accomplishments were undistinguished, except for his support of civil rights. Indeed, the world will never know what Kennedy would have accomplished, as his term in office was cut short on November 22, 1963.

Kennedy had planned a visit to Texas to win delegates for his renomination. White House aides were uneasy about this decision because a few weeks earlier, when UN Ambassador Adlai Stevenson had visited Dallas to celebrate United Nations Day, he had been physically attacked by a screaming mob led by Major General Edwin A. Walker, a John Birch Society member removed from his army command for indoctrinating his troops abroad with right wing propaganda.

On November 21, handbills were distributed throughout Dallas carrying Kennedy's photo under the headline: "WANTED FOR TREASON AGAINST THE UNITED STATES." Next day, when Kennedy was scheduled to arrive in the city, a full-page ad appeared in the Dallas *Morning News*, placed by a right wing "American Fact-Finding Committee." It accused the president of being pro-Communist.

Jackie Kennedy expressed alarm for her husband's safety. He only shrugged and said, "If someone wants to shoot me from a window with a rifle, nobody can stop it." When they arrived in Dallas, the Kennedys were taken on a tour of the city in an open limousine with Texas Governor John Connally and his wife. Spectators lining their route cheered. "No one can say Dallas doesn't love and respect you, Mister President," said Mrs. Connally.

"You sure can't," he agreed.

Seconds later the motorcade swept past the Texas School Book Depository, where former U.S. Marine Lee Harvey Oswald was concealed on the sixth floor with a high-powered rifle. To the horror of millions of Americans watching the event on NBC-TV, Oswald opened fire.

The president reached for his throat. "My God," he gasped, "I'm hit!"

Other shots killed him and severely wounded Governor Connally in the front seat. Spectators screamed, ran, and dived to the grass. The motorcade sped ahead, with Jackie Kennedy holding her blood-spattered husband and weeping.

Two hours later, Vice President Lyndon B. Johnson took the oath of office as the new president.

The assassin Oswald escaped, but he was caught after killing a policeman who stopped him. Two days later, while in police custody, he was shot and killed by Jack Ruby, a Dallas nightclub owner. This assassination was also seen by millions on a live TV newscast. Ruby was convicted of murder and sentenced to death, but he died of cancer in prison.

The reverberations of the tragedy were profound. The whole nation and much of the world were plunged into grief at the loss of the young president who had symbolized the era of a new, American Camelot, who had filled the nation with new vigor and an exciting idealism. The young were especially devastated because Kennedy had answered their need for heroes.

"For a time," writer Norman Mailer said, "we felt the country was ours." He added sadly, "Now it's theirs again."

But Kennedy's great contribution remained behind—the exciting new spirit of idealism he'd inspired in the country. He set the tone for the sixties—galvanizing great change by encouraging American youth to get involved in solving the nation's problems.

3

Turning the South Around— the Freedom Riders

*T*housands of angry white Southerners, including students, are gathered on the campus of the all-white University of Mississippi in Oxford on September 30, 1962. They are there to prevent the enrollment of the first black student, even though James Meredith's right to enter "Ole Miss" has been upheld by the Supreme Court.

Governor Ross Barnett has vowed to "stand in the doorway" to bar Meredith's admission. However, in a private phone call to Attorney General Robert F. Kennedy, the president's brother, Barnett promised, "There won't be any violence . . . no one will be armed." But Robert Kennedy considers Meredith's life to be in danger, and he has ordered two hundred federal marshals to protect him.

The sullen mob spits and jeers at the marshals as they escort Meredith to the administration building. One marshal is hit by a homemade firebomb that fails to explode. A second bomb crashes against an army truck, sending it up in flames. One marshal is hit by an uncapped bottle of acid and badly burned. The marshals use tear gas to move back the violent mob.

A newsman on the scene turns his car radio loud as President Kennedy broadcasts an appeal to the university's white students. "The eyes of the nation and all of the world are upon you and upon all of us," the president reminds them. "And the honor of your university—and state—are in the balance."

But the enraged rioters stone the newsman's car, smashing its windows.

Some rioters begin shooting at the marshals, who dive for cover. The two hundred National Guardsmen who rush onto campus are met with a hail of bricks and firebombs. One brick breaks the commander's arm. Snipers fire at the guardsmen's jeeps, wounding thirteen men. The mob also sets faculty cars ablaze to hinder the arrival of sixteen thousand federal troops sent by the president.

The mob attacks them with bricks, rocks, and firebombs. Advancing through curtains of gasoline flames, the troops at last drive off the rioters. When the fifteen-hour seige is over, two men are dead, over eighty wounded.

All this happens because a young, black American citizen named James Meredith believed that the Constitution gave him the right to seek an education at the University of Mississippi.

The stormy civil rights events of the sixties were precipitated by a Supreme Court ruling on May 17, 1954, in the case of *Brown v. Board of Education*. Racial segregation in public schools was held to be unconstitutional by the ruling, which required all to be integrated. Millions of infuriated southern whites feared that this nullification of traditional, discriminatory Jim Crow laws would create a mingling of blacks and whites leading to intermarriage.

In July of that year, White Citizens' Councils were formed in Mississippi to resist the court's decision, which was labeled a plot to "Communize our government." Senator James Eastland told them, "You are not required to obey any court which passes out such a ruling. In fact, you are obligated to defy it."

For five years, White Citizens' Councils in the South organized resistance against all attempts to abolish Jim Crow laws. President Eisenhower was forced to send federal troops to occupy a high school in Little Rock, Arkansas, to compel the admission of black students.

In 1957 an eloquent black leader, the Reverend Martin Luther King, Jr., organized the Southern Christian Leadership Conference (SCLC) to mount peaceful demonstrations demanding civil rights.

As the sixties dawned, four black freshmen at a Greensboro, North Carolina, college decided to challenge a local law that forbade them to join whites at the town's eating places. On February 1, 1960, inspired by Dr. King's demonstrations, the four bought toothpaste at the local Woolworth's, then ordered coffee at the lunch counter. When the waitress refused to serve them, they quietly kept their seats until the store closed.

Next day they returned with sixteen other black students, who also sat and waited for counter service until closing time. One day later they returned with fifty students, including sympathetic whites from a nearby women's college. By the weekend, several hundred well dressed black and white students, many carrying Bibles, were demonstrating at Woolworth's and also at an adjacent Kress store.

The news story won national attention. "Sit-in" demonstrations began to spread to northern as well as southern restaurants that refused to serve blacks. In some southern states, blacks were arrested for declining to leave restaurants that had denied them service.

All through 1960, protests were mounted by young people of both races against discriminatory practices, not only in restaurants, but also in hotels, parks, playgrounds, swimming beaches, libraries, and theaters. Almost a hundred thousand civil rights activists sought to integrate public places in over a hundred southern and border-state cities. Between 1960 and 1963, some twenty-four thousand demonstrators were arrested by the police.

Although the demonstrations were generally peaceful, many were met with violence. In Jacksonville, Florida, one person was killed and seventy injured during a three-day riot instigated by white supremacist Ku Klux Klansmen, who pistol-whipped a sixteen-year-old boy. At a sit-in in Houston, Texas, one black was stabbed. Another was flogged with a chain by three white men who carved the initials "KKK" on his chest and stomach.

In Atlanta, 235 middle-class black college students formed the Student Nonviolent Coordinating Committee (SNCC) in April 1960. Joined by white sympathizers, they sought to change the unjust treatment of blacks through peaceful demonstrations. But they encountered bombs in Georgia, brutality in Alabama, and murder in Mississippi.

Meanwhile, Congress was being prodded into legislating peaceful change by enforcing the right of blacks to vote. The Civil Rights Act of 1960, signed by President Eisenhower, provided for federal voting referees in states that barred blacks from the polls by one subterfuge or another.

Segregationists, enraged by what they considered a federal assault on states' rights, retaliated with a campaign of violence. Black people's churches, schools, and homes were bombed and burned. Southern police arrested civil rights demonstrators on pretexts of "impeding traffic" and "endangering the public safety by inflammatory slogans and speeches."

SNCC students in the north decided to challenge southern state laws that compelled blacks to sit in the back of public buses. In May 1961, joined by white activists, they organized "Freedom Rides" through the south for that purpose.

When the first contingent arrived in a Greyhound bus in Montgomery, Alabama, they were besieged at the bus terminal by several thousand furious Alabamans wielding metal pipes, baseball bats, and other weapons. "Here they come!" screamed a brunette in a yellow dress. "Get those niggers!"

Local police had been notified in advance with a request for protection. But when the bus door swung open, not one officer was visible. Students who tried to enter the terminal were seized and thrown over a rail to a cement parking lot ten feet below the station. Others were pursued and clubbed, punched, or thrown to the ground.

John Seigenthaler, an administrative assistant to Attorney General Kennedy who was sent along as an observer, was knocked unconscious. Twenty-two of the Freedom Riders were injured. Police did not arrive until the riot had raged for twenty minutes. Ambulances phoned for failed to arrive. President Kennedy had to send hundreds of U.S. marshals to restore order.

Alabama Governor John Patterson insisted that it was all the fault of the Freedom Riders. "I have no use," he snapped, "for these agitators or their kind."

In March 1963, SNCC and other civil rights groups began a drive to register black voters in the Mississippi delta. By now many impatient black activists wanted to answer southern white violence with black violence. But Martin Luther King, Jr., urged blacks not to lose faith in the eventual redemption of white racists through the example of Mahatma Gandhi's nonviolent campaign of civil disobedience in India.

In April, he led a five-day march of three hundred Freedom Riders from Selma to Montgomery, Alabama, which Dr. King called "the most segregated city in America." In Birmingham, they were joined by twenty thousand others. As they marched through the city, singing "We Shall Overcome," the anthem of peaceful black demonstrators, Birmingham police, led by Safety Commissioner Eugene "Bull" Connor, assaulted men, women, and children in the procession.

They were beaten with clubs and shocked with electric cattle prods.

When some marchers knelt to pray, they were attacked by police dogs. Firemen turned powerful fire hoses on marchers, knocking them down and sweeping them along the streets with such force that the streams stripped bark from trees and tore bricks from walls. More than fifty men and women were severely injured. Almost 2,500 marchers, including Dr. King, were jailed.

While driving in a car, demonstrator Mrs. Viola Liuzzo, a white mother of five, was shot and killed that night by rifles fired from a pursuing car full of white men.

The nation was shocked by TV newscasts showing the police attack on the marchers. A fresh cry arose for federal action against southern racism. It intensified when Governor George Wallace of Alabama vowed to stand in the doorway of the University of Alabama to prevent two black students from registering. Wallace had been elected with the campaign promise, "Segregation today, segregation tomorrow, segregation forever!"

President Kennedy angrily federalized the state's National Guard, who were ordered to protect the black students when they attempted to enter the university. Wallace made the gesture of standing in the doorway, but he stepped aside when ordered.

"When Americans are sent to Vietnam or West Berlin we do not ask for whites only," Kennedy declared. "It ought to be possible, therefore, for American students of any color to attend any public institution they select without having to be backed up by troops. . . . One hundred years of delay have passed since President Lincoln freed the slaves, yet their heirs, their grandsons, are not fully free."

On June 12, 1963, the field secretary for the National Association for the Advancement of Colored People (NAACP) in Mississippi, Medgar Evers, was shot in the back and killed.

In August Dr. King organized a dramatic march on Washington, D.C., "for Jobs and Freedom." One of the largest demonstrations in American history, it attracted over two hundred thousand people, both black and white. The rally was climaxed by King's famous speech, "I have a dream," delivered at the Lincoln Memorial.

"I have a dream," he cried eloquently, "that one day on the red hills of Georgia the sons of former slaves and the sons of former slave owners will be able to sit down together at the table of brotherhood. I have a

Black student James Meredith (lower right) is told by Mississippi Lt. Gov. Paul B. Johnson, Jr., that he cannot enter the University of Mississippi. Meredith was accompanied by federal marshals, but patrolmen would not let him within three blocks of the Ole Miss campus.

Police dogs were used to break up this racial demonstration in Birmingham, Alabama. Birmingham was one of many U.S. cities, north and south, in which racial violence erupted in the sixties.

Three Birmingham police restrain a black woman during racial protest marches. When Martin Luther King, Jr., began a campaign to end Birmingham's discrimination against blacks, the police commissioner used fire hoses and electric cattle prods on demonstrators.

dream that even the state of Mississippi, a state sweltering with people's injustices, with the heat of oppression, will be transformed into an oasis of freedom and justice. I have a dream that my four little children will one day live in a nation where they will be judged not by the color of their skin but by the content of their character."

President Kennedy was so moved by the speech that he asked Congress for an all-embracing civil rights law that would ban discrimination in the use of all public facilities, including hotels, motels, and restaurants, and would authorize the attorney general to sue on behalf of any person discriminated against. Blacks then traveling through the South had to search an average of 174 miles before finding a decent public accommodation that would admit them for food or lodging.

Dr. King's leadership of the civil rights movement made him suspect to FBI Chief J. Edgar Hoover, who believed that both the civil rights and anti-Vietnam movements were "Communist-inspired." To "safeguard national security," he pressured Attorney General Robert Kennedy into letting him wiretap the phones of Dr. King, hoping to find evidence that would discredit the black leader.

White racist anger in the South climaxed that year on September 15, when four young black girls in Sunday school were killed in a bombing of their church. The FBI traced the murders to the Ku Klux Klan.

Blacks mourned with whites when President Kennedy was assassinated in November. Kennedy's pending new Civil Rights Act was pushed through Congress by the new president, Lyndon B. Johnson. And in January 1964, the Twenty-fourth Amendment was passed, making it illegal to deny any citizen the right to vote in a federal election for failure to pay a poll tax—the device southern states had used for a century to keep blacks from voting.

Spring saw the formation of a black Council of Federated Organizations (COFO), which was a coalition of the Council of Racial Equality (CORE), SNCC, NAACP, and SCLC. When COFO announced a new "Freedom Summer" campaign in Mississippi, the state reacted with alarm. "Outsiders who come in here and try to stir up trouble," threatened the *Neshoba Democrat*, "should be dealt with in a manner they won't forget."

The new Freedom Riders, black and white, came from all over the country—some eight hundred college students, including sixty from the

Boston area and eighty from California. Setting up "freedom schools" in Mississippi, they registered black voters and shared the physically dangerous part of every black person's life in that state.

Enraged segregationists destroyed almost forty black churches and beat up hundreds of summer workers, who were also arrested and jailed by police. Mississippi newspapers published the names of newly registered voters, identifying blacks by omitting the usual prefix Mr., Mrs., or Miss. Many of these blacks were visited by their employers, who threatened to fire them if they dared exercise their franchise and go to the polls.

In June 1964, the Klan held a meeting in Neshoba County, then went to the Mt. Zion Church, where two COFO civil rights workers, white Michael Schwerner, 25, and black James Chaney, 21, had been organizing a freedom school. The Klansmen beat up three black men at a church meeting, then returned later to set the church on fire.

Schwerner, Chaney, and another white civil rights worker, Andrew Goodman, 21, drove to Neshoba County to investigate the church burning. After talking to blacks in the community, they drove back through the town of Philadelphia. There they were arrested by Deputy Sheriff Cecil Price on a charge of speeding and suspicion of burning the church. Jailed at 4:00 P.M., they were told six hours later by Price that they could be released by paying twenty-dollar fines. Paying, they drove off into the night.

They were not seen again alive.

Their disappearance aroused a hue and cry up north. The FBI received information that they had been murdered by Klansmen. Americans for the Preservation of the White Race (APWR) urged Philadelphians not to cooperate with FBI investigators, suggesting that COFO had killed its own three civil rights "agitators," in order to blame the South. Mississippi Senator James Eastland called their disappearance "a publicity hoax."

But FBI reward offers for information led them to the bodies of the three young men, who were found buried underneath an earthen dam. Evidence provided by the informant, a KKK member, revealed they had been brutally murdered by the White Knights of the Ku Klux Klan chapter of Mississippi. The Imperial Klan Wizard, along with the sheriff, deputy sheriff, former sheriff, and a city policeman, were all arrested.

On July 2, President Johnson signed the Civil Rights Act of 1964, the most sweeping civil rights legislation in American history. In addition to outlawing segregation in public facilities and schools, it also provided new job opportunities for blacks through an Office of Economic Opportunity (OEO). A new Job Corps for youths aged 16 to 21 benefited mostly unemployed black teenagers.

Vice President Hubert Humphrey called the new law a "quiet revolution," claiming it would end poverty in America forever. But while the OEO was helpful, it only scratched the surface of the problem. Funds provided for the program amounted to less than two percent of the money spent on the military.

Even so, Senator Herman Talmadge of Georgia bitterly opposed the new civil rights law, crying, "God forbid, Mister President, that our rights and freedoms are in such jeopardy that they must be preserved under the heels of storm troopers."

In the South, some ten million white Americans lined up behind the leadership of Alabama Governor George Wallace, who defied the federal government to enforce its civil rights edicts. In 1965 a Louis Harris poll in the South showed Wallace's defiance to have the support of seventy-nine percent of white Southerners.

In March 1965, angered by southern violence against Freedom Riders, President Johnson declared war on the Ku Klux Klan as a "hooded society of bigots." Some Klan leaders were arrested and charged with over a dozen of the seventeen racial murders that had occurred in the previous two years. The Klan was also found to have hatched plans to assassinate President Johnson and to blow up the White House.

"Jews and Niggers are part of the Communist conspiracy," declared Robert Shelton, Imperial Grand Wizard of the Klan, who described blacks as "poisonous as rattlesnakes." He charged, "Negroes are making preparations for setting up a black supremacy state with you and I to be their slaves. The Bible proves the Nigger is inferior to us white Anglo-Saxons. The Jew is inferior, too. God is a segregationist."

"People laugh at them in their sheets and robes," said Richmond Flowers, Alabama attorney general. "The average Klansman is of low intelligence and with no economic or social standing in the community. . . . Because of apathy an effective education program is absolutely necessary to inform the responsible citizens of our communities just what kind of a vicious, perverted organization the Klan really is."

Freedom Riders continued to risk their lives by venturing south. During a civil rights protest march in 1965, Reverend James Reeb, 38, a white Unitarian minister from Boston, was beaten to death by a furious white mob in Selma, Alabama. President Johnson went on TV to appeal to Congress for a new civil rights bill that would absolutely guarantee southern black suffrage.

"No law that we now have on the books . . . can insure the right to vote when local officials are determined to deny it," he pointed out. "In such a case our duty must be clear to all of us. . . . There is no issue of states' rights or national rights. There is only the struggle for human rights."

Congress responded by passing the Voting Rights Act of 1965, which suspended for five years all literacy tests and other pretexts used to keep blacks from voting. Federal examiners were sent to all districts where less than fifty percent of the population were registered to vote. Anyone trying to intimidate a citizen from registering or voting was arrested.

Several southern states immediately challenged the new act as an infringement of states' rights, but the Supreme Court upheld its constitutionality. In Mississippi the number of registered black voters jumped suddenly from only thirty-five thousand to two hundred thousand. Within the next two years, some two hundred black candidates were elected to office in the South.

Mississippi Klansmen shot and killed black farmer Vernon Dahmer, leader of the Hattiesburg NAACP, and burned down his house with his ten-year-old daughter in it.

"If our enemies . . . continue to resist, they must be physicially destroyed," Imperial Wizard Samuel Holloway Bowers, Jr., instructed Klan units, "before they can damage our Christian Civilization further and destroy us."

But by 1966, FBI infiltration of the Klan made its members aware that their secret plans of murder and arson were no longer secret. Thousands were frightened into leaving the Klan. There were further defections in 1967, when the seven Klansmen who had killed Schwerner, Goodman, and Chaney were tried in federal court and sent to prison.

In June 1966, three years after becoming the University of Mississippi's first black graduate, James Meredith marched alone from Tennessee to Mississippi to get out the Southern black vote. Almost as soon as he set foot in Mississippi, he was shot and wounded in an ambush. Martin Luther

King, Jr., and nearly every other black leader sped to Mississippi with fifteen thousand black followers to continue Meredith's march. They were attacked by whites hurling stones and bottles. Shots were fired into the leaders' headquarters.

"There is a complete reign of terror here," Dr. King said.

Stokely Carmichael, the new chairman of SNCC, scorned nonviolent tactics as futile. He issued a call for "Black Power"—a new militant cry for blacks to reject the dream of integration and to "organize black community power to end these abuses." Carmichael's call alienated many white liberals who had worked with black leaders in the civil rights movement. It also spurred militant action by blacks, in some cases creating a revolutionary spirit.

But at least up north, many voters were reflecting a new acceptance of racial equality. In 1966 Massachusetts elected Edward Brooke to the U.S. Senate—the first black senator in eighty-five years. The following year, Thurgood Marshall became the first black appointed to the Supreme Court. A month later, Carl B. Stokes of Cleveland, Ohio, and Richard G. Hatcher of Gary, Indiana, were elected the first black mayors of major U.S. cities.

Spurred by the Black Power movement, black university students began to demand a voice in shaping university policy. At Howard in 1968, they agitated for the university to become "the center of Afro-American thought." At Northwestern they insisted upon sharing power in the awarding of increased admissions and scholarships to students from black ghettos. At San Francisco State they demanded that a bachelor's degree be awarded for Black Studies.

On May 2, 1968, Dr. Ralph Abernathy led a Poor People's March to Washington. The demonstrators protested the impoverishment of most black Americans in a country spending seventy-nine billion dollars a year for military appropriations. In front of the Lincoln Memorial, they built a shantytown called Resurrection City, camping there for two months. Millions of TV viewers heard their grievances on newscasts.

"Few who watched failed to learn," noted former Attorney General Ramsey Clark. "The poor people . . . spoke of hunger in America, of welfare robbing people of their dignity, of racism and schools that failed to teach. They reminded us that the law spoke of equal justice, while they had no rights."

That month the Supreme Court ruled that plans for desegregating America's schools must be carried out, and that plans must be shown "realistically to work" and "to work now."

Robert Kennedy, by then a U.S. senator from Massachusetts, charged that both the Surplus Commodity Distribution of Food Stamp programs were such well kept secrets that they were reaching only eighteen percent of poor families, while four million poor schoolchildren were being left out of the free or low-cost school lunch program.

Making a Freedom Ride of his own in his state of South Carolina, Senator Ernest Hollings toured muddy, unpaved ghettos where he saw ragged women and children crowded into sagging shacks without heat, running water, or electricity. Most were hungry. "This is when the thought first struck me," he reported, "that it might be cheaper to feed the child than jail the man." Dr. Kenneth Aycock, state health official for South Carolina, estimated that there were at least three hundred thousand hungry people in the state, eleven percent of its population.

But the other senator from South Carolina, conservative Strom Thurmond, said, "You had them back in the days of Jesus Christ, you have got some now, and you will have some in the future. You will always have some people who are not willing to work."

Senator Hollings replied, "The hungry are not able-bodied men sitting around drunk and lazy on welfare. They are children. They are abandoned women, or the crippled, or the aged."

When the Poor People's March permit expired, Reverend Abernathy and many followers refused to leave Resurrection City until Congress passed legislation providing jobs for the poor, a low-cost housing program, better medical care, larger welfare payments, and a guaranteed minimum income. They were arrested and jailed for an "illegal demonstration."

Resurrection City was torn down.

The failure of the Poor People's March signaled the collapse of Dr. King's crusade to persuade white America to respond to black needs by nonviolent protest marches and peaceful civil disobedience. New, militant black leaders now urged violence, arson, and guerrilla warfare as the only way to compel concessions to black demands.

Even up north, white communities were turning a deaf ear to the pleas of needy blacks. In 1969 New York State slashed welfare payments, giving families on relief only sixty-five cents a day per person for three meals and every requirement except rent. Yet this was generous compared to Florida and Texas, where the relief allotment per person came to only eight cents a day.

Investigating hunger in Mississippi for the Field Foundation, Dr. Raymond Wheeler reported, "Slow starvation had become part of the southern way of life. . . . The children here get up hungry, go to bed hungry, and never know anything else in between. They are hungry all the time. . . . Malnutrition impairs their performance for life."

In campaigning for the presidency in 1968, Richard M. Nixon sought southern votes by privately promising southern leaders he would not enforce civil rights laws if elected. Taking office in 1969, he kept his pledge by opposing school busing as a means of integration. He also sought to kill the Office of Economic Opportunity that had been set up to provide vocational training and jobs for the ghettos. Four members of the U.S. Civil Rights Commission resigned in protest.

Nixon's attorney general, John Mitchell, went to Congress to argue against renewing the Voting Rights Act of 1965 that had more than doubled black voter registration in the South.

It was not surprising that many black Americans who had shared Martin Luther King's wistful dream of racial equality became gradually disillusioned during the sixties.

Midway in the decade, their frustration began to explode.

4

"Burn, Baby, Burn!"— the Ghettos Explode

*A*ll day long on August 12, 1965, an angry rumor flashes around the black ghetto of Los Angeles's Watts district. Police are reputed to have beaten up a black motorist for a traffic violation and clubbed down a pregnant black woman who protested. No one doubts the gossip, because for years white police have been accused of using deliberate brutality to spread fear in the Watts ghetto, as a technique of control.

Just before midnight, an angry mob of seventy-five black youths begins hurling bricks at passing cars driven by white motorists. Squad cars with wailing sirens and flashing red lights disperse the mob. But the rioters return as soon as the police leave, and they set five cars ablaze.

All next day, the mood of Watts is sullen. A crowd of four hundred gathers in the street. Trouble is in the air.

"Whitey's no good!" one man yells. "He talks about law and order. It's *his* law and *his* order—not mine!"

Other speakers work up mob passions by articulating bitter black grievances: "We're forced on welfare rolls to survive because we can't get jobs. We get fourth-rate education in run-down schools. We're charged higher prices in Watts for food, clothes, and liquor than they charge in white neighborhoods. We're forced to live in a ghetto filled with poverty, sickness, vice, and crime. Police harass and beat up black motorists. Over sixty percent of all arrests in L.A. are made in Watts—which has less than fifteen percent of the population!"

Another outburst of violence erupts after midnight. This time mobs are led by "war counselors"—youths who communicate with each other through public telephone booths. Their attacks are directed principally against white property in the ghetto. Shops owned by blacks who hastily soap "Blood Brother" or "Soul Brother" on their windows are spared.

Throngs surge through the streets, overturning cars and setting them afire. Business buildings are torched until two whole blocks are blazing, lighting up the ghetto.

"Burn, baby, burn!" yell excited rioters.

Firemen and any whites who enter Watts are driven off by sniper fire and hurled rocks and bottles. Looters break into white-owned stores, running out with arms full of clothing and merchandise. Riot police form a skirmish line and fire warning shots over rioters' heads. Many racing looters refuse to halt when ordered, and some are shot down in flight.

Sniper fire is reported from a tenement. White police break in and rout its residents with blazing guns.

"You shot right into a house full of babies!" one woman screams at them. "Just because I'm a Negro doesn't mean I don't love my babies just as much as you love your white ones!"

The riot rages for six days, as up to ten thousand ghetto-dwellers join the tumultuous mobs. When the flames finally die down in Watts, thirty-four people are dead—twenty-eight blacks, three Mexican-Americans, one Japanese, and two white policemen. Injured: 875. Arrested: nearly four thousand. The destruction of 209 buildings, with damage to 789 more, in what is now grimly called "Charcoal Alley," is estimated at over 200 million dollars. Whole blocks lie in rubble and ashes.

Helmeted troops patrol the wrecked streets with loaded weapons. Hungry ghetto residents queue up in breadlines.

An angry President Johnson excoriates the rioters. "Neither old wrongs nor new fears can ever justify arson or murder. A rioter with a Molotov cocktail [firebomb] in his hands is not fighting for civil rights any more than a Klansman with a sheet on his back and a mask on his face. They are both . . . lawbreakers."

Gun sales in Los Angeles soar by one thousand percent in a single month. Whites are stunned and frightened by the dangerous racial polarization in their city.

Tension built steadily in black communities all through the sixties. Millions were gradually embittered by President Johnson's abandonment of his War on Poverty to spend America's wealth instead on the Vietnam War and by the intense white backlash against the enforcement of civil rights laws.

A study of seventy-six race riots by sociologists Stanley Lieberson and Arnold R. Silverman found that most broke out in northern ghettos over-crowded by jobless blacks who had immigrated from the rural South. Rioters, in effect, pushed aside nonviolent black leaders who had failed to win social justice by negotiating peacefully with the white power structure.

Their spontaneous uprisings were directed less against white persons than against white-owned property and hostile guardians of that property—police, firefighters, and National Guardsmen.

One of the first serious riots of the decade took place in New York City's Harlem in July 1964, when a fifteen-year-old black youth was shot to death by an off-duty white police lieutenant. Jesse Gray, leader of a Harlem rent strike against slumlords, appealed to a furious crowd for "a hundred dedicated men who are ready to die for Negro equality."

A crowd of blacks descended on the precinct station, where police blocked their entry. Rocks and bottles were hurled down from rooftops. The police began to make arrests, and an officer ordered the people to go home.

"*You* go home," one black cried. "We *are* home!"

When police charged the crowd, scattering blacks began shattering store windows, looting, and setting fire to trash-filled garbage cans. The police swung nightsticks and fired at blacks on the rooftops. Before the night was over, fifteen people had been shot, one fatally, with 116 injured, including a dozen policemen. Violence continued for several days, touching off other large-scale riots in Brooklyn and Rochester, New York.

In the hope of easing tension between blacks and police, New York City appointed its first black precinct commander.

Some blacks flocked into the Black Muslim movement founded by Elijah Muhammad, who preached hatred of, and separation from, the white race. His disciple, Malcolm X, scorned the Freedom Riders for ignoring black oppression in northern ghettos, and he opposed as a fraud Dr. King's campaign for integration.

"Why was it that when Negroes did start revolting across America," Malcolm X demanded, "virtually all of white America was caught up in surprise and even shock?" He predicted a future with "more racial violence than Americans have ever witnessed." Breaking away to form a separate Black Muslim cult in 1964, Malcolm X was assassinated a year later in what was believed to be a cult feud. Fulfilling his prediction, from 1965 through

1968 Americans witnessed the most destructive racial violence in the nation's history.

Leading another militant black movement was the Black Panther Party, organized in the summer of 1965 by SNCC chairman Stokely Carmichael in an Oakland, California, ghetto.

To develop racial pride and erase the stigma whites had attached to blackness from slavery days, the Panthers created the slogan "Black is beautiful!" Rejection of the white culture was emphasized by Afro hairstyles, dashiki robes, Black Power handshakes, and celebration of history's black heroes.

"We have to wage a psychological battle for the right of black people to define their own terms, define themselves as they see fit and organize themselves as they see fit," Carmichael declared in a speech at Berkeley, adding, "We are concerned with getting the things we want, the things that we have to have to be able to function. . . . Will white people overcome their racism and allow for that to happen in this country?"

Black Power alarmed many black leaders as well as the white community. "We of the NAACP will have none of this," Roy Wilkins said firmly. "It is the father of hatred and the mother of violence. Black Power can mean in the end only black death."

Racial tensions soared. On a hot July day in 1966, Chicago police refused to allow fire hydrants to be turned on so that black children could cool off in the water. Fierce riots broke out in the ghetto, requiring Mayor Richard Daley to call in the National Guard.

The cry "Black Power!" rang out in ghettos wherever blacks felt mistreated. When a white woman unwittingly drove a white Cadillac through a tense Atlanta ghetto, a black nine-year-old threw a brick that smashed her rear window. His friend protested, "Hey, man, that's a lady!"

The attacker replied, "Hell, she's white, ain't she?" After a moment's reflection, his friend picked up a brick and smashed her side window.

Chicago police put a riot control program into action. When trouble broke out, massive sweep arrests cleared the streets, and judges set exorbitant bail to keep those arrested in jail for a month or more. Chicago's major black newspaper, the *Daily Defender*, charged the police with harassment, verbal abuse, beatings, and unjustified shootings.

"We want an immediate end to police brutality and the murder of black people!" the Black Panthers demanded.

A huge crowd listens as Black Muslim leader Malcolm X speaks in New York's Harlem. The Black Muslim movement advocated black separatism. After his 1964 break with the movement, Malcolm X was murdered.

Flames engulf a building in Detroit during racial riots. Fifteen hundred National Guardsmen backed by tanks were called in to quell the firebombing, looting, and related violence.

The worst race riots of the decade occurred during the summer of 1967 in Newark, New Jersey, and Detroit, Michigan. Newark was seething that July because of black complaints against the police, and because, in addition to twenty-four thousand unemployed black adults, twenty thousand jobless black teenagers had no place to go and nothing to do.

An angry mob formed when white police were seen clubbing and kicking a black cabdriver as they dragged him into a police station. A firebomb was thrown against the station wall and burst into flame. A barrage of rocks followed. Police charged out, clubbing everyone within reach. That triggered a four-day riot of rock-hurling, firebombing, window-smashing, looting, and car-burning. Newark's 1,300-person police force had to be reinforced by 475 state troopers and four thousand National Guardsmen.

The streets echoed with continual gunfire, most of it aimed at looters. Many stray bullets struck innocent people. Rumors of black snipers made the young, inexperienced guardsmen nervous and trigger-happy.

When they mistook one of their own men for a sniper, they poured fire into a housing project. A number of black men, women, and children were killed.

"You have now created a state of hysteria," Newark's chief of police raged at the guardsmen.

State troopers shot at blacks standing on their own porches. Guardsmen shot into a passing car, killing a ten-year-old boy. An eleven-year-old boy, whose mother sent him out with the garbage, was shot and killed. Guardsmen and state troopers rode around in jeeps, firing into stores with "Soul Brother" signs in the window. Some seized black youths, put a pistol to their heads, forced them to say foul things about their race, then pulled the trigger on an empty chamber.

When the Newark riot finally ended, at least twenty-one blacks had been killed, including six women and two children, and over ten million dollars worth of property had been burned or looted.

The Detroit riot took place a few weeks later, sparked by police raids on after-hours drinking clubs, during which eighty-two blacks were arrested. A mob rioted in protest, hurling bricks through shop windows, then looting. Firebombs flew, and a high wind swept flames through the city. Fire fighters rushing to the scene were driven off by a hail of stones.

Proclaiming a state of emergency, Governor George Romney rushed in

National Guardsmen. "These poor kids were scared," observed Police Commissioner Ray Girardin, "and they scared me." Spraying bullets wildly at real or imagined snipers, the inexperienced guardsmen killed many innocent people, as in Newark.

Some black snipers shot at police, firemen, and guardsmen, as the latter's Patton tanks rumbled through the streets with machine guns blazing, strafing buildings suspected of harboring snipers. "I'm gonna shoot anything that moves and is black," one guardsman told a reporter grimly.

When some blacks were shot dead as snipers, they were found to be unarmed. Many suspects were taken to police stations, beaten to force confessions, then taken off to hospitals. Over 7,200 people were arrested, and over forty persons were killed.

Flying over Detroit in a helicopter, Governor Romney said, "It looked like the city had been bombed . . . with entire blocks in flames." Damage was estimated at over two hundred fifty million dollars.

By September 1967, there had been 162 more ghetto riots, resulting in eighty-three deaths. President Johnson appointed a National Advisory Commission on Civil Disorders, headed by Illinois Governor Otto Kerner, to probe the problem.

The commission put the primary blame on police racism and repression, and they secondarily blamed the neglect of black needs for jobs, decent housing, and educational opportunities.

"The urban disorders of the summer of 1967," said the Kerner report, "were not caused by . . . any organized plan of 'conspiracy.' " The typical black rioter was found to be not a hoodlum or criminal, but a young high school dropout without a job.

President Johnson appealed to angry blacks to seek peaceful means of redressing their grievances: "Let us remember that it is the law-abiding Negro families who have really suffered the most at the hands of the rioters. . . . Whose neighborhood is made a shambles? Whose life is threatened most?"

But by 1968, most blacks were convinced that America operated under two separate sets of laws—one for blacks, one for whites. "Our nation is moving toward two societies," warned the Kerner report, "one black, one white—separate and unequal." Northerners were irked by its finding that prejudice was not just a southern failing but was operative substantially throughout the North as well.

A new wave of fiery black riots was touched off on April 4, 1968, with the assassination of Martin Luther King, Jr., in Memphis by a white convict named James Earl Ray, who had escaped from the Missouri State Penitentiary a year earlier.

Ironically, the martyrdom of the black leader who had preached nonviolence resulted in the worst violence the nation had known since the Civil War, and his death did more to compel the government's attention to black grievances than his life had been able to do.

Black wrath exploded across the nation following King's assassination. Racial rioting struck sixty-three cities in twenty-nine states. Before it was over, at least forty-six people had been killed, over 2,600 injured, and more than twenty-one thousand arrested. Damage to property was estimated at sixty-seven million dollars. A dusk-to-dawn curfew was imposed in some cities for several nights in an attempt to restore some semblance of order.

"Police control problems exceeded anything ever before experienced," noted former Attorney General Ramsey Clark. "Traffic stopped, stores closed, windows were smashed, there was looting, arson, and finally deadly violence—all to honor the fallen prophet of nonviolence. In recurring waves for several days, as if we had been seized by a nationwide fever, there was more rioting, looting, and arson."

In Washington, D.C., over seventy buildings and cars were set on fire, and police made over four thousand arrests. A machine gun was set up on the steps of the Capitol, and troops were called out to guard the White House.

In Chicago, Mayor Richard Daley ordered his police, "Shoot to kill arsonists, shoot to maim looters!" They began patrolling Chicago's ghettos with loaded shotguns.

Black crowds gathered in the ghettos to listen to furious speakers denounce white America. "We must move from resistance to aggression," cried Black Panther and SNCC leader H. Rap Brown, "from revolt to revolution!" Congress was stampeded into passing the 1968 Anti-Riot Act to punish "the outside agitator" who crossed state lines to "stir up trouble" and "cause riots."

The ghetto riots of the sixties reflected black rage at the deterioration of the inner cities where they were forced to live. Whites fleeing to the suburbs had left the ghettos to crumble around the poor, jobless, and hungry. By 1968 New York City had a million people on its welfare rolls, the vast majority of them black.

Congress had passed a Housing and Urban Development Act to provide "a decent home and a suitable living environment for every American family." But *The New York Times* urban affairs reporter John Herbers criticized the several hundred units New York had bought. "At what a price!" he wrote scornfully. "The crooks in the central city have had a field day with it. Much of the housing is junk, built on questionable sites, fostering the old pattern of segregation and serving the moderate income more than the very poor." The program was later abolished as "a hundred-billion-dollar mistake."

In April 1969, black leaders organized a National Black Economic Development Conference. They issued a Black Manifesto that declared, "Racist white America has exploited our resources, our minds, our bodies, our labor. For centuries we have been forced to live as colonized people inside the United States, victimized by the most vicious, racist system in the world."

The manifesto demanded that the government spend half a billion dollars for specified measures that would give black communities control over their own lives.

Significantly, in 1969 SNCC substituted the word "National" for "Nonviolent" in its name. "As long as people in the ghettos of our large cities feel they are victims of the misuse of white power," warned Stokely Carmichael, "without any way to have their needs represented . . . we will continue to have riots."

But at the end of the decade, ghetto riots subsided, primarily because the majority of American blacks, who suffered most from the violence, wanted to "cool it." They thought the riots had only made things worse for black America by stiffening white opposition to ghetto grievances.

As black political leaders began to gain influence in the big cities that had been abandoned by whites fleeing to the suburbs, and as many of these cities began electing black mayors, there was a growing feeling in black America that maybe, after all, Martin Luther King, Jr., had been right.

Maybe more could be gained by working nonviolently within the system for needed changes, than by burning it down.

5

THE NIGHTMARE OF VIETNAM

"An eight-year-old or a nine-year-old can kill you just as quick as a twenty-five- or twenty-six-year-old man," Army Sergeant Thomas Murphy explains to a war correspondent who asks why it is necessary to kill Vietnamese children. Guerrilla warfare is unnerving to American troops, who are never sure which Vietnamese civilians are friendly and which are enemy Viet Cong.

But being ordered to shoot first and ask questions afterward has a demoralizing effect on many GIs.

Marine Corporal Ronnie W. Wilson, 20, writes home to his mother in Kansas, "Mom, I had to kill a woman and a baby. Why must I kill women and kids?"

The 1960s were the decade that saw over fifty thousand Americans die in a country halfway around the world, killed in a war few Americans understood. It was a war, moreover, that tore America apart between flag-waving patriots and defiant dissenters. How did the United States get involved?

The war had its origin in the struggle of the Vietnamese people to free themselves from French colonialism. The French, establishing their rule in Southeast Asia in 1883, had carved Indochina into five powerless parts—Cambodia, Laos, and three Vietnamese provinces.

The French colonial ruling class had sought to recreate an Asiatic France in Indochina by means of native labor. They gave themselves the right to slap awkward Vietnamese waiters who spilled soup or rickshaw coolies who dared argue about the fare.

Anti-French sentiment led to the rise of a revolutionary movement under a resourceful leader named Ho Chi Minh. During World War II, the Japanese invaded Vietnam, ousting the French. When the French sought to return after the war, Ho's party, the Vietminh, called for a patriotic revolt. His forces seized the northern part of the country, which was proclaimed the Democratic Republic of Vietnam.

The French fought the Vietminh unsuccessfully for eight years. Ho's forces were skilled guerrilla fighters, and they had the support of almost the entire country. The Vietnamese regarded Ho as a great patriot, Communist or not, and trusted him to free them from the French.

Finally, in 1954, the Vietminh defeated the French decisively at Dien Bien Phu, winning control of three-quarters of the country. The French were forced to sue for peace at Geneva, in a conference attended by the Vietminh, the French, the British, the Russians, the Chinese, and the Americans.

The Geneva Accords ending the war were signed by the Vietminh and the French, and they were approved by Great Britain, the Soviet Union, Cambodia, Laos, and the French puppet regime in Saigon, capital of the southern zone of Vietnam. The treaty divided Vietnam in half at the Seventeenth Parallel, but only temporarily. Country-wide elections were to be held in two years to determine one unified goverment for all of Vietnam. Election preparations were to begin in one year.

The United States, however, withdrew from the conference. Secretary of State John Foster Dulles pledged that the U.S. would not interfere with the Geneva Accords settlement, but he secretly planned to sabotage the scheduled elections. He knew, as President Eisenhower later acknowledged, that the Communist leader, Ho Chi Minh, would have been easily elected with about eighty-five percent of the national vote.

Dulles maneuvered to transform the temporary southern zone into a separate and permanent nation—an American client state called South Vietnam. Catholic politician Ngo Dinh Diem was put in place as its head, despite the fact that ninety percent of the Vietnamese were Buddhists.

Diem was financed and armed by the United States, and the CIA helped him crush opposition.

By April 1960, Diem's regime was so widely detested that even eighteen conservative South Vietnam nobles, including some former government ministers, challenged his rule in a public petition. They protested that the jails were overflowing with political prisoners and that Diem's bureaucracy was corrupt and inefficient. They predicted "soaring waves of hatred and resentment of a terribly suffering people standing up to break their chains."

In December a secret meeting was held in South Vietnam at which all of Diem's opponents united in a coalition called the National Liberation Front (NLF). Their armed guerrilla units were known as Viet Cong.

When President Kennedy was elected, he sent Vice President Lyndon Johnson to Saigon to report on the situation. Johnson informed Kennedy that the United States had only two choices—either admit that supporting Diem and Saigon had been a bad mistake and get out of Vietnam or commit major American forces to keep Diem in power.

Kennedy ordered an intensification of American aid for Diem, which soon amounted to almost two million dollars a day. He also increased the ten thousand military "advisers" sent to Diem to twenty thousand, declaring they would shoot back if fired upon.

According to former Undersecretary of State George Ball, Kennedy was impelled to this decision by the humiliating failure of his attempt to overthrow Fidel Castro in a disastrous CIA-sponsored invasion of Cuba he authorized shortly after taking office. The president felt that he could not afford a second failure of U.S. foreign policy in Vietnam.

But despite massive increases in American aid, Diem was not able to control more than a third of South Vietnam. The rest of that zone remained in the hands of the Viet Cong, while all of North Vietnam was united under Ho Chi Minh.

General Thomas Harkins, the U.S. commander in Vietnam, nevertheless assured reporters in 1962 that the war would be "over by Christmas."

Robert Kennedy, visiting South Vietnam that year, also declared, "We will win in Vietnam and we shall remain here until we do."

Despite training by the American military advisers, Diem's Army of the Republic of Viet Nam (ARVN) troops were no match for the Viet Cong. Diem also had his hands full with the Buddhist leaders, who organized bitter demonstrations against his attempt to establish Catholicism as the official religion of that Buddhist land.

In May 1963, Diem's troops killed seven Buddhist demonstrators. In June, when five hundred students gathered to protest religious discrimination, sixty-seven were injured in clashes with government forces. Three days later, a seventy-three-year-old Buddhist monk drenched himself with gasoline and set himself on fire in the street. A news photo of his immolation made front pages all over the world, stirring international indignation at the Diem regime.

When a second monk committed suicide by fire the next month, Diem's Special Forces raided Buddhist pagodas, killing scores of monks and jailing hundreds. Diem closed all schools and universities, arresting four thousand students and declaring martial law.

Kennedy despaired of the Diem regime for having "gotten out of touch with the people." He informed Senate Majority Leader Mike Mansfield that he planned to withdraw all U.S. troops from Vietnam after he was reelected in 1964. To do so sooner, he feared, would provoke a Republican campaign accusing him of "appeasing Communism."

On September 2, 1963, Kennedy gave the nod to Ambassador Lodge in Saigon, and the CIA secretly encouraged a military junta to stage a coup and get rid of Diem. On November 2, the Diem regime was overthrown. In a truck taking him to prison, Diem was shot by one of the rebel officers, who pronounced the fallen ruler's death as an "accidental suicide."

A series of military dictatorships rapidly came and went in Saigon, until Washington was finally able to stabilize the regime with General Nguyen Van Thieu as president. Meanwhile, Ho Chi Minh sent several thousand North Vietnamese troops into South Vietnam to aid the Viet Cong.

On November 20, Kennedy told White House aide Michael Forrestal, "I want you to organize an in-depth study of every possible option we've got in Vietnam, including how to get out of there." He expressed strong doubts about the wisdom of getting further mired down in a civil war in Indochina.

After Kennedy's assassination on November 22, 1963, his successor, Lyndon B. Johnson, at first also vowed not to get "our boys" involved in an Asian war. But his determination not to "lose Vietnam" led him to increase steadily the amount of troops and money sent to Saigon.

A young marine in Vietnam wipes away tears as he kneels beside a body wrapped in a poncho. Other casualties lie along the road.

These flag-draped caskets bring the bodies of eight American soldiers and a navy man back to the U.S. from Vietnam. Fifty-seven thousand Americans died in the war in Indochina.

⌐By the summer of 1964, Johnson was convinced that the only way the war in Vietnam could be won was with American troops and air power.⌐ *The New York Times* revealed that he secretly promised the Saigon regime to bomb North Vietnam as soon as the 1964 fall elections were out of the way. James Reston reported that Washington officials were "talking casually about how easy it would be to 'provoke an incident' in the Gulf of Tonkin which would justify an attack upon North Vietnam."

In August 1964, the U.S. Navy did report such an attack upon two destroyers, the USS *Maddox* and the USS *Turner Joy*, by three North Vietnamese P.T. boats. On August 6, Johnson asked Congress for a resolution authorizing him "to take all necessary measures . . . to prevent further aggression."

Senators Wayne Morse and Ernest Gruening warned their colleagues, "Those who vote for this will live to regret it." But save for them, the whole Senate endorsed the Gulf of Tonkin Resolution. In a subsequent investigation, officers of the USS *Maddox* admitted that North Vietnamese PT boats had *not* fired any shells or torpedoes at the American destroyers. CIA operative Ray Cline also confirmed that there was no evidence of any attack on the USS *Turner Joy*.

Senator William Fulbright, heading the Senate Foreign Relations Committee, angrily accused the administration of having deliberately lied to his committee about the alleged attacks.

But Johnson, armed with the Gulf of Tonkin Resolution as his authority to fight an all-out undeclared war, prepared to bomb North Vietnam and build up the American military presence in South Vietnam to over half a million troops.

His secret plans, however, could not be revealed until after the 1964 elections. Running for a presidential term in his own right, Johnson assured voters that he had no intention of allowing the United States to get bogged down in a land war in Southeast Asia or to engage in any rash military actions.

Attacking his Republican opponents led by Senator Barry Goldwater, Johnson declared on August 12, "They call upon us to supply American boys to do the job that Asian boys should do. They ask us to take reckless action which might risk the lives of millions and engulf much of Asia and certainly threaten the peace of the world. Moreover such action would offer no solution at all to the problem of Vietnam." On October 21, in Akron, Ohio, he repeated his pledge that American boys would not be sent to fight in Vietnam.

But in February 1965, after election to a term of his own, Johnson ordered continuous bombing of territory held by the North Vietnamese below the Twentieth Parallel. Next month Assistant Secretary of Defense John McNaughton defended the American presence in Vietnam as necessary "to avoid a humiliating U.S. defeat." In an operation called "Rolling Thunder," 105 American bombers flew over North Vietnam, bombing ammunition dumps.

The new president, Nguyen Van Thieu, took power in South Vietnam, presiding over the arrival of new thousands of American troops. By July, Johnson had committed a hundred thousand GIs to the battle, making the United States a full belligerent in the land war in Asia that he had sworn to avoid. He did so because he was now convinced that the South Vietnamese ARVN troops were an ineffective fighting force who could not win their own war.

Under a secret program called Operation Phoenix, the CIA established forty-one interrogation centers where South Vietnamese forces tortured suspected Viet Cong. CIA Director William Colby's legal adviser in Saigon, Robert F. Gould, admitted, "Everybody who was there accepted torture as routine."

Colby himself acknowledged that over twenty thousand political prisoners were murdered in two-and-a-half years. The Saigon regime proudly claimed the number of victims to be forty thousand. TV cameras were on hand to record South Vietnam's police chief personally execute a Viet Cong prisoner on a Saigon street with a revolver shot to the head. American viewers were horrified at this graphic view of the brutality of the war.

But the Viet Cong, too, committed atrocities, primarily against village chiefs who had bought their appointments from the Saigon military. Many of these village officials and their families were kidnapped, murdered, and mutilated. The VC also blew up buses along Saigon-controlled highways.

During 1966, Johnson used massive American air power against North Vietnam. Ho Chi Minh's deputy minister of health reported that the bombings had hit 180 hospitals and medical centers. The U.S. Air Force also sprayed the chemical Agent Orange as a defoliant to destroy rice crops and rubber trees and to "eliminate Viet Cong hiding places." After the war, many GIs who had been within reach of these sprays developed cancer. Some of them subsequently sued the chemical company that had been the primary manufacturer of Agent Orange, as well as the government, and a settlement was won.

American bombs fell not only on North Vietnam but also on villages in South Vietnam suspected of aiding the Viet Cong. The Marines told *The New Yorker* reporter Jonathan Schell that in one South Vietnamese province, seventy percent of the villages had been destroyed by American air raids.

By February 1967, an estimated 1,750 U.S. planes had been lost in the war. The Defense Department announced that over 6,600 American troops had been killed, over 37,000 wounded.

By March, there were 427,000 GIs in Vietnam. Throughout the year, U.S. military headquarters in Saigon issued progressively lower estimates of Viet Cong strength, creating the impression that American military operations in Vietnam were succeeding. But CIA analyst Sam Adams found that the actual enemy strength was over twice as great as reported by General William Westmoreland's headquarters. He sent his figures to General Earl Wheeler, chairman of the Joint Chiefs of Staff.

Wheeler cabled Westmoreland, "If these figures should reach the public domain they would, literally, blow the lid off Washington. Please do whatever is necessary to insure that these figures are not repeat not released to news media or otherwise exposed to public knowledge."

On November 22 Westmoreland told the press that the ranks of the Viet Cong were steadily thinning. But Secretary of Defense Robert S. McNamara split with the Joint Chiefs of Staff over their insistence that a military solution to Vietnam could succeed. He resigned, explaining years later that he and Westmoreland had "differed in our judgments on the progress of the war." In January 1968, by which time there were 475,000 U.S. troops fighting in Vietnam, Westmoreland's headquarters again issued optimistic reports about American war gains.

President Johnson assured the American people, "The enemy has been defeated in battle after battle."

National Security Adviser Walt Rostow promised, "The Viet Cong are going to collapse within weeks. Not months, but weeks."

A shock awaited Americans. During Tet, the Vietnamese lunar new year, the Viet Cong suddenly opened a surprise offensive in South Vietnam. On January 29, 1968, over two hundred thousand Viet Cong and North Vietnamese troops attacked thirty-seven city and provincial capitals with mortars and rockets. Invading Saigon itself, they seized key points in the city, including part of the U.S. Embassy compound. For five days, heavy fighting continued in the city and its suburbs.

The Pentagon rushed additional troops and weapons to South Vietnam, bringing the forces there to 510,000 by mid-February. They finally drove the Viet Cong out of Saigon and Hue, the second most important city in South Vietnam.

Westmoreland was summoned home to explain the Tet disaster to stunned Americans. When Johnson decided not to risk running for reelection, Westmoreland was transferred to the Joint Chiefs of Staff, and General Creighton W. Abrams replaced him in Saigon.

The killing in Vietnam went on. In 1968 alone, another fifteen thousand U.S. soldiers died, with ninety-two thousand more wounded.

When one Marine veteran, Lt. Colonel William R. Corson, retired, he accused fellow officers in Vietnam of having lost all sense of human values. He quoted one officer who explained why it had been necessary for U.S. forces to demolish the city of Ben Tre during the Tet offensive: "We had to destroy Ben Tre in order to save it."

"This is the language of madness," Colonel Corson said, "a madness which, if allowed to continue, will destroy not only the people of Vietnam but also the moral fabric and strength of America."

By that time, the United States had dropped more bombs on Vietnam than had been dropped in all of World War II.

To continue his policies, Johnson selected Vice President Hubert Humphrey to run for the White House in 1968. In October, just before the election, he ordered a halt to all bombing of North Vietnam, to help Humphrey. But Richard M. Nixon won the presidency by promising voters that he had a secret plan to end the war within six months.

His plan proved to be "Vietnamizing" the war by having U.S. units train and arm the ARVN to replace them. American forces were gradually withdrawn as the ARVN were dispatched to take over more of the fighting.

Shortly after his inauguration, Nixon ordered the bombing of suspected enemy hideouts in neutral Cambodia that triggered the uproar at Kent State and other college campuses.

Abandoning his promise to bring peace within six months, Nixon now insisted that the American intervention had to continue until there was "peace with honor." The *Washington Post* observed, "What President Nixon means by peace is what other people mean by victory."

But Nixon insisted, "For the United States, this first defeat in our nation's history would result in a collapse of confidence in American leadership not only in Asia but throughout the world."

Arnold Toynbee, the eminent British historian, pondered why three American presidents and millions of Americans had permitted the costly, unpopular war to drag on and on all during the sixties and even afterward. He judged their thinking to be: "It's a mistake, it's immoral, it's devastating for us. But America has never lost a war, and we are determined not to lose this one."

Toynbee summed it up: "Pride, personal and national."

6

"HELL, NO, WE WON'T GO!"— THE RESISTANCE MOVEMENT

*D*uring his trial for draft resistance in 1965, nineteen-year-old Tommy Rodd tells the court, "I am forced by my conscience to stand as representative of the suffering millions of Vietnam. I am forced to stand for the girl child burned to death in Bien Hoa, for the refugee cold and hungry in a camp on the outskirts of Saigon . . . for the thousands with no legs, thousands more with no eyes. . . . My word from them to this government, to this country, is this: 'Stop the war!' "

He is sentenced to four years in federal prison.

The antiwar movement was deeply upsetting to many parents, university administrators, and government officials. What was the matter with college kids, anyhow? Why weren't they content to work off their excess energy as students in the fifties had—staging panty raids on coed dorms and seeing how many kids could squeeze into a telephone booth? Why couldn't they behave themselves and be like the "Silent Generation" youths who had minded their own business, pursued their diplomas, then sought well paying jobs with the Establishment or become contented wives and mothers?

Instead, many sixties youths preferred to wear torn blue jeans, beards, headbands, and love beads as they sought to stop the war in Vietnam and racism at home. "Doing their own thing," they refused to conform to the expectations of corporations, government, and parents.

The opening gun in the resistance movement was fired in June 1962, when radicalized middle-class student leaders from fifty-nine campuses gathered at Port Huron, Michigan, to organize Students for a Democratic Society (SDS). After debate they adopted the Port Huron Statement, prepared for them by Tom Hayden, twenty-two-year-old editor of the University of Michigan campus daily who had been jailed in Georgia as a Freedom Rider.

SDS asserted that life in the United States was frustrating; that the system was rigid and obsolete; that the nation's leaders mouthed hypocritical platitudes; and that job opportunities were both overrated and corrupting to ideals.

Condemning America's cold war against Communism as a bankrupt foreign policy, SDS also criticized most Communist parties as undemocratic, subservient to Moscow, and unwilling to allow political freedom. SDS vowed to work nonviolently for a "New Left," using the campus as a fulcrum to promote mass resistance to the Establishment, with the goal of making the government and the economy more responsive to human needs.

Although SDS never represented more than a small fraction of the student body in the sixties, its members were an elite group in the forefront of organizing protest demonstrations. In four years they grew rapidly in strength to 151 chapters in thirty-seven states, with a following of some twenty-eight thousand active supporters.

The Defense Department began to increase its draft calls late in 1961. In May 1964, as it became clear that draftees might be sent to Vietnam, SDS joined with the Student Peace Union, the War Resisters League, and the Quakers in the May Second Movement, which had as its slogan, "Hell, no, we won't go!"

In the 1964 campaign between President Johnson and Republican Senator Barry Goldwater, students viewed Goldwater as a dangerous cold warrior who might unleash a nuclear war with the Soviet Union. At Berkeley they set up tables on campus to campaign against him. Influenced by Republican Senator William Knowland, powerful owner of the *Oakland Tribune*, the university banned this activity.

Led by SDS, a thousand students picketed the university, demanding the right to speak out on campus against politicians, the Vietnam War, the university, the government, or anything else. When police arrested Jack Weinberg for passing out leaflets and collecting contributions, over two thousand students surrounded the police van and refused to let it leave.

Mario Savio, a philosophy major who had been a Freedom Rider in Mississippi, emerged as leader of the demonstration when he jumped up onto the roof of the squad car to proclaim a two-day Free Speech rally. He demanded Weinberg's release and an end of the ban on political activity.

"There is a time," Savio cried, paraphrasing American philosopher Henry David Thoreau, "when the operation of the machine becomes so odious, makes you so sick at heart, that you can't take part . . . and you've got to put your bodies upon the levers . . . and you've got to make it stop. And you've got to indicate . . . that unless you're free, the machine will be prevented from working at all."

SDS then led sit-in protests in various campus buildings. When police were summoned to take them to detention centers, the students went limp and had to be carried. Indignant at the arrests, the student body, supported by many faculty members, carried out Savio's warning. A general strike brought the huge university to a virtual standstill.

SDS's Free Speech movement compelled University of California President Clark Kerr to offer new, liberal rules for student protest and to promise that none of the eight hundred sit-down demonstrators holding the university buildings would be punished.

The winds of change swept from Berkeley through the campuses of America. Under SDS leadership, students everywhere began organizing and demonstrating for five principle demands—university reform; equal rights for blacks; a priority for human values over financial concerns; an end to the draft; and getting out of Vietnam.

Where college adminstrations showed a willingness to negotiate reasonable demands, most demonstrations were nonviolent. Campus disorders occurred chiefly when police and the National Guard were called in and used violence against demonstrators.

Some youths asked for a change in the draft law to allow them to serve their country in the Peace Corps instead of the army. Conscience, they insisted, did not permit them to participate in an undeclared war that millions of students, teachers, and ministers considered morally wrong.

"Today's protesters against the Vietnam War," declared Senator Fulbright, "are in good historical company. . . . It is an expression of national conscience and a manifestation of traditional American idealism."

Many eighteen- to twenty-year-olds refused to be drafted to fight a war waged without their political consent. Why were they considered old enough to die for their country, they demanded, but not old enough to vote in it?

In January 1965, a federal grand jury handed down indictments against Dr. Benjamin Spock, the famous adviser on child-rearing; the Reverend William Sloane Coffin, Jr., Yale University chaplain; and three other dissidents for "a continuing conspiracy to aid, abet, and counsel violations of the Selective Service Law." A Boston court sentenced each of them to two years in jail.

"My main defense," Dr. Spock told reporters, "was that I believed a citizen must work against a war he considers contrary to international law." He cited the Nuremberg Tribunal verdict at the end of World War II, which held that every citizen ordered by his government to commit "crimes against humanity," as the Nazis had done, had a higher duty to his moral conscience and to mankind to disobey such orders as criminal. Dr. Spock pointed out that an American magistrate had sat on that tribunal, binding the United States to its ruling.

The U.S. Court of Appeals in Boston later reversed the convictions of Dr. Spock and the others, holding that the antiwar defendants had not received a fair trial. The court agreed with them that "vigorous criticism of the draft and of the Vietnam War is . . . protected by the First Amendment, even though its effect is to interfere with the war effort."

Dr. Spock and Rev. Coffin rededicated their efforts to helping young war resisters. "It seems to me absolutely tragic," Spock said, "that young Americans will continue to die in Vietnam . . . and that young men have been imprisoned for being opposed to it and doing as their consciences dictated." Spock was again convicted in June 1968 of conspiring to counsel draft resisters.

When youths began burning draft cards in front of TV cameras at antiwar rallies, Senator Strom Thurmond hastened a bill through Congress providing five years in prison and a ten thousand dollar fine for burning a draft card or inciting this act.

"It wouldn't be so bad if these people didn't make a public protest with their cards," Senator Everett Dirksen said on TV, "but just went out behind the barn and burned them."

The American Civil Liberties Union (ACLU) called the bill unconstitutional, holding that it violated the right of free speech because burning a draft card was simply a symbolic way of dramatizing a protest against injustice.

The first antiwar march on Washington was organized by SDS in April 1965. Over twenty thousand demonstrators picketed the White House, then held a rally at the Washington Monument and marched four abreast from the Mall to the Capitol singing "We Shall Overcome."

Harvard student David Goldring recalled, "When we got up on the Capitol steps I looked back, and all the way to where the road dipped, the Mall was solid with people. Oh, man, was that exciting! I was just delirious! More than ever before, I got the direct physical knowledge of a movement we were all part of. It was just a grand day!"

"No one is quite the same after he has marched in a demonstration, however tame," wrote Andrew Kopkind in *The New York Times Magazine*.

That same month the University of Michigan became the first major university to hold an anti-Vietnam "teach-in"—a huge campus rally of students and faculty to disseminate facts about the war that had been suppressed by the government. Teach-ins spread rapidly to campuses all over the country, many exposing university cooperation with Pentagon war research.

Students demonstrated against the invasion of campuses by recruiters from the military, the CIA, and corporations aiding the war effort, especially the manufacturers of napalm, the liquid fire that burned victims alive.

"The protesters feel," observed University of Toledo sociologist Joseph W. Scott, "that the hypocrisy of industry in supplying napalm in the name of peace-seeking is exceeded only by that of the universities in their willingness to provide military manpower to carry on the war."

University of Pennsylvania students exposed their university for conducting germ war research for the Pentagon.

Berkeley held the largest teach-in on October 16, 1965, with thousands of students and professors pouring in from seventy-one cities and twenty-eight states. After a full day of open-air classes, some fifteen thousand dissenters marched on the Oakland Army Terminal, where men and supplies were being shipped to Vietnam. The marchers were turned back by an armed phalanx of police and National Guardsmen.

Student activism, led by SDS, gathered force steadily during the middle and late sixties. Something new had happened: For the first time in American history, college students were becoming a force for social change.

In November 1965, Baltimore Quaker Norman Morrison set himself aflame, in imitation of the Buddhist monks in Vietnam, a hundred yards from the window of Secretary of Defense Robert McNamara's office in the Pentagon. His aim was to make the American people realize what napalm bombs were doing to Vietnamese men, women, and children. One week later, a Hunter College student immolated himself for similar reasons.

Shock waves ran through the TV-viewing public.

As hundreds of American deaths in Vietnam became thousands, Senator Fulbright decided that the time had come for a public debate on Vietnam. It began two months later at a Senate Foreign Relations Committee hearing. Americans watching on TV heard experts like General James Gavin, Marine General David Shoup, and former Ambassador George Kennan assert that the administration's escalation of the war had been a blunder. Fifteen senators urged President Johnson to end the war. The hearings led new millions to protest U.S. foreign policy.

The president, aware that intellectuals were the backbone of the resistance, sought to cajole them into muting their opposition with a "White House Festival of the Arts." But many prominent intellectuals refused to attend. Lewis Mumford, president of the American Academy of Arts and Letters, declared that artists and writers had "a special duty to speak out openly in protest" against the war. Johnson told his consultant, Professor Eric F. Goldman, that he had had "enough of these people." He added, "Don't they know that I'm the only president they've got and a war is on?"

The Yippies (Youth International Party) were an antiwar, anti-Establishment group who sought to discredit the government through mockery. Their leaders were Jerry Rubin and Abbie Hoffman.

In December 1965, Rubin led a satirical demonstration in San Francisco against General Maxwell Taylor, U.S. commander in Vietnam. Arrested and sentenced to a month in jail, Rubin shouted in the courtroom, "Our act was a political protest. Our punishment is political. We are today political prisoners."

At the same time, University of Michigan students organized a sit-in protest at the Ann Arbor draft board. Draft administrator Lewis B. Hershey ordered them drafted immediately. The ACLU challenged his order in court. Didn't the government consider it an "honor" to serve one's country in the Armed Forces? Then how could it at the same time be a punishment? Wouldn't all draftees have the right to ask what they had done to be so punished? The administration pressured General Hershey to rethink his punitive decree.

When David Earl Gutknecht's draft board in Minneapolis classified him 1A (immediately draftable) as a "delinquent" for throwing his draft card at the feet of a federal marshal, he refused induction and was given a four-year prison term. He fought the case up to the Supreme Court, which reversed his conviction and declared illegal attempts by draft boards to intimidate war protesters by labeling them delinquents. Gutknecht's victory prevented thousands who joined the resistance from being similarly punished.

The resistance raised a new battle cry: "Make love—not war!" Rather than go to jail, many draft resisters sought political refuge in Canada and Sweden. Some dissenters disapproved, considering flight a "cop-out" from the antiwar struggle. But speaking in Toronto, lawyer William Kunstler declared, "I would hope, myself, that every American of draft age came across the border here or went to Sweden; then they wouldn't have to fight anybody's wars."

March and April 1966 saw tremendous antiwar demonstrations, parades, and rallies all over the country, sparked by the Fulbright hearings and revelations of indiscriminate U.S. air attacks on North Vietnam. The World Council of Churches opposed State Department policy, demanding that direct negotiations be opened with the Viet Cong. Pro-war advocates protested that such criticism was "dangerous treason."

The weekly paper of the entertainment world, *Variety*, revealed that the Johnson administration was putting intense pressure on TV news programs not to show American troops setting fire to Vietnamese villages, South Vietnamese troops killing or torturing prisoners, U.S. soldiers wounded in battle, or antiwar or antidraft demonstrations. Nevertheless, for the first time in history, war was brought into American living rooms, and many Americans were shocked by its bloody reality.

The Senate Foreign Relations Committee reported that American munitions firms were prospering as never before. Ohio Senator Stephen Young found some corporations making million-dollar profits on Pentagon contracts. "The economy of the United States," observed historian Arnold Toynbee, "has become dependent on war orders to a startling extent."

Opposition to President Johnson by noisy demonstrators grew so intense that he was afraid to have the presidential plane land at commercial airports. Instead he moved around the country from air force base to army camp. Wondering whether his bombing of North Vietnam might provoke Hanoi's supporter, the Soviet Union, to nuclear war, he told his daughter Luci, "You may not wake up tomorrow, honey. Your daddy may go down in history as the man who started World War III."

In April 1967, a sensation was caused by the popular world heavyweight boxing champion, Muhammad Ali, 25. Ali, whose motto, "Float like a butterfly, sting like a bee," had delighted millions of sports fans, refused to be drafted, claiming exemption by reason of his Muslim faith.

"The real enemy of my people is right here," said the black champion. "Why should they ask me . . . to put on a uniform and go ten thousand miles from home, drop bombs and bullets on brown people in Vietnam while so-called Negro people in Louisville are treated like dogs and denied simple human rights? I am not going to help murder and kill and burn other people simply to help continue the domination of the white slave masters over the dark people the world over." He was tried and convicted, and on June 20 he was sentenced to five years in prison and a ten thousand dollar fine.

But some three years later his conviction was overturned on religious grounds upon appeal to the Supreme Court.

More and more universities were revealed to have accepted Pentagon grants for war research. At Pennsylvania State, more than twenty faculty members prepared to march in commencement exercises wearing gas masks.

The board of trustees hastily agreed to cancel that university's contract with the Pentagon for research in chemical-biological warfare.

SDS led a drive to wipe out all forms of university cooperation with the military. Demonstrations and sit-ins demanded that recruiters for the military and corporations with Pentagon contracts be barred from the campus. At Claremont Men's College in California, students not only drove the recruiter for napalm manufacturer Dow Chemical off campus, they literally chased him out of town. In April 1967, some eight hundred Columbia students drove Marine recruiters off campus. The protesters were attacked in turn by two hundred right wing students.

Anti-Vietnam demonstrations also included burning draft cards, setting the American flag afire, sitting in at induction centers, lying down in front of troop trains, and breaking into draft centers and burning files. Joining students in their protests were many antiwar ministers, priests, rabbis, doctors, professors, and scientists, including Nobel Prize winners.

On April 15, 1967, a Spring Mobilization to End the War in Vietnam attracted three hundred thousand protesters to New York's Central Park, where 175 youths defiantly threw their draft cards into a bonfire. Picket signs proclaimed, "Burn Draft Cards, Not People."

Some twenty thousand demonstrators left the park to march through the streets, shouting, "Hey, hey, LBJ, how many kids did you kill today?" and "Hell, no, we won't go!" Some New Yorkers cheered, applauded, and chanted with them.

Others, infuriated, climbed on top of cars to shout, "Bomb Hanoi!" Construction workers threw down wet concrete and white paint on the marchers, who were also hooted at by American Nazi Party members.

Fifty mounted police rode into the marchers, scattering them as hundreds of police on foot waded into the crowd, clubbing demonstrators who tried to escape.

Next month a Brooklyn dermatologist, Captain Howard Levy, refused to train medical corpsmen for service in Vietnam. He branded the Green Berets—special U.S. guerrilla forces—fighting there "liars and thieves and killers of peasants and murderers of women and children." Court-martialed, he introduced proof at his trial that the Green Berets tortured prisoners and paid bounties to Montagnard tribesmen for the ears of Viet Cong they killed.

He was sent to prison for three years. Dr. Arthur Blank, who served in Vietnam for over a year as chief psychiatrist at a Third Division hospital, declared that Dr. Levy's opposition to the war was widely shared by army doctors.

"The Gallup poll has told us that the percentage of Americans who think our involvement in Vietnam is a mistake is now approaching a majority," Dr. Blank said. "Yet the army is asked to carry on as if this were not so. The government tells the generals: You must never allow a soldier to say what perhaps a quarter of the U.S. Senate may say."

More and more middle-class youths joined the demonstrations. "The war in Vietnam is fundamental to the radicalization of youth everywhere," said the famous Swedish sociologist Gunnar Myrdal. "It has started young people everywhere thinking about causes and events."

SDS called for an escalation of antiwar strategy "from protest to resistance." Folksinger Joan Baez, along with artists, professors, Quakers, and clergymen who founded the Committee of Draft Resistance, urged all Americans to "organize and encourage resistance to, disruption of, and noncooperation with all the war-making machinery of the United States."

Some 320 scientists, writers, professors, and ministers, including Nobel Prize winner Linus Pauling and Episcopal Bishop James A. Pike, pledged to raise funds for the movement.

A new peace mobilization in October brought to Washington another fifty-five thousand demonstrators representing 150 antiwar groups. The apprehensive administration put twenty thousand armed forces on standby alert at nearby military bases. Addressing the mobilization Dr. Spock denounced President Johnson for campaigning as a peace candidate then "betraying us within six months."

When some of the demonstrators sought to invade the Pentagon, soldiers and federal marshals beat many severely with rifle butts and nightsticks. Some 128 were arrested, including the mobilization's organizer, David Dellinger, and author Norman Mailer, who later described the "seige of the Pentagon" in his book *Armies of the Night*.

Antiwar demonstrations took place simultaneously in Oakland, Boston, Cincinnati, Chicago, and a dozen other cities. At Oakland's mobilization, four thousand demonstrators tried to block the entrance to the induction center. Along with reporters covering the event, they were Maced and beaten by police. Two dozen had to be hospitalized.

Don Brice, president of the News Directors Association, charged, "These attacks were not only unprovoked, but . . . some members of the Oakland Police Department were deliberately selecting news people as targets for this treatment."

California Governor Ronald Reagan said of the incident, "The work of the Oakland Police Department . . . was in the finest tradition of California's law enforcement agencies. The officers displayed exceptional ability and great professional skill." He added, "The taking of alleged grievances to the streets cannot and will not be tolerated." One antiwar lawyer sent him a copy of the Bill of Rights by special delivery.

A unique situation arose when draft card burner Don Baty publicized his resistance by seeking sanctuary in a Methodist church. The Reverend Finley Schaef refused to turn him over to U.S. marshals, insisting, "He has committed no crime in refusing by conscience to kill." The marshals climbed over the bodies of some one hundred nonresistant sympathizers protecting Baty at the altar. Seized, handcuffed, and carried off, he raised two fingers defiantly in the "V" peace sign. In jail he went on a hunger strike, and he had to be carried into court.

"I am not simply a number to be handcuffed, ordered around, tried, and sent off to a penitentiary," he told the judge. "I am Donald Baty, a young human being, struggling to cope with a bewildering world." He was sentenced to four years in prison.

In December 1967, some forty antiwar groups initiated a national Stop the Draft Week. There were mass arrests in five cities for trying to close down induction centers. Those incarcerated included Dr. Spock and 585 peaceful demonstrators in New York City. The ACLU accused New York police of using unnecessary violence in making the arrests. "By Friday afternoon," the ACLU report stated, "the police had completely lost their ability to distinguish between disorderly conduct and free assembly."

When gangs of pro-war longshoremen attacked the antiwar demonstrators, police arrested only the demonstrators. "One important factor in peace demonstrations," stated Algernon D. Black, chairman of the New York Civilian Complaint Review Board, "is that the police—perhaps to a higher percentage than the general population—are likely to have strong nationalistic and militaristic feelings favoring any war in which the United States is involved. They tend to have some prejudices against pacifists and conscientious objectors and all war protesters."

By the end of that turbulent year, Senator Robert Kennedy painted a dramatic picture of an American society tearing itself apart over the war:

"Demonstrators shout down government officials, and the government drafts protesters. Anarchists threaten to burn the country down, and some have begun to try—while tanks have patrolled American streets and machine guns have fired at American children. . . . Half a million of our finest young men struggle, and many die, in a war halfway around the world; while millions more of our best youth neither understand the war nor respect its purposes, and some repudiate the very institutions of a government they do not believe."

General David Shoup, retired Marine commandant, declared that the administration's excuses for fighting in Vietnam were "a bunch of pure, unadulterated poppycock," and that the real issue was a civil war between Vietnamese nationalists and the side the U.S. was backing—"those crooks in Saigon."

After the powerful Tet offensive at the end of January 1968, Americans no longer believed the administration's assurances that there was "light at the end of the tunnel," with victory not far off. More than 1,300 clergymen signed a defiant statement pledging to support draft resisters, and they invited arrest for "aiding and abetting" them.

At a January luncheon of fifty women invited to the White House, actress Eartha Kitt created a sensation by publicly denouncing the war policies of Lady Bird Johnson's husband.

"You send the best of this country to be shot and maimed," Kitt accused. "They rebel in the streets. . . . They don't want to go to school because they're going to be snatched off from their mothers to be shot in Vietnam!" Lady Bird wept.

With the war escalating to a cost of thirty thousand Americans killed and over a hundred thousand wounded, Senator Eugene McCarthy of Minnesota suddenly announced in early 1968 that he would try to prevent the president's renomination by seeking to become the Democratic candidate himself. All over the country, enthusiastic antiwar "McCarthy kids" rallied to his banner in what became known as "the children's crusade." The Americans for Democratic Action (ADA) endorsed McCarthy's candidacy, a humiliating slap at Johnson. A Gallup poll showed that half the American people now considered U.S. involvement in Vietnam a mistake.

On March 12, 1968, McCarthy scored a stunning upset by winning the New Hampshire Democratic primary election. Three days later, Senator Robert Kennedy abruptly announced that he, too, would, as a peace candidate, oppose the president for renomination.

These unexpected challenges to a sitting president from within his own party were almost unprecedented in American history. Johnson was forced to realize what columnist Walter Lippmann, a respected adviser of presidents, had tried to tell him: "To wage a land war on the Asian continent is a colossal mistake. To wage it with an army of drafted men is a colossal mistake. It is one of the principal causes of disunity of the American people."

Swallowing his pride, Johnson made a decision that stunned the country. In a March 31 TV broadcast, he announced that he would not seek reelection, and that he was curbing the bombing of North Vietnam. He urged Ho Chi Minh to enter peace talks with the United States.

McCarthy's young supporters were jubilant. College students marched through New York's Greenwich Village clapping, shouting, and singing, "Good-bye, Lyndon! Good-bye, Lyndon! We're glad to see you go!" Campaigning for McCarthy and Kennedy, they saw hope of creating change by working within the system instead of outside it.

Many in the resistance disagreed. That same month, in the underground newspaper *Berkeley Barb*, Yippie leader Jerry Rubin urged students to revolt against universities who cooperated with the military-industrial complex. "I think the thing to do," he wrote, "is to get a traveling Yippie guerrilla theater band roaring through college campuses burning books, burning degrees and exams, burning school records, busting up classrooms, and freeing our brothers from the prison of the university. We'll probably get beat up or arrested, because physical force is the final protector of law and authority in the classroom. The universities cannot be reformed. They must be abandoned or closed down. . . . We can learn more from any jail than from any university."

When Columbia University graduate student Mark Rudd became president of SDS in March 1968, he won a vote to raise student resistance to the level of confrontation. The following month, he led a strike at Columbia to demand that a proposed eleven million dollar gym be open to the poor of surrounding Harlem. With the cry of "Student Power!" SDS founder Tom Hayden led a contingent in staging a sit-down strike in one building.

61

The Columbia revolt quickly escalated into a protest against university authoritarianism and cooperation with the war effort. Some eight hundred students seized and barricaded five buildings for five days. "We are fighting to recapture a school from business and war," student James S. Kunen wrote in the *Atlantic Monthly*, "and rededicate it to learning and life."

Columbia President Grayson Kirk called a thousand policemen onto campus to drive out students holding the buildings. Over seven hundred protesters were arrested, and 150 students and faculty were injured. Outraged, five thousand students and faculty responded to SDS's call to shut the university down.

Kirk was compelled to cancel classes and exams for the remainder of the school year. The strikers held their own "teach-ins," which they labeled "the free university." In a second police action that injured sixty-eight more resisters, another two hundred students were arrested. The university suspended seventy-five students as ringleaders and flatly rejected SDS's demands for a student voice in administration policy.

Kirk's use of police polarized the campus, radicalizing many students who at first had disapproved of SDS's confrontation tactics. Kirk complained, "Our young people, in disturbing numbers, appear to reject all forms of authority."

He was answered by Harold Taylor, former president of Sarah Lawrence College, who said, "If the university and its present leadership fails to act, either to stop the war, reform the archaic curriculum, grant legitimate student rights, take its students seriously, take a stand against racism and racial injustice, what else can serious people do, students or anyone else, but move . . . into protest and resistance?"

The Columbia student strike eventually won some of its demands, and Dr. Kirk was compelled to resign. The Columbia example was quickly copied on other campuses.

When the president of San Franciso State University agreed to discuss the grievances of student resisters, he was fired on orders from Governor Ronald Reagan. Over two thousand students staged a protest demonstration. Acting president S. I. Hayakawa called in police, who attacked and dispersed the rally, beating up spectators in the process. Infuriated, the student body and faculty went on strike, compelling Hayakawa to shut down the college.

Antiwar demonstrators burn their draft cards outside Selective Service headquarters in Massachusetts. In addition to antidraft protests, two hundred thousand men either evaded the draft or deserted the war effort.

Judge Julius Hoffman presided over the court case involving "The Chicago Eight." William Kunstler was one of the defense attorneys, and U.S. Attorney Thomas Foran prosecuted. Five men were convicted of crossing state lines to incite a riot during the 1968 Democratic National Convention in Chicago. They were David Dellinger, Thomas Hayden, Rennard Davis, Jerry Rubin, and Abbie Hoffman.

Dellinger

Hayden

Davis

Rubin

J. Hoffman

Kunstler

Foran

A. Hoffman

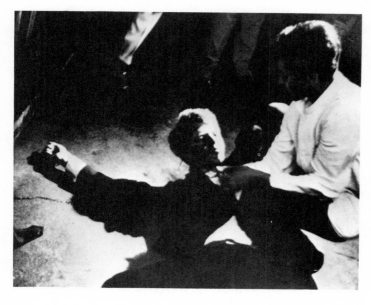

Senator Robert F. Kennedy lies on the floor at a Los Angeles hotel after he was shot the night of his California primary victory. The murders of the Kennedy brothers and civil rights leader Martin Luther King, Jr., led to a great loss of faith within American society.

The student crisis sharply dramatized the serious generation gap between young and old and made it clear that the nation's best educated young people could no longer be ignored in blueprinting the shape of the future society.

In May 1968, two priests, the brothers Philip and Daniel Berrigan, led seven other Roman Catholic dissenters in breaking into the draft office at Catonsville, Maryland. They burned six hundred draft files with napalm, then gave themselves up for arrest.

Father Dan had visited Hanoi and observed how napalm bombs dropped by U.S. bombers had set North Vietnamese children afire. "I went to Catonsville and burned some papers," he said, "because the burning of children is inhuman and unbearable."

Defense lawyer William Kunstler told the jury, "They were trying to make an outcry, an anguished outcry to reach the American community before it was too late. I think this is an element of free speech to try, when all else fails."

But a jury found the Berrigans guilty, and they were sentenced to three-and-a-half years in prison. Father Dan jumped bail to continue his resistance in the anti-Vietnam underground. More than three hundred people risked jail to shelter him as he moved from one family to another, meeting with peace groups. It took the FBI four months to apprehend him.

On June 5, 1968, Robert Kennedy, campaigning for president in opposition to the war, was shot in Los Angeles by Sirhan Sirhan, a Jordanian-born American. He died approximately 25 hours later.

The Harvard *Bulletin* noted, "It was . . . 'the year the golden college stuff stopped.' Following hard on the assassinations of Martin Luther King and Robert Kennedy, that Commencement was marked by a pervading bitterness." The country mourned, and antiwar violence escalated.

One resistance group bombed the New York draft office, another bombed the draft board office in Lancaster, Pennsylvania. Draft board offices in Berkeley and in Madison, Wisconsin, were also firebombed, and a fire was set inside Selective Service headquarters in the capital.

A Yippie flier told students, "Disobey your parents. Burn your money. . . . All our institutions are man-made illusions. . . . Break down the family, church, nature, city, economy. . . . What is needed is a generation of people who are freaky, crazy, irrational, sexy, angry, irreligious, childish, and mad. People who burn draft cards, burn high school and college degrees."

Yippies and other student anarchists called for the abolition of all government, to be replaced by a society in which everyone did his or her "own thing." They envisioned communes like the utopian societies set up during the nineteenth century, whose members would love and help one another. But most of the earlier idealistic experiments had quickly crumbled, and so did most of the hippie and Yippie communes set up in the sixties.

Vice President Hubert Humphrey, campaigning in 1968 on the "politics of joy," sought to avoid any mention of Vietnam. But he could not live down his enthusiastic cry the previous year, after visiting Saigon before Tet: "This is our great adventure and a wonderful one it is!"

The National Mobilization Committee to End the War in Vietnam determined to block his nomination at the Democratic Convention in Chicago in August 1968. SDS members came to Chicago from all over the country, along with Yippies led by Abbie Hoffman and Jerry Rubin. The Yippies alarmed Mayor Richard Daley by spreading rumors that LSD would be put in the city's water supply to "turn on" Chicagoans.

Daley turned Chicago into an armed camp. The Convention Hall amphitheater was ringed with barbed wire and barricades, like a fortress. Illinois National Guardsmen were mobilized, with army troops and armored personnel carriers standing by.

The New York Times noted, "The Convention thus became, before it even convened, the first national [U.S.] political convention in memory to require the protection of troops."

The vast majority of demonstrators who came to Chicago were peaceful. But all week long, scenes of violence swirled across the nation's TV newscasts, showing young people being attacked, clubbed, and dragged bleeding into police vans. Daley's blue-helmeted police officers swung nightsticks furiously at everyone in their path, then deliberately beat TV camera operators filming these scenes.

Demonstrators were scattered by tear gas hurled by National Guardsmen in gas masks. Ordered to leave the area, thousands of demonstrators sat down where they were, chanting, "Hell, no, we won't go!"

The police charged wildly into the sitting protesters, clubbing those on the ground as well as those who tried to flee. Weeping people hurt in the crush cried for help. Police cracked heads right and left, kicking victims as they crumpled. People who tried to shield fallen friends were also clubbed and kicked. Arrested demonstrators were hit with nightsticks as they were dragged along the ground.

Reporter Nora Sayre declared, "I saw seven policemen beating one girl—long after she had fallen; a row of sitting singers whose heads were cracked open by a charge of running cops." A medic wearing a white coat and Red Cross armband was grabbed and beaten to the ground, his face bloodied.

A few enraged demonstrators fought back by throwing firecrackers and blazing trash bins at the police. Some hurled rocks, while others threw sawhorses set up to block traffic. From a few upper-story windows of the Hilton Hotel, ashtrays, bricks, and other debris were hurled down at the police.

When one well dressed woman indignantly protested the brutality of police in arresting demonstrators, policemen sprayed Mace in her face, clubbed her to the ground, dragged her to a paddy wagon, and threw her in. Nearby, police on motorcycles charged into the crowd, knocking people down and running over them. Some victims were ten- to twelve-year-old children.

Inside the Convention, Senator Abraham Ribicoff was made aware of what was going on outside the hall. From the rostrum he denounced Mayor Daley for using "Gestapo tactics." Purple with rage, Daley shouted back a profane defiance.

By the time the "Battle of Chicago" was over, it had caused seven hundred civilian and eighty-three police injuries, with 653 people jailed. Out of three hundred reporters assigned to cover the events in Chicago, sixty-five had either been injured or arrested or had their equipment smashed. The Chicago Newspaper Guild charged that the police had "conspired with each other to wage planned mayhem on men serving as the public's eyes and ears."

The New York Times blamed the Daley regime—and by implication the Johnson-Humphrey forces supporting it—for causing the disorders. The right of assembly had been denied to protesting groups, and excessive, indiscriminate police force had stifled antiwar dissent.

The final verdict on the 1968 Chicago riot was pronounced by President Johnson's own National Commission on the Causes and Prevention of Violence. The Walker Report, named after the commission's director, summed up its findings succinctly by describing the events in Chicago as "a police riot."

Nevertheless, eight leaders of the Mobilization were indicted for conspiracy to cross state lines to "incite a riot," while not a single Chicago police officer was indicted for assaulting demonstrators, reporters, and innocent bystanders. As the Walker Report noted, "There has been no public condemnation of these violaters of sound procedures and common decency by either their commanding officers or city officials."

U.S. Attorney General Ramsey Clark declared, "Hundreds of thousands of young people . . . have seen a raw demonstration of police capacity for violence, and they will never forget it."

Ironically, opinion polls found that most Americans who had watched the riots on TV were indignant not at the police, but at the TV networks for showing them this violence. And they preferred to blame the youthful demonstrators who had been attacked, rather than the police who had attacked them. America's despairing young dissenters saw this bias as just one more example of adult hypocrisy responsible for the "generation gap." A bitter new slogan arose among many youthful dissidents: "Never trust anyone over thirty!"

That conviction grew as the Johnson forces at the Convention swept aside Eugene McCarthy's antiwar candidacy, securing the nomination for Hubert Humphrey, even though he had neither entered nor won any state primary elections, as McCarthy had. This was the final straw that shattered the unity of the Democratic party. Millions of Democrats abandoned the party, assuring the election of Republican Richard M. Nixon, who promised that he had a plan to end the war quickly.

As a backlash against these stormy events, and against ghetto riots, millions of "middle Americans" supported a third-party candidate—Governor George Wallace of Alabama. He promised that if his American Independent Party won the election, he would keep peace in the streets with "law and order" if it took "thirty thousand troops . . . with two-foot-long bayonets."

As his running mate, Wallace chose retired Air Force General Curtis

LeMay, who had his own plan for ending the Vietnam war: "Bomb 'em back to the Stone Age!" Asked whether that plan included nuclear bombs, LeMay replied, "If it was necessary."

Worried by Wallace's appeal in the South, Nixon lured conservative southern voters with a "southern strategy," promising to sabotage school integration, support big military appropriations, and impose "law and order." He vowed to listen to "the great Silent Majority . . . the forgotten Americans, the non-demonstrators."

At the last moment in the campaign, Humphrey broke with Johnson's Vietnam policy in the hope of winning back defecting Democrats. But it was too late. Nixon won a narrow victory, and America changed direction, moving to the right. Some who voted for him believed his promise to end the war quickly; others voted for him as a backlash against upsetting demonstrations of all kinds—antiwar, antidraft, antisegregation.

Impatience with the war soared as Johnson finished his term. By this time, the student resistance had even reached down into sixty percent of all high schools and junior high schools, according to a survey by the National Association of Secondary School Principals. Almost 215,000 pre-college students were now active in antiwar demonstrations, and almost 3,700 had been arrested one or more times while demonstrating.

One month after President Nixon took office, a third annual mobilization of Clergy and Laymen Concerned About Vietnam convened in Washington. The Reverend William Sloane Coffin; Mrs. Coretta King, wife of the slain civil rights martyr; and other antiwar leaders met with Nixon's adviser, Henry Kissinger. He assured them that the new president intended to "wind down the war" as quickly as possible. But Nixon persisted in continuing the war throughout the whole four years of his first term.

When Ohio high school students wore black mourning bands to class to signify sorrow over the war, three who refused to remove them were suspended. But in February 1969, the Supreme Court ruled that students were entitled to freedom of expression of their antiwar views during school hours.

"Students in school as well as out are persons under our constitution," wrote Justice Abe Fortas. "They are possessed of fundamental rights which the state must respect."

Nixon labeled all dissenters "young criminals posturing as romantic revolutionaries . . . a severe internal security threat." He ordered the FBI to keep closer tabs on them.

In April 1969, the University of California at Santa Barbara refused to allow Jerry Rubin, one of the defendants in the Chicago Eight trial, to speak on campus. When students staged protest demonstrations, a few hotheads set fires, and police were called in. One student was killed by police while he was trying to put a fire out, and four others were wounded by shotgun blasts.

"If it takes a bloodbath," Governor Reagan declared angrily, "let's get it over with. No more appeasement!"

Another campus crisis erupted that month at Harvard, where SDS demonstrators seized an administration building and ousted nine deans. They demanded that Harvard end its partnership with the military establishment and stop expanding its space at the expense of poor urban neighbors. The university summoned police.

As students fled, *The New York Times* reported, "they were beaten and kicked by the policemen, many of whom had removed their badges [to prevent identification]. There was no excuse for the savage club-swinging that marred the police activity."

A thousand Harvard students staged a three-day protest demonstration.

Early 1969 also saw campus disorders spread to MIT, Howard, Sarah Lawrence, and other universities. The chief grievances were "perversion of a university's purpose" to serve military ends, and the refusal of administrations to give students a voice in shaping university policy.

Racism was the issue at Cornell in April, when a burning cross was thrown on the porch of the black girls' cooperative. Black students took over Willard Straight Hall with rifles and shotguns. After the administration negotiated a settlement of their demands, the black students, brandishing their weapons, made a dramatic exit in front of TV news cameras.

When students demonstrated to demand job opportunities for blacks in the construction of campus buildings at the State University of New York at Buffalo, New York Governor Nelson D. Rockefeller declared, "I think that students have assumed a share of social responsibility in the life of our community, and I applaud them for it."

The ACLU observed in April, "Students' protests have in great degree been motivated by extraordinary selflessness, idealism, and altruism."

This view of student demonstrations was not shared by President Nixon, who warned, "We have the powers to strike back if need be, and to prevail. The nation has survived other attempts at insurrection. We can survive this."

The resistance sought to dramatize the fact that the thousands of GIs who had died in Vietnam were not mere armed forces serial numbers, but people's sons with names. They organized a candlelight procession across Arlington Memorial Bridge in Washington. Each marcher wore a placard bearing the name of one of the dead. One by one these were dropped into an open coffin.

In June, a group of Quakers from Philadelphia attempted to read, from the steps of the Capitol, the list of Americans killed in Vietnam. They were arrested, photographed, fingerprinted, and charged with unlawful assembly; some were jailed. Senator Jacob Javits denounced their persecution, and a General Sessions judge ruled the Quakers' demonstration peaceful and nondisruptive.

By June 1969, a Harris poll showed students in revolt on two out of three American campuses. Another poll revealed that, prior to the use of police against students, ninety percent of students had held a favorable opinion of police. Now, ninety percent instead considered them brutal and unfair. A Gallup poll that month also found most students convinced "that society as a whole is seriously ill and that changes are imperative."

The student body president of the University of Colorado told the state's Board of Regents, "You brought us up to care for our brothers . . . not to run away from injustice, but to recognize it and fight and destroy it. And now you castigate us . . . because we think and care."

Like President Nixon, California Governor Ronald Reagan saw the student revolt as subversive. At the 1969 National Governors Conference, he called for a "full and complete investigation into the instigators of campus unrest." The governors rejected his proposal.

On June 9, the National Commission on the Causes and Prevention of Violence, headed by Dr. Milton Eisenhower, branded as false the view that campus unrest was the result merely of a "conspiracy of student radicals."

The CIA nevertheless secretly spied on college student movements, hoping to discover Communist links to their demonstrations. When CIA Director Richard Helms delivered a report of this investigation to National Security Adviser Henry Kissinger in the White House, he warned, "This is an area not within the charter of this agency. Should anyone learn of its existence, it would prove embarrassing for all concerned."

In June 1969, former Secretary of Defense Clark Clifford suddenly declared in the influential *Foreign Affairs Quarterly* that he was convinced America's military course in Vietnam had been both wrong and hopeless. He called for one hundred thousand troops to be withdrawn by December, with all combat forces pulled out of Vietnam by the end of 1970.

When the Chicago Eight were put on trial in September, Nixon was determined to make an example of them, to discourage further antiwar demonstrations. The defendants were Yippies Abbie Hoffman and Jerry Rubin, SDS founders Tom Hayden and Rennie Davis, Black Panther leader Bobby Seale, pacifist David Dellinger, chemistry professor John Froines, and sociologist Lee Weiner.

The trial commanded national attention because it pitted the government squarely against leaders of the resistance. The judge was diminutive Julius J. Hoffman, who denied almost every motion made by defense attorneys William Kunstler and Leonard Weinglass, while favoring almost every motion made by the prosecution.

The defendants considered Judge Hoffman's rulings so blatantly biased that they displayed open contempt for his court, making a shambles of the proceedings during the entire twenty-one weeks of the trial. Abbie Hoffman—no relation to the judge—accused both the court and the government of a political conspiracy against the Chicago Eight.

He set the tone of the trial by announcing, "I should plead guilty by reason of sanity." He explained to the jury, "The institutions of America were crumbling. . . . All we had to do was sit there, smile and laugh, and the whole thing would come tumbling down because it was basically corrupt and cruel."

Telling the district attorney, "I've never been on trial for my thoughts before," he blew kisses at the jury.

Judge Hoffman snapped humorlessly, "The jury is directed to disregard the kiss thrown by the defendant Hoffman."

Although the jury dismissed the conspiracy charge, they found Dellinger, Hayden, Davis, Hoffman, and Rubin individually guilty. First sentencing each of them to prison terms of four years for contempt of court, Judge Hoffman added five concurrent years and a five thousand dollar fine each for their "crimes." He denied bail, calling the defendants "too dangerous to be at large."

Jerry Rubin told him, "Julius, you have radicalized more young people than we ever could!"

Demonstrations against the trial erupted in Washington, Boston, Chicago, and other cities. Yale historian Staunton Lynd declared, "The government says the defendants conspired to riot. I, on the contrary, say they organized a process of petitioning just as Sam Adams and Tom Jefferson did before them."

State bar associations were upset by the judge's conduct on the bench. An appeals court overturned Judge Hoffman's denial of bail, and the defendants were released from jail. Later, the appeals court overturned all the judge's contempt sentences and also set aside the rest of his sentences on all charges because of his prejudiced conduct on the bench.

The American Bar Association praised the reversal of Hoffman's sentences and deplored the trial as a government attempt to restrict the free movement of political dissenters around the country.

President Nixon had withdrawn twenty-five thousand troops from Vietnam in June. On September 16, 1969, he announced withdrawal of another thirty-five thousand. But these token withdrawals from a force of over half a million did not satisfy the antiwar movement, which laid plans for new demonstrations in Washington and other cities on October 15. A poll showed that now fifty-seven percent of the public favored a total withdrawal of *all* troops by a specified date.

The October 15 Vietnam Moratorium attracted huge turnouts all over the country. Over three hundred thousand peaceful demonstrators marched on Washington. In a forty-hour vigil, placards with the names of dead American soldiers and destroyed Vietnam villages were carried past the White House.

The president let it be known that he would not look out the window; he would watch the televised football game instead. When the crowds joined folksinger Pete Seeger in singing "Give Peace a Chance," Dr. Spock cried, "Are you listening, Nixon?"

Watching from the Justice Department, Attorney General John Mitchell muttered to his wife, Martha, "It looks like the Russian Revolution!"

Four days later, Vice President Spiro Agnew attacked leaders of the antiwar movement, calling them an "effete corps of impudent snobs who characterized themselves as intellectuals." Commenting on their plan to stage an even bigger antiwar demonstration on November 15, Agnew snapped that "hard-core dissidents and professional anarchists" were out to "destroy their country's strength."

On November 3, Nixon went on TV with more angry denunciations of the demonstrators. He insisted that any swift withdrawal from Vietnam "would be a disaster. It would lead to defeat and humiliation for the United States."

The November 15 demonstration was organized by the Student Mobilization Committee—the "New Mobe"—and the Vietnam Moratorium Committee. Twelve coffins filled with the names of dead soldiers were borne through Washington in a huge candlelight procession. A crowd estimated at half a million gathered at the Washington Monument to hear stirring antiwar addresses by Dr. Spock, Senator George McGovern, Senator Eugene McCarthy, and Dave Dellinger. It was the largest gathering for peace ever held in the United States.

The President left town before the event.

In December the country first learned of the atrocities committed by U.S. troops at the Vietnamese villages of Mylai and Songmy the previous year, which had been kept secret by high-ranking officers of the Americal Division. As many as six hundred civilian men, women, and children had been rounded up, huddled together, then killed by automatic weapon fire. Some families had been blown up in their huts with hand grenades. Other huts were set on fire, and the families were shot as they came running out.

Public outrage led to the arrest and court-martial of 1st Lt. William Calley for having ordered these criminal acts. Calley called the actions "legal and justifiable acts of war. . . . They were all enemy." He was convicted of the massacre, but the U.S. Army paroled him.

As Christmas approached, the president sought to appease bewildered and angry Americans by announcing the withdrawal of another fifty thousand troops. At the same time, a new draft lottery was held, supposedly a fairer system to decide which draftees would be sent to Vietnam as replacements. More than ten thousand draft resisters had already fled to Canada and Sweden. The army admitted there had been over 73,000 desertions.

By the end of the sixties, student militancy had achieved some, but not all, of its goals. Most university administrators were listening and responding to demands for change. Many scrapped ROTC programs and Pentagon research grants and began recruiting more minority students. Student representatives were added to faculty committees and were even allowed to sit on some university governing boards.

Students had also stirred up the whole country over the war in Vietnam, in the process toppling one president and forcing another to begin "winding down" the war.

Those were no small achievements for a minority group that, prior to the sixties, had been totally powerless.

7

A DIFFERENT LIFE-STYLE— THE COUNTERCULTURE

*I*n April 1969, the *Berkeley Barb*, the underground newspaper, demands that a dusty, unused three-acre plot owned by the University of California be made into a "people's park." Adopting the plan enthusiastically, hundreds of counterculture Berkeleyites and San Franciscans—hippies, Yippies, street people, students, and poor local residents—raise a thousand dollars; plant trees, shrubs, and flowers; and install benches, a children's sandbox, and swings.

At dawn on May 15, University Chancellor Roger Heyns sends bulldozers and 250 police to destroy the park. Some seventy-five people sleeping there are kicked out, and an eight-foot cyclone fence is erected around the area. Angered, 1,800 Berkeley students march on the park to reclaim it. A three-hour battle with police ensues. The police fire shotguns loaded with birdshot at students and street people, who fight back with stones. More than sixty people are shot and hospitalized, while an innocent bystander watching the clash is killed.

The fighting goes on for three days. Governor Reagan calls out over two thousand National Guardsmen with gas masks and rifles. When demonstrators stage a funeral march for the dead bystander, a helicopter sprays them with searing tear gas. The crowds grow to thirty thousand and are driven off by the guardsmen. More than 150 people are hurt, including police, and there are nine thousand arrests. Guardsmen surround the fence to prevent further attempts to reopen the People's Park.

Over 170 outraged university faculty members boycott classes in protest against Chancellor Heyns's and Governor Reagan's use of force. *Newsweek* publishes a photograph showing three female students sitting on the ground facing rows of gas-masked guardsmen with uplifted rifles and fixed bayonets.

"When youthful citizens can be wantonly gassed and beaten, all because of a small, unauthorized park, what has happened to America?" the editors ask. "What has happened to our sense of perspective, our tradition of tolerance, our view of armed force as a last—never a first—resort?"

What has happened is the emergence of a formidable counterculture that perplexes and alarms the Establishment.

Like their parents, most teenagers in the fifties were basically content with the status quo. They prepared to take their place in the social order without questioning the values of the government or business world. Middle American teens wore ducktails and ponytails, and they drove fast, flashy cars, racing each other at intersections and in drag races. Cruising Main Street was a favorite pastime. Conformity was the order of the day.

Middle America looked askance at a small group of disillusioned fifties dissidents who had adopted radical life-styles, dressing and behaving in defiance of middle-class standards. The Beatnik movement was antisocial and anarchistic. Rejecting all traditional values, the Beats, or Beatniks, offered instead an "anything goes" philosophy—"Do your own thing . . . and do it *now!*" Although the Beats were only a handful of society's dropouts, they were forerunners of the sixties' youth revolution.

The rebellious example of the Beats spread first to college students, who became increasingly dissatisfied with the rigidity of a university system that seemed to process them like so many cookies in a bakery. Many were inclined to experiment with new life-styles, including using drugs.

They began rebelling against their Middle American lives in the suburbs; against spending evenings exposed to puerile TV programs; against preparing for conventional nine-to-five jobs; against being required to be neat, well-groomed, and "properly" dressed. Out of this rebellion came the hippie explosion.

As the decade wore on, civil rights fights and anti-Vietnam clashes radicalized many young people. Losing respect for authority, they saw it as unjust, autocratic, often brutal, and mindless. They identified the Establishment, or "square world," with the older generation, whom they saw as polluting the earth and exploiting oppressed people.

At first most youths were enthusiastic supporters of President Kennedy, sharing his goal of a "New Frontier." After his death, many were hopeful that President Johnson's "Great Society" program would end poverty and racial discrimination and bring about world peace. They became alienated when instead the government expended its energy and treasury on the Vietnam War. The assassinations of John F. Kennedy, Martin Luther King, Jr., and Robert Kennedy left the young despairing of a society they saw as violent. Many felt driven to drop out and form a culture of their own—a counterculture.

A clarion call for college revolt came from SDS, whose leaders began organizing college reform movements, civil rights drives, antipoverty programs, and antiwar demonstrations.

The counterculture began to spread among the "Now generation," so-called because they demanded gratification of their needs now, not in the distant future. Many adopted the credo of Yippie Abbie Hoffman, who urged them to "question authority!"

Their new life-style rejected the conservative clothing, short haircuts, clean-cut appearance, social drinking, moral codes, conventions, conformism, racial prejudice, economic goals, and Sunday Christianity of their elders. They waged, in effect, a cultural revolution.

"If adults admired their long hair more, the young would probably cut it off themselves," wryly observed social critic Marya Mannes. "The only thing apparently intolerable to them is our approval."

Long hair became the most visible symbol of young people's right to look the way they pleased. The challenge was quickly met by school authorities, who insisted that the hair be cut. More than half the court cases concerning student appearance involved long hair. The others involved beards, miniskirts, desert boots, and other violations of Middle America's dress code.

What was at stake was youth's demand for recognition of its right to individuality. But sarcastic adults pointed out that, for most teens, the hippie style was just as much a regimented dress code as the conventional style they rejected. Said one teacher, "They're just substituting one uniform for another."

For the hippie look, young people wore patched and torn blue jeans, funky dresses, beaded headbands, fringed jackets, ragged T-shirts, shirts made of scrap material, and mod boots or sandals. Some went barefoot.

People's Park, owned by the University of California, was taken over by a group of local residents. In this photograph, workmen begin building a fence around it as helmeted police watch.

Self-expression was a way of life in the sixties. This student belonged to a guerrilla protest group en route to a campus demonstration.

They decorated themselves with yards of love beads made of shells, eucalyptus balls, peacock feathers, American Indian ornaments, and peace symbols. Girls went braless, and both sexes sometimes painted their bodies and faces with psychedelic colors. The more outrageous their appearance, the more they shocked adults—and the more they enjoyed the sensation they created.

Ironically, while this dress revolution was going on, most sixties employers refused even to allow women employees to wear slacks to work. Nevertheless women by the millions were wearing a sixties fashion—thigh-high miniskirts whose creator, Mary Quant, described their significance in one word: "Sex." Women wore miniskirts with another innovation, pantyhose—combined panties and stockings that let a woman wear miniskirts without revealing the tops of her stockings.

Fashion designers and manufacturers watched the counterculture carefully to latch onto the "latest thing," in order to create excitement among the fashion-conscious middle class. When the hippies began painting themselves, Coty Originals came out with washable body paint in green, blue, and mauve. When some hippie girls began going topless at rock concerts, fashion designer Rudi Gernreich came out with the topless bathing suit, predicting that in five years every American woman would wear one. Many of his other fashions were inspired by hippies, as well.

"What I do," he explained, "is watch what kids are putting together for themselves. . . . The generation feels defeated; nothing seems to make any difference. The look in clothes expresses an anti-attitude, the result of being bored—bored by being told what to do, bored by the hopelessness of the bomb and the abstractions of government, bored by sexual discovery in high school. And so if you're bored, you go for the outrageous gestures. Everything else seems to have lost any meaning."

Many school authorities, sensing defiant dress and grooming as a rejection of authority, barred students who failed to present a conventional appearance. When these controversies would end up in court, youthful defendants sought to convince judges that the way they wore their hair or dresses was a symbol of social protest protected by the First Amendment.

In 1967 a high school sophomore named Davis was expelled for his "exceptionally long, shaggy hair." When he appealed his case to a federal district court, the judge ruled against him, demanding, "Just what does the wearing of long hair symbolize? What is student Davis trying to express? Nothing, really."

The Supreme Court refused to hear an appeal of a similar case, leading maverick Justice William O. Douglas to observe sarcastically, "I suppose that a nation bent on turning out robots might insist that every male have a crew cut and every female wear pigtails."

Only two years later, as the sixties wound to an end, a federal court decided in favor of long-haired teenager Tom Breen, ruling that the due process clause of the Constitution protected his hairstyle from being regulated by public school officials without clear proof that regulation was necessary. Noting that no court would think of upholding a haircut rule for adults, the judge saw no reason to do so for youngsters.

Another appeals court in California ruled in favor of Gregor Meyers's long hair because "whether a given hairstyle is 'extreme' or not is a matter of opinion." But other court rulings favored a school's right to ban long hair as "distracting."

Eventually, nationwide acceptance of long hair, as it spread to adult males, made the whole question obsolete.

The right to wear beards in school found courts equally divided. In 1967, when one male teacher sympathetic to the counterculture revolution came to class with a beard, the principal disciplined him, but an appeals court overruled the school. Yet when California student Kevin Akin, 15, protested his exclusion from high school because of a neatly trimmed beard, the court ruled against him out of concern that all his fellow students might follow his example. Nevertheless, a 1969 court ruling set aside a state junior college regulation against beards as a violation of the Fourteenth Amendment.

A similar controversy involved the right of girls to wear slacks to school. Although most schools tried to ban them, courts in New York State and Alabama found "no danger to school decorum" and held that allowing slacks for boys but not for girls was sex discrimination. Girls' slacks, as well as jeans, soon became commonplace in the classroom.

It is part of any cultural revolt to develop its own unique slang, partly to confound those it opposes, partly to develop a bond of community among the cultists. Hippie slang, some of it borrowed from ghetto terms, became almost a foreign language to adults.

To understand something, in counterculture parlance, was to "dig" it. School dropouts and others whose vocabulary was limited found difficulty in articulating their meanings. Often they would begin their sentences: "Man, like, I mean, y'know. . . ." Teens tended to bid each other good-bye with "hip" counterculture clichés like, "See ya later, alligator."

"Too much" meant excessive. "Heads" referred to drug-users. "Pigs" meant cops. "Far out" meant an admirable reach beyond the comprehensible. "Vibes" signified the ambience of an event or place. "Groovy" meant great. A "pad" was a place in which to "crash" or sleep. "Tuning in" meant taking drugs, particularly LSD, or "acid." "Out of sight" meant terrific. "Bread" was money. "Making it" meant being successful; "making out" meant making love. "Getting your head straight" meant coming out of a drug fantasy. Getting high on drugs was known as "freaking out," getting "stoned," "spaced out" or "zonked," "tripping," or "blowing your mind." A "roach" was a marijuana cigarette butt. A "bummer" meant a bad trip. A "be-in" meant a gathering of counterculturists, particularly those using drugs. "To rap" meant to discuss. Approval was voiced with "Right on!" Throbbing rock music was described as "heavy sounds." An "ego trip" denoted vain behavior. A young hippie seeking to persuade people to love instead of fight one another was a "flower child."

Popular slogans of the day were: "Make love, not war"; "Give peace a chance"; and "Black is beautiful." Recognizing that power was the decisive factor in changing society, the counterculture raised the slogans of "People Power" and "Black Power."

Marijuana (pot, grass, or Mary Jane), LSD, speed, and other hallucinogenic or mind-altering drugs were used by many young people primarily as a way of escaping from the disillusionment of the times, turning away from Middle America to focus inward on one's self. When police, government, and medical authorities condemned pot as endangering health, the counterculture refused to believe them.

"The one thing that contributes most to young people experimenting with marijuana," declared Harvard social scientist Bruce Jackson, "is that this is the one subject that the older generation has made it a point to consistently lie about."

Many youths felt that the older generation, while objecting so strenuously to their use of drugs, were being hypocritical because of the social acceptance of drinking, another mind-altering habit; smoking, possibly more addictive and harmful than pot; and the widespread adult use of prescription drugs.

In 1958, there had been less than ten thousand arrests throughout the country on drug charges. By 1968, that figure had soared to 162,000, with hundreds of thousands more taking drugs but avoiding detection by the law. In addition, the age level of those arrested dropped drastically. In 1958, only thirty-five percent of those arrested had been under twenty-five; in 1968, almost seventy-seven percent were.

"Drug abuse is increasing in epidemic proportions," declared John F. Ingersoll, director of the Justice Department's Bureau of Narcotics and Dangerous Drugs, "and has become a fact of life, if not a way of life, to a sizable segment of our youth population, where we can least afford it to take root."

Grammar and high school youngsters experimented with different ways to "get high," including sniffing model airplane glue, eating morning glory seeds and baked banana peel scrapings, and smoking catnip, all of which were alleged to be hallucinogenic.

The high priest of the sixties drug culture was Professor Timothy Leary, fired from Harvard with Professor Richard Alpert for LSD experiments with students. In Milbrook, New York, they founded the League for Spiritual Discovery to "introduce the sense of psychedelic celebration." Prescribing LSD even for seven-year-olds, Leary coined the motto "Turn on, tune in, drop out," meaning that one should use drugs, get in touch with psychedelic experience, and drop out of the square world.

"Laws are made by old people," Leary told Dane Archer in a 1968 interview, "who don't want young people to do exactly those things young people were meant to do—to make love, turn on, and have a good time."

The use of drugs accentuated the growing generation gap between young people and their parents, leading to a sharp rise in teenage runaways. In 1969, authorities estimated the number to be over half a million, almost double that of just four years earlier. FBI Director J. Edgar Hoover blamed a lack of communication between teens and parents on problems like drugs, sex, the draft, and the Vietnam War.

Many school dropouts and runaways headed for two counterculture meccas—East Village in New York City and the Haight-Ashbury district of San Francisco.

Haight-Ashbury had been a magnet for fifties Beatniks and artists forced out of other San Francisco neighborhoods by high rents. Early in the sixties, the area began to fill with bearded hippies, women in funky dresses, and spaced-out floaters who patronized "head shops" selling psychedelic art and drug accessories. LSD, which California made illegal in 1965, was freely available on the streets of Haight-Ashbury.

In January 1967, the "World's First Human Be-In" was organized by Haight-Ashbury heads in Golden Gate Park. Timothy Leary and Beat poet Allen Ginsberg addressed some twenty thousand costumed flower children who rang bells, chanted, danced ecstatically, took drugs, and handed flowers to police officers. The event was widely publicized by the media, attracting a hundred thousand or more young people to Haight-Ashbury that year for a "Summer of Love."

Time magazine reported that "teenyboppers" and tourists were overrunning Haight-Ashbury, which had become "the vibrant epicenter of the hippie movement." A special clinic had to be opened to take care of teens on bad drug trips. A counseling service for runaways helped reunite them with anxious parents.

The overcrowding of Haight-Ashbury led many hippies to move away to other parts of San Francisco as well as to communal farms in northern California. Taking drugs—especially "dropping acid" (LSD)—remained a common bond among them.

The hippies were replaced in Haight-Ashbury by dope pushers, petty criminals, Hell's Angels, and other tough types, a far cry from the middle-class flower children. By the end of 1968, crime had doubled in the district, which went downhill rapidly. The president of the San Francisco Board of Supervisors sighed that Haight-Ashbury now looked "like East Berlin."

The basic philosophy of the counterculture was first laid down in SDS's Port Huron Statement, which asked, "What is really important? Can we live in a different and better way? If we wanted to change society, how would we do it? . . . we oppose the depersonalization that reduces human beings to the status of things. . . . We would replace power rooted in possession, privilege, or circumstance by power and uniqueness rooted in love, reflectiveness, reason and creativity."

The Yippies added another dimension. Mocking the absurdities and pretensions of the Establishment, they sought to discredit it by ridicule. Their Voltaire-like satire often succeeded in provoking laughter at American institutions, but it offered no constructive blueprints for building a better society.

The Yippies called for the abolition of all government. Abbie Hoffman told young Americans, "Everything seems meaningless. Socialism, Communism, Capitalism, all irrelevant. What is the Kremlin? I don't know. . . . Churches? What do they mean? There's a sign on the door with twenty different don'ts: don't wear slacks, don't do this, don't do that. That's where churches are at. Revolutionary? What does that word mean? *Dash* is a revolutionary detergent. How do you know what anything means in this system?"

The Yippies resisted American values by opting for a more joyful, spontaneous life-style. They demonstrated scorn for the Establishment's reverence of money by visiting the gallery of the New York Stock Exchange and showering brokers on the floor with dollar bills during peak trading hours.

Hoffman and Jerry Rubin mocked the Democratic Convention in 1968 by choosing a pig as the Yippie candidate. They showed reporters a spray they called their answer to Mace, alleging that it caused police to "develop love feelings toward demonstrators." They also gravely announced a plan to join a march on Washington and "levitate" the Pentagon off its foundation, destroying its power by destroying its gravity.

On Easter Sunday in 1967, Yippies and hippies staged a "Flower Power Love-In" in New York's Central Park. Over ten thousand people, many of them in body paint, joined a celebration that featured rock bands. Pot was smoked, flowers and peace buttons were exchanged, some draft cards were burned, and chants of "Flow-er Pow-er" floated on the spring breeze.

The Yippies sought to repeat this idyll the following March by staging a "Yip-In" celebration of Spring at New York's Grand Central Station. The station was packed with dancing and singing celebrants and floating balloons. Some Yippies removed hands from all four of the station's clock faces, and dancers jumped up on the information booth. Suddenly a phalanx of police charged the crowd, swinging nightsticks indiscriminately. At least a dozen people fell, seriously hurt.

"They drove the kids up the inclined ramp of the 42nd Street entrance," reported *Washington Post* reporter Nicholas Von Hoffman, "banging them in the knees, the groin, the stomach and head."

On the West Coast, notable leaders of the satirical counterculture were the "Merry Pranksters" led by Ken Kesey, author of the best-seller *One Flew Over the Cuckoo's Nest* and a hero of the psychedelic movement. In 1964 he, Neal Cassady, and other Pranksters left for a wild odyssey around America in a funky bus painted with swirling Day-Glo mandalas. They wore costumes, shirts painted white and red, and faces painted in Day-Glo colors, creating a sensation wherever they traveled.

Some older middle-class and professional Americans were also alienated by the Establishment. Rejecting the principle of competition as the American Way, they opted for a different life-style—cooperation, with an emphasis on personal growth and development. The spur for this movement came from California where, in 1961, innovative and experimental courses were first offered at a Big Sur center called Esalen.

Founded by Michael H. Murphy, who had spent almost two years in study and meditation at an ashram in India, Esalen had as its avowed aim to "devise ways of extending man's human potential." During the next seven years, as many as two hundred thousand Californians participated in Esalen activities, which included encounter groups, body awareness classes, sensitivity training, and Gestalt therapy workshops, all designed to "turn on" people without the use of drugs. Participants could also soak nude by sunlight or starlight in stone baths fed by hot mineral springs and be massaged to the sound of ocean waves crashing below.

Centers like Esalen began to spring up around California, then spread to the East Coast as well. The techniques of the human potential movement were unique, designed to free people from restraints imposed upon them by conventional society. In body awareness sessions, for example, participants would roll over each other and gently stroke each other, to give them a sense of the joy of the human body.

Dr. Abraham Maslow, president of the American Psychological Association, called Esalen potentially "the most important educational institution in the world."

Michael Murphy said, "Experiments have been tried here that couldn't have been tried in many other places. Some of these were failures. We hosted certain programs in the late sixties I wouldn't get anywhere near again."

Zen Buddhists also influenced the West Coast, teaching a Western approach to Eastern religion and mysticism. They won followers who set up Zen temples, monasteries, and retreats that attracted many intellectuals, including scientists. Another counterculture development was the American Indian peyote cult, which offered this hallucinogenic drug to adherents. Many were middle-class youths who had broken with their families and were seeking to join and relate to a counterculture family.

Urban drug communes were run by "diggers"—hippies who operated soup kitchens in tenements. Young potheads adrift in the cities turned to them for food and a floor space on which to crash in sleeping bags. Rural hippie communes were founded by society dropouts who pursued a simpler life close to the soil, with "brothers and sisters" who shared cooperative toil.

Counterculture youth were attracted by *t'ai chi chuan*, Sufi dancing, meditation, and the occult. Venerating the environment, they experimented with surviving on natural foods.

A darker side of the counterculture was represented by the Hell's Angels, who in packs of forty rode on Harley-Davidson 74s. One of their slogans was, "Never trust a man who hasn't done time." The summer of 1965 made them infamous in California, after a series of weekend invasions of towns where they roughhoused people and initiated fights.

They wore long hair and beards, sleeveless denim or black leather jackets with the death's-head insignia, pirate-style gold rings in their ears, and sometimes a swastika insignia. They enjoyed frightening "square" communities. Wherever Hell's Angels congregated, police cars gathered warily.

The counterculture of the sixties, in both its peaceful and violent aspects, represented a sharp break with the past.

8

THE ROCK 'N' ROLL REVOLUTION

*M*ore than any other superstar, Elvis Presley was responsible for making rock 'n' roll the music of sixties youth.

His hip-swiveling movements as he accompanied his rock songs on guitar provoked shrieks, tears, and hysterics in young female audiences. Parents disapproved not only of his music, which they viewed as encouraging immorality, but also of his long sideburns, pegged pants, and sultry expression.

Shortly before the dawn of the sixties, I had dinner with Elvis in his Beverly Hills hotel suite, where he was staying while making a movie. I was surprised to find young Presley a polite, modest, deeply religious vegetarian who didn't drink or smoke and who was lonesome for his parents in Tennessee.

That did not prevent 1,500 Presley fan clubs from seeing him as a sex symbol, mobbing him wherever he gave concerts. His early records, "Heartbreak Hotel," "Hound Dog," and "Blue Suede Shoes," were gigantic sellers. Fans flocked to the music stores whenever he released a new record, keeping him on top of the charts more frequently than any other performer in the history of recorded music.

"He represents youth, and the kids can identify with him," film producer

Dave Weisbart told me. "In his singing style Elvis often expresses the loneliness and yearning of all teenage kids as they break from childhood and become adults. It has a defiant note in it, sure. All kids are a little defiant when they break their apron strings. But it's anything except delinquent. . . . Elvis is simply a kid who is emotionally honest—and honestly emotional."

When I asked Elvis about criticism that his act ought to be "cleaned up," because his rock music was an immoral influence on youth, he replied, "Tell me this, sir. Does it make sense to blame it on music if a boy beats up another boy, or robs a place? Of if a teenage girl gets into trouble? Music gives people enjoyment. How can it make them do bad things? . . . Wasn't there any delinquency before I came along with my guitar?"

"Many parents object to your singing technique," I pointed out, "because they feel that in voice, lyric, and manner there are sexual overtones that get the kids all worked up."

"When grown-ups were kids," Elvis replied, "*their* parents had the same objections to 'sexy' music and dancing like the Charleston, the Black Bottom, and the Lindy Hop. I don't recall ever hearing that songs and dances of the twenties and thirties ever made any delinquents. Rock 'n' roll is just today's version of jazz."

The sixties revolt of youth was mirrored by a dramatic revolution in the music they listened and danced to. The era saw the rise, primarily, of rock 'n' roll, with its sexual and drug overtones, but also of folk music and protest songs.

A radical departure from traditional contact dancing, with partners in each other's arms, developed with a new song and dance called "The Twist." Introduced in 1960 by singer Chubby Checker, it started people dancing apart. Facing each other, they gyrated their bodies rapidly from side to side in a kind of sexy shimmy. When screen star Zsa Zsa Gabor was photographed doing the Twist at New York's "in" discotheque, the Peppermint Lounge, the dance became a new rage.

Much of Middle America was shocked by the erotic tone of the dance. It was barred in Tampa, Florida. But some psychiatrists approved, finding it excellent therapy to make dancers forget personal anxieties. In the tense sixties, that was no mean accomplishment.

Two years later, dancers adopted the Latin-beat Bossa Nova, imported from Brazil. Other energetic dances that were briefly popular in the sixties included the Watusi, the Frug, the Jerk, and the Monkey.

Much of Middle America continued to listen to music from car radios and jukeboxes. One sixties record company that scored hit after hit was Motown Records, which popularized the "Motown sound," featuring black performers. Motown introduced Stevie Wonder rendering "Fingertips" (1962); Marvin Gaye singing "How Sweet It Is" (1964) and "Mercy Mercy Me" (1965); the Temptations harmonizing "Where Did Our Love Go?" (1964); and the Isley Brothers crooning "This Old Heart of Mine" (1966). Their hit "Shout" had dancers raising their arms in the air and yelling "Shout!" on cue.

Black performers introduced "soul music"—music with a distinctive black flavor that achieved international popularity. The leading exponent was Aretha Franklin, whose best-selling album *Lady Soul* appeared in 1961. Subsequently she made the hit records "I Never Loved a Man," "Respect," and "Natural Woman." She called soul music a marriage of gospel and blues, of heaven and hell. The top male soul singer was James Brown, who introduced "Papa's Got a Brand-New Bag" in 1965 and "It's a Man's Man's Man's World" in 1966.

Teenagers doted on radio disc jockeys like Wolfman Jack, who howled like a banshee as he played his favorites. He delighted listeners by growling comments like, "Oh, we're gonna rock 'n' roll ourselves to death, baby!" Wolfman, who was Brooklynite Bob Smith, appealed to teenagers because he was so unconventional that American radio stations were afraid to use him. He had to broadcast from a powerful Mexican station that penetrated car radios from Los Angeles to New York.

Early in the decade, rock 'n' roll became the favorite music of teenage America. Enthusiasts called it "blues with a beat." But the talented musician and band leader Duke Ellington sensed its threat to more traditional music. "Rock 'n' roll," he insisted, "has nothing to do with music."

That view was vehemently shared by most of the adult population, who were incensed by what they considered the indecency of its lyrics, its throbbing beat, and the erotic gyrations performed by its vocalizers. Resenting the peace-shattering volume at which rock was played on records and radio by their youngsters, parents warned their progeny that it would damage their eardrums, leaving them deaf by age thirty. In household after household, a familiar cry of parental anguish could be heard: "Turn that @#$%&**$** thing down!"

But for most teens, rock was a form of escape from adolescent problems and frustrations, as well as a wonderful way to wage war between the generations. One corporation vice president sighed, "My kids are really very different from me. They have different points of view in music, for instance. See, they were interested in the Beatles up to Janis Joplin, whom I couldn't stand. After hearing her, I suggested that a wire brush [properly applied] . . . would produce the same sort of screaming. And they looked at me as if I was . . . an old -----, which I was!"

On the other hand, the younger generation ridiculed square music like that performed by the Osmond Family, Lawrence Welk, and Liberace. About the only music that appealed across the generation gap was the old song "Tiptoe Through the Tulips," as sung falsetto by long-haired Tiny Tim, who accompanied himself on a ukulele. The performance was so ridiculous that it tickled both young and old.

The decade began with two big 1960 hits by Elvis—"It's Now or Never" and "Stuck On You." Next year he scored with "Are You Lonesome Tonight?" In 1962 he made the charts with "Return to Sender." At one point, he was awarded a gold record every day.

The next rock 'n' roll sensation to emerge in the sixties were the Beatles of Britain—John Lennon, Paul McCartney, and George Harrison, who began playing in 1957, performing in Liverpool and Hamburg and joined later by Ringo Starr. The "Fab Four" drew their inspiration from Elvis's rock 'n' roll, and also from country music and blues. Lennon and McCartney wrote most of the group's songs, which strove for a "new sound." The Beatles elevated the primitive power of rock from a barbaric tom-tom beat to a sophisticated art form.

In January 1962, they won an audition for a recording contract with Decca, but—to Decca's subsequent everlasting regret—were rejected. Only one year later, they were taking Britain by storm, with English youngsters wearing wigs to imitate their "mophead" hairstyles. Their fame and music quickly spread across the Atlantic. Of the fifteen best-selling hits in 1964, the Beatles were represented by no less than four—"I Want to Hold Your Hand," "She Loves You," "Can't Buy Me Love," and "A Hard Day's Night," from their film of the same name.

Americans first saw them on January 3, 1964, singing "She Loves You" on a tape run on Jack Paar's TV show. Ed Sullivan, impressed, imported the Beatles for a live appearance on his top-rated TV variety show the following month. American teenagers went wild over them, and the cult of "Beatlemania" was born.

Their first film, *A Hard Day's Night*, synthesized the new music with new film concepts. The movie was a pseudo-documentary about a popular rock band (read the Beatles) whose members' lives revolved around music, and who built an ecstatic following of screaming fans from whom they finally had to flee. The film accented the Beatles' high sense of comedy and their charm.

In 1964, the film was echoed in real life as teenagers mobbed the British foursome wherever they appeared during their first major American tour. In Cleveland they were actually dragged offstage by worshipful fans, and they had to be rescued by police, who captured two hundred ecstatic fans in a huge net. In Colorado and elsewhere, entrepreneurs bought the bed linen the Beatles had used in hotel stops and cut it into three-inch squares that were sold to Beatlemaniacs for ten dollars each. When they landed in Toronto for a concert three hours past midnight, the Beatles had to run a gauntlet of seventeen miles of waiting fans shivering in the cold night air.

Foreign nations took note of the phenomenon. *Izvestia*, official voice of the Kremlin, commented, "The reason for the immediate cult of the Beatles is youth looking for idols to replace those worshipped by their parents." President Sukarno of Indonesia scoffed, "Beatlemania is a mental disease."

Looking back on the Beatles, one film reviewer recalled her own reactions as a "teenybopper": "Puberty and the Beatles hit me at about the same time, and it was years before I recovered. . . . The yearning of those 'Yeah! Yeah! Yeah!'s' and the urgency of that high note in 'I Want to Hold Your Hand' touched something deep and restless in my preteen bosom. Suddenly I couldn't get enough of them. . . . My school was in absolute pandemonium. The girls couldn't talk about anything else. . . . My bedroom walls were papered in Beatle Centerfold Modern, and they shook with the fury of Beatle records. . . . We memorized the Beatles' jokes, copied their clothes, and imitated their Liverpudlian slang. . . . [At their concerts] we were in the same place, breathing the same air, sharing the same moment with the Beatles themselves, and the ecstasy was indescribable."

Many adults also liked the Beatles for their charm, sense of humor, exuberance, and music. One reviewer commented that they created "an explosion of joy at being young and alive."

Among their most popular hits were "Sgt. Pepper's Lonely Hearts Club Band," "Let It Be," "Eleanor Rigby," "Help," "Yesterday," "I Feel Fine," "We Can Work It Out," and "All You Need Is Love." Their records spread their fame around the world, and they gave sold-out concerts in country after country. Beatle T-shirts, motor scooters, sneakers, pillows, and lunch kits added to their income, selling by the millions.

Author Tom Wolfe described the frenzy of teenyboppers who jammed the Cow Palace in San Francisco when the Beatles took their tour there in 1965: "The whole front section of the arena becomes a writhing, seething mass of little girls waving their arms in the air . . . like a single colonial animal with a thousand waving pink tentacles. . . . [The Beatles] have brought this whole mass of human beings to the point where they are one, out of their skulls, one psyche, and they have utter control over them. . . . Thousands of teeny bodies hurtling toward the stage . . . a solid line of cops, fighting to hurl the assault back . . . the girls start fainting . . . and getting tromped on. . . ."

In 1966 John Lennon declared, "Christianity will go. It will vanish and shrink. We're more popular than Jesus now. I don't know which will go first—rock 'n' roll or Christianity." Cardinal Cushing agreed that the Beatles *were* more popular than Christ. But later Lennon had second thoughts about the propriety of his assertion, and he retracted it.

Early in 1970 the Beatles broke up—and broke millions of fans' hearts—when the other three objected that Lennon's marriage to Yoko Ono was interfering with the unity of the group. There was no scarcity of other British rock groups eager to replace them. Thanks to the enormous success of the Beatles, a "British invasion" of rock stars had been launched.

The most successful of these groups was the Rolling Stones, whom *Time* magazine called "perverted, outrageous, violent, repulsive, ugly, incoherent, a travesty. That's what's good about them." The group went in for wild escapades that made headlines like "STONES ABDUCT PREMIER'S WIFE FOLLOWING HEROIN BUST" and "STONES THROW TV SETS OUT THE WINDOW."

Mick Jagger, the lead vocalist, was an impatient, surly, middle-class British youngster who was responsible for much of the band's popularity. Among the tunes he and the Stones popularized were "Satisfaction," "Gimme Shelter," "Honky Tonk Woman," "Jumpin' Jack Flash," "Time Is on My Side," and "Let's Spend the Night Together."

Unlike the Beatles, the Stones reflected the darker, more cynical side of human nature. When one of their songs, "Sympathy for the Devil," inspired an outbreak of wild violence at their 1969 concert in Altamont, California, the Stones dropped it from their repertory. But they also sang songs opposing racism, injustice, and the war in Vietnam.

Other top British rock bands of the sixties were The Who, Cream, Jethro Tull, Pink Floyd, the Animals, and the Moody Blues. Peter Townshend of The Who originated the frenzied ploy of smashing his guitar onstage at the end of a concert.

A pseudo rock band called the Monkees were actually mostly actors chosen to play a rock group in a TV show based on *A Hard Day's Night*. Invading the recording charts as a real rock group, they scored hits in 1967 with "I'm a Believer" and "Daydream Believer." One critic labeled their music "junk" but added, "Which is all right. In the fatuity of their enthusiasm lay their very charm."

The year 1965 saw the emergence of the American rock group the Grateful Dead in San Francisco's Haight-Ashbury district. It had the early patronage of a reputed LSD chemist named Owsley, and under its leader, Jerry Garcia, it developed a drug-related style called "acid rock." The band attracted a large underground following of "Dead Heads" who flocked to the group's often free concerts. The Grateful Dead were one of the most prominent rock bands openly opposed to the Vietnam War.

What became known as the San Francisco Sound came out of the psychedelic bands that played to the hippies of Haight Ashbury—the Grateful Dead, the Diggers, Jefferson Airplane, Big Brother and the Holding Company, Quicksilver Messenger Service, Moby Grape, Country Joe and the Fish, It's a Beautiful Day, the Charlatans, the Peanut Butter Conspiracy, Dan Hicks and His Hot Licks, and others. In 1967 this movement had its first commercial hit with the Jefferson Airplane's "Somebody to Love," sung by lead vocalist Grace Slick.

Two of the most influential singers of the sixties were Jimi Hendrix and

Janis Joplin, whom one of *The New York Times* critics labeled "the king and queen of gloriously self-expressive music." They had a huge following among the youth culture exploring itself through drugs and experiencing itself through rock music.

Jimi Hendrix, a brilliant rock composer and guitarist who scored with such hits as "Are You Experienced," "Axis: Bold as Love," and "Electric Ladyland," had been a poor black high school dropout in Seattle. He played electric guitar in a number of rhythm and blues bands, but his career first began to soar in a 1966 tour of England with his own rock group, Experience. The flamboyantly dressed Hendrix broke attendance records with his dramatic, dazzling music, singing lyrics like "Excuse me while I kiss the sky" and "Stone free, to do as I please." A favorite with Hendrix fans was the Beatles' classic, "Lucy in the Sky with Diamonds," the initials of which drug-wise youths believed signified LSD.

Hendrix interacted with his guitar as though it were a lover. His music strongly influenced Peter Townshend of The Who and Eric Clapton, who declared, "From the time I met him, my music changed incredibly."

Hendrix galvanized the American scene when he returned in June 1967 for a gig at the Monterey Pop Festival. He gave a stunning performance of moaning, screaming, heartrending sound that made him, at 24, a superstar of rock. He told the roaring audience, "I could sit up here all night and say thank you, thank you, thank you, you know. . . . What I want to do, I'm going to sacrifice something right here that I really love. . . . This is just for everybody here, this is the only way I can do it, okay? . . . Don't get mad, don't get mad, no."

And then he burned his guitar onstage.

The same bill that night also catapulted to rock stardom a middle-class white "soul belter," Janis Joplin, also 24. The driving force of her extraordinary energy was a miserable childhood in Port Arthur, Texas. "In high school, do you know they once threw things at me in the hall?" she said. "I don't know why. I was strange, sure. It was like the whole environment turned on me, as if the trees said, 'Go home.' They hurt me in Port Arthur." She released her anger and frustration in the song "Kozmic Blues."

Wearing jangling bracelets, funky dresses, and floppy hats, she poured out her anguish in fervent blues, stamping her feet and shaking her hair and body. She got her start singing with a high-intensity electric rock

Bob Dylan has been called the most influential songwriter of his generation. Elusive and enigmatic, he emerged in the sixties as an uncompromising spokesman for the counterculture.

In August 1969, half a million rock music fans filled a field near Bethel, New York, for several days of entertainment. Stage is at far left.

band, Big Brother and the Holding Company, in San Francisco bars and coffeehouses.

"I don't know what happened," she said. "I just exploded."

Starring in a New York concert, she screamed at her youthful audience, "What are you doing in your seats? This is a rock 'n' roll concert!" Her fans surged to their feet and, in an adoring rush, almost swept her off the stage.

The Monterey Pop Festival established her as a superstar along with Hendrix. She was such a smash hit that she was featured in a Monterey Jazz Festival three months later. When she began screaming her first number, "Ball and Chain," people began dancing wildly and prancing in snake lines through the arena. Nothing like it had ever happened in the festival's ten years. Adults as well as teenagers were carried away.

Hendrix said, "The drug scene was opening up things in people's minds, giving them things they just couldn't handle. Well, music can do that, you know, and you don't need any drugs."

But the intensity with which he and Joplin lived and performed led both to depend heavily on both alcohol and drugs. On September 18, 1970, Hendrix died in London of a drug overdose. Sixteen days later, Janis Joplin was found dead on the floor of a Los Angeles motel room, fresh needle marks on her left arm and a supply of heroin nearby. After meteoric careers that had lifted them to superstardom, earning as much as sixty thousand dollars in a single night, both died at age twenty-seven.

The sixties also gave rise to folk rock, developing the folk music of Woody Guthrie, Pete Seeger, and the Weavers into songs of social significance with a rock beat. The artists who worked in this genre were not the hippies who specialized in drug, acid, or hard rock, but jeans-clad singers, sometimes barefoot, who adapted folk music to the mood of the sixties, expressing dissent from a war-oriented society. Their greatest support came from the sixties flower children, many of them into drugs but all dedicated to advocating peace and love. The folk troubadors mirrored their hopes and desires.

The guru of sixties folk music was Bob Dylan, whose "Blowin' in the Wind" became the early anthem of the peace movement. It was Dylan's line—"You don't need a weatherman to tell which way the wind blows"—

that inspired the revolutionary Weathermen movement to give itself that name.

Dylan's lyrics were intelligent, sensitive, and inspiring, enormously appealing to the college crowd. Significantly, he took his stage name from one of his idols, poet Dylan Thomas.

Joan Baez, another popular folk-rock singer, refused to pay income tax for defense spending. She marched with Martin Luther King, Jr., in Mississippi, sang for striking farm workers in Santa Monica, and was arrested at the Oakland Draft Induction Center. Her courage as well as her music inspired thousands of college-age fans. Cartoonist Al Capp depicted her as "Joanie Phonie" in his *Li'l Abner* comic strip, and she was barred from performing in Carnegie Hall.

Other folk-rock stars included Barry McGuire, who sang of impending nuclear doom in his hit, "Eve of Destruction"; Peter, Paul, and Mary, who had hits with Dylan's songs and with "Puff, the Magic Dragon," "All Over This Land," and "If I Had a Hammer"; Sonny and Cher, who scored in 1965 with "I Got You, Babe"; and the 5th Dimension, who epitomized a generation of flower children with the melodic song hits from the musical comedy *Hair*—"The Age of Aquarius" and "Let the Sunshine In."

Time magazine called composers Paul Simon and Art Garfunkel the greatest living rock poets. They wrote and performed the haunting music for *The Graduate*, a film starring Dustin Hoffman, in a role dramatizing the sexual ambivalence of American youth. The theme song of that film, "Mrs. Robinson," became a 1968 hit.

Folk-rock singer and composer Arlo Guthrie, son of the famous Woody Guthrie, scored a hit with his anti-draft song, "Alice's Restaurant."

Toward the end of the decade, some folk-rock artists began singing country and western music. The Byrds had a hit in "Sweetheart of the Rodeo," Bobbie Gentry with "Ode to Billie Joe," and Johnny Cash with the album *Johnny Cash at San Quentin*.

What was called the greatest musical festival in history took place near Woodstock, New York, on a Catskill Mountains farm in August 1969. The Woodstock Music and Art Fair established rock 'n' roll as the official music of youth. Traffic jams twenty miles long forced some of the celebrants to abandon their cars and walk miles to the festival. There was a six-hour delay before the three-day entertainment could begin, with musicians air-lifted to the stage. Food and water were in short supply.

The festival starred Janis Joplin, Joan Baez, Arlo Guthrie, Joe Cocker ("With a Little Help from My Friends"), Sly and the Family Stone ("Higher"), Crosby, Stills & Nash, sitarist Ravi Shankar, The Who ("Summertime Blues"), Canned Heat, the Grateful Dead, and Jimi Hendrix, who closed the festival with a psychedelic, strobe-light, rock version of the national anthem.

Drugs flowed freely among half a million rain-soaked young people who jammed together in the farm's six hundred muddy acres for a long week-end of music, fraternizing, lovemaking, Yoga exercises, and nude bathing in a nearby pond. Two deaths from drugs were reported. A local paper headlined the event: "THE BIGGEST DRUG AND SEX ORGY SINCE THE ROMAN EMPIRE."

"The Woodstock Nation," as the celebrants called themselves, felt bonded by rock, drugs, brotherhood, and defiance of the Establishment. A trun-cated film version of the festival spread the message of "joyous rebellion" across the nation. The reviewer in *Variety* called the screen version "a pop-cultural and sociological celebration beyond belief," adding, "Not all films can be like it, of course, but once in a lifetime is satisfaction enough."

Closing out the decade in December 1969 was another huge musical festival—Altamont, in the Speedway outside of San Francisco. Attracting a crowd of three hundred thousand, it starred the Rolling Stones. Unlike Woodstock, this festival was anything but peaceful because of the use of tough, black-jacketed Hell's Angels as "guards" to "keep order." Five people died from accidents, suicide, and clashing with the Angels. One Angel was tried for murder. Altamont closed the rock era of the sixties on a note of revulsion.

One of the surprise hits of the sixties was Merle Haggard's "Okie from Muscogee," which expressed a redneck view of the rock, drug, and anti-Vietnam counterculture. No one was more surprised than Haggard, who had written the song tongue-in-cheek, only to have its satirical lyrics taken seriously by hand-clapping blue collar and rural Americans.

The California life-style was celebrated by the Beach Boys of Los Angeles, who romanticized carefree sunny days on the Coast with bikini-clad girls and perfect waves in such hits as "Fun Fun Fun," "California Girls," "Help Me, Rhonda," "Catch a Wave," "All Summer Long," "Surfin' Safari," and "Little Surfer Girl."

Other California groups included the Mamas and the Papas ("California Dreamin' "), the Doors ("Light My Fire"), Buffalo Springfield ("Bluebird"), and Creedence Clearwater Revival ("Proud Mary").

The rock music of the sixties was more than just a heavy-beat revolt against traditional pop melodies. Millions of frustrated, angry youths felt that it was "their" music because it frankly celebrated sex, drugs, and an alternate life-style. It encouraged emotionalism and eruptions of energy, providing a deafening explosion of sound that excited the feelings of the young while irritating the older generation.

Rock expressed defiance of the conventional society youth resented, exactly as ragtime had done it for the young people of the World War I, jazz for the youths of the twenties, and swing and folk music for the young of the thirties.

It was part of growing up in the sixties.

9

THEY CHANGED AMERICA'S THINKING—ARTISTS AND WRITERS

*T*he counterculture, which disdained TV as the "boob tube," nevertheless tuned in regularly to one CBS program that made its debut in 1967—the "Smothers Brothers Comedy Hour." Dick and Tom Smothers delighted antiwar activists by mixing their songs and comedy with ridicule of the Vietnam War and the Johnson administration for waging it.

CBS grew increasingly upset with the Smothers Brothers, especially when they invited as guests two folksingers who were secretly blacklisted for their public opposition to the war—Joan Baez and Pete Seeger. CBS executives then demanded the right to censor a tape of every Smothers Brothers broadcast before it could go on the air, in order to water down or eliminate any material that would anger the White House.

The stars resisted and exposed to the media the network's attempt to censor them. CBS cancelled the show in April 1969.

Like everything else in the turbulent sixties, the thinking of millions of Americans underwent significant changes that both reflected and affected the society. The underground press, published on a shoestring, enjoyed enormous influence among the young, especially college students and hippies. Unlike the advertising-supported Establishment press, rebel journals thumbed their collective noses at shibboleths of the old order. They celebrated the "new morality," a fresh perspective on achieving a more satisfying life-style.

On the West Coast, the chief manifestation of the counterculture was the *Berkeley Barb*, the underground paper published in northern California. On the East Coast, it was the *East Village Other*, published in New York City. In 1967, a new magazine called *Rolling Stone* became the voice of the drug/rock culture.

Although the circulation of the counterculture press was small, its influence was widespread. Dr. Eugene Schoenfeld, a Berkeley physician, began writing medical advice for hippies in a column called "HIPpocrates" for the *Berkeley Barb*. By the end of the decade, it was syndicated in fifteen underground papers, as well as in newspapers around the world.

The underground press introduced innovations in the art world, such as Pop Art, which first appeared in 1961. Pop artists filled canvases with the artifacts of our daily lives, like hamburgers, cigarette packs, Coke bottles, and cornflakes boxes magnified to giant size. Enlargements of Popeye and other comic strip characters were also painted by such serious artists as Roy Lichtenstein. Andy Warhol won fame with a huge representation of a can of Campbell's tomato soup.

At first the conventional art world ridiculed Pop Art as absurd and worthless, until some critics perceived it as a satiric look at the shallow, commercial culture that dominated the lives of most Americans.

The next art innovation was Op Art, so called because it presented unsettling optical illusions that surprised the eye. This developed into psychedelic or LSD art, often created under the influence of hallucinatory drugs, which was baffling at first to the older generation. But psychedelic posters, many of them advertisements for rock concerts, quickly became collectors' items. Their bright fluorescent colors, drug-inspired images, and distorted lettering gave viewers the dizzying effect of a trip on LSD.

The posters became so popular among the young that poster stores opened to sell them as room and dorm decorations. In 1967, one West Coast artist sold fifty-seven thousand of his posters in a single month. By the end of the decade, American youths had spent an estimated twenty million dollars on this form of Op Art.

The outstanding name in psychedelic art was Peter Max, whose posters could be found everywhere. His unique colors, style, and designs also appeared on linen, clocks, glassware, tableware, clothes, phone books, album covers—and even on city buses. This transformation of art and product design became so widespread that Max declared, "We are now on the verge of a golden age of infinite peace and beauty. The revolution has been won; it's happened. . . . The things I've learned under Yoga— a message of love, harmony, unity, and symmetry—I try to change into art for the masses. . . . The business people are a vehicle through which I distribute my very intimate ideas."

Max was chiefly responsible for the spread of Op Art to products and to Madison Avenue advertising. An art revolutionary who made a Capitalistic fortune out of the counterculture, he became the "in" artist of the smart set.

In the sixties, the baby boom of post-World War II came of age, creating a demand for another form of art—comic books. During the fifties, these had come under fire as a bad influence on children. But in 1961 they won a huge following with the introduction of such characters as Spider Man and the Incredible Hulk. Superman and Batman, carryovers from earlier decades, shared the riches that flowed out of young people's pockets during the comics' "golden age." Pop Art, both in itself and through the techniques borrowed from it by comic book artists, helped raise the comics to a new level of acceptability. Youngsters thrilled to the adventures of such new comic book heroes as the Fantastic Four, Captain America, the X-Men, and Aquaman.

During the sixties, "Batman" became a TV series so popular that the term "Batmania" was coined to describe the addiction of viewers. Later on, *Superman*, also a TV series, was to become a theater movie so successful that it was followed by sequels.

A few comics of the sixties appealed to a more sophisticated audience. *Mad*, a satirical magazine founded in 1952 to mock "sacred cows" and the media, became a sixties favorite with counterculture youth. Another popular comic was "Peanuts," drawn by Charles Schultz and enjoyed by adults as well as children. Beginning as a modest fifties comic strip, it developed into a sixties smash hit as millions identified with its all-too-human characters—Charlie Brown, Snoopy, Lucy, and others in the "Peanuts" gang. They became so popular that fifty million dollars worth of merchandise tied in with the characters was sold during 1969 alone.

A Yale cartoonist named Garry Trudeau began a cartoon strip called "Doonesbury," which won syndication in 1969. It appealed to intellectuals because it dealt satirically with adults who strove to be part of the counterculture. Those who appreciated it were sophisticated members of the counterculture able to laugh at themselves.

More and more people in the sixties grew worried that the cold war might expand into nuclear war. Their anxiety was reflected in a 1960 film, *On the Beach*, which emphasized the horror of being among the few who might survive in a world devastated by a nuclear holocaust. In 1962 the film *Fail-Safe* made people worry about whose finger was on the nuclear button.

The following year, *Dr. Strangelove, or How I Learned to Stop Worrying and Love the Bomb*, mocked the military-industrial complex as insane, frightening audiences about the dangers of accidental nuclear war.

Hollywood also mirrored other political controversies of the sixties. *Judgment at Nuremberg* (1961) dealt with the trial of the Nazi war criminals by an international tribunal. It had a significant message for youths soon to be faced with being drafted for the Vietnam War—that one had a moral obligation to God to refuse to obey orders to commit crimes against humanity. This defense was frequently cited by draft resisters.

The Russians Are Coming, The Russians Are Coming (1966) poked fun at cold war hysteria, in effect pleading with Americans to look at the Russians as ordinary people like themselves, rather than as faceless enemies. That same year, *Doctor Zhivago*, the film version of a Soviet novel, echoed the message by relating a love story played against the Russian Revolution.

Films in the sixties created sympathy for ethnic groups at home and abroad. *Exodus* (1961) glorified the struggle of persecuted Jews to found a homeland in Israel. *Lawrence of Arabia* (1962) created sympathy for Arabs in their struggle for freedom against the Turks. *West Side Story* (1961) revealed the plight of Puerto Rican immigrants in a gang-ridden New York ghetto.

Hollywood also dramatized the injustice of racial prejudice. *To Kill a Mockingbird* (1962) aroused anger against southern lynch mobs. Sidney Poitier won an Academy Award for his performance in *Lilies of the Field* (1963), the story of a vagabond black Baptist who helps a group of immigrant nuns to build a mission in the Southwest. Poitier also addressed the racial issue in four other films during the sixties—*In the Heat of the*

Night, exposing southern racism; *To Sir with Love*, dealing with ghetto education; *Guess Who's Coming to Dinner*, a film depicting the dilemma of white liberals when a black becomes engaged to their daughter; and *The Lost Man*, the story of a militant black leader hunted by police after a daring robbery.

Spy scares engendered by the cold war were reflected in sixties films. In *The Manchurian Candidate* (1962), Americans are captured by a Communist power, brainwashed into becoming robots, then programmed to return home and commit an important political assassination. The film led millions of Americans to suspect that when John F. Kennedy, Martin Luther King, Jr., and Robert Kennedy were later assassinated, the real-life assassins had to be members of an international conspiracy.

The spy syndrome inspired a whole series of theater and TV films. The first James Bond film, *Dr. No*, was screened in 1963, the year of President Kennedy's assassination. It was followed by a long series of Bond movies and their imitators. The year 1966 alone saw no less than twenty-three spy films and ten TV spy series, including "The Man From U.N.C.L.E." Americans welcomed the spy entertainments as an escape from the stormy real-life events that assailed them almost every night on TV newscasts.

Horror films provided another form of escapist entertainment. Rapt audiences screamed at *Psycho* (1960). Seeking to cash in on the success of this Alfred Hitchcock movie, Hollywood rushed out a series of cheap horror films with such titles as *Werewolf in a Girl's Dormitory*, *The Beast of Yucca Flats*, *Teenage Zombies*, and *Beach Girls and the Monster*.

TV jumped on the bandwagon with its own horror shows but softened them with humor for family audiences. Two of the most popular were "The Addams Family," featuring weird characters, and "The Munsters," a Frankenstein takeoff.

Hollywood also took swipes at the Establishment. *Elmer Gantry* (1960) exposed the hypocrisy of religious evangelism. *The Music Man* (1962) mocked the gullibility of small-town America in falling for the pitch of smooth-talking con men. *Bye Bye Birdie* (1963) had fun with the teenybopper groupie syndrome, while ridiculing baffled parents who asked, "What's the Matter With Kids Today?" *Hud* (1963) took swings at oil-rich Texans.

Other notable films of the era included *The Miracle Worker* (1962), *My Fair Lady* (1964), *Mary Poppins* (1965), *The Sound of Music* (1965), *A Man for*

All Seasons (1967), *Georgy Girl* (1967), *Funny Girl* (1969), *Butch Cassidy and the Sundance Kid* (1969), and *Oliver!* (1969).

Some counterculture audiences preferred to patronize an underground cinema. Andy Warhol experimented with filming armpits, people sleeping, boiling golf balls, and men blowing bubbles, in uncut films that ran on endlessly. *Scorpio Rising*, a 1963 film that was shown at New York's Museum of Modern Art, presented viewers with half an hour of homosexual symbols.

Most critics agreed that the film genius of the decade was Sweden's director Ingmar Bergman. His films *Smiles of a Summer Night*, *The Seventh Seal*, *Wild Strawberries*, *Through a Glass Darkly*, *Winter Light*, and *Persona* were intellectual favorites.

One sixties film with tremendous impact was *Bonnie and Clyde* (1967), a curious blend of comedy and horror. This portrayal of a real-life criminal pair of the thirties romanticized crime as fun, creating compassion for the two bank-robbing lovers as they are gunned down. An enormous box office success, the film also stimulated a revival of thirties fashions.

Moral distinctions were similarly blurred by *The Wild Bunch* (1967), which sentimentalized Old West outlaws. Both *Bonnie and Clyde* and *The Wild Bunch* used slow motion depictions of bloody killings in a kind of "ballet of death," pandering to an audience lust for violence. *The Wild Bunch* was followed by other new-style Westerns that glorified outlaws, furthering the sixties breakdown of Establishment standards of absolute right and absolute wrong.

Because of the increase of violence and sex in films, widespread parental protests led Hollywood to establish a movie ratings system in 1968. Parents were guided by a film's "G" rating, meaning suitable for all ages; "M" (parental guidance advised); "R" (no one under 16 admitted alone); and "X" (no one under 16 admitted).

Another film that created a sensation in the sixties was *2001: A Space Odyssey* (1968). In addition to appealing to science fiction fans, it attracted youths on drugs. "Everyone sees it stoned, or tripping," one teenager said. "Usually the first five rows anyplace *2001* is playing are full of heads, I mean guys really crashing their brains, but they can't get much more than a light-show effect out of it, from my experience."

The drug culture led movie exhibitors in the sixties to revive Walt Disney's 1940 film, *Fantasia*, which drew young crowds who reveled in its early display of celluloid psychedelia.

One of the most influential films of the sixties, which spoke directly to alienated youth, was *Easy Rider* (1969). Depicting the persecution by redneck America of two long-haired, drug-dealing motorcycle hippies, it stirred bitter anger among the young people who flocked to see it. *Easy Rider* was the first authentic mass-audience picture about the youth counterculture. It sharpened the conflict between "them" (square adults) and "us" (hippie youth), branding Americans who were intolerant of a different life-style as brutal, immoral, and unjust.

Another counterculture film of the sixties was *M*A*S*H*. Its black humor depicted the Korean War—and by implication all such wars—as bloody insanity. *M*A*S*H* was considered such an affront to the U.S. Army that at first it was banned on all American military bases. But it delighted antiwar youth of the sixties by debunking war's "glory."

Because it came directly into the home, TV during the sixties was considerably blander than the movies. The networks feared offending family audiences. Americans who sat glued in front of the "boob tube" had their minds dulled by such simple-minded situation comedies as "The Beverly Hillbillies"; "Mr. Ed," which starred a talking horse; "Gomer Pyle," a slapstick comedy about a dumb marine: "I Dream of Jeannie," a childish fairy tale about a sexy genie; and "Gilligan's Island," a foolish takeoff on *Robinson Crusoe*. It was small wonder that the chairman of the Federal Communications Commission, Newton Minow, blasted the networks' TV programming as "a vast wasteland."

All programs were heavily censored, except for violence. Those who sought more adult, risqué TV fare tuned in Jack Parr on NBC's "Tonight Show" at 11:00 P.M., when youngsters were presumably in bed. In 1960, when NBC censors clipped some of his "blue" material as offensive, Paar walked off the show for three weeks. Two years later he quit and was replaced by Johnny Carson, who continued to host the show over twenty years later.

The "Tonight Show" broke the TV taboo against frank sexual discussions. It paved the way for a prime-time NBC comedy show called "Laugh-In," which joked about pregnancy, sex, marijuana, and other TV taboos. A censor was assigned to the set to cut anything too controversial before the tape was aired. The show captured a lot of the lighthearted, irreverent spirit exemplified by the Yippies. Another comedy show also appealing to sixties youth was "Sonny and Cher," a team that in song and wit often reflected the changing times.

If counterculture youth in the sixties were infuriated by police actions against their demonstrations, the older, traditional generation approved of such "law and order." TV programming catered to them with shows glorifying law enforcement—"The FBI," "Dragnet," "The Mod Squad," "The Untouchables," "Burke's Law," and "Ironside." Police were portrayed as lovable nice guys in the situation comedy "Car 54, Where Are You?"

Soap opera moved into prime time with "Peyton Place," which riveted millions of viewers, who became more involved with the melodramatic happenings of fictional characters than with the melodramatic real happenings on the streets of the nation.

In 1966 publishers appealed to the TV soap opera crowd with a barrage of Gothic novel paperbacks. Bearing melodramatic titles like *Thunder Heights* and *Flowers of Evil*, they often involved eerie castles, witches, vampires, and ghosts. For many readers, vicarious identification with the heroines of the TV soaps and Gothic novels offered the only romantic excitement in otherwise dull lives.

War spirit was aroused by TV series like "Combat" and "Rat Patrol," and war was made a laughable experience in situation comedies like "McHale's Navy" and "Hogan's Heroes."

The space race inspired such popular extraterrestrial TV shows as "Star Trek," "The Invaders," "The Twilight Zone," "The Outer Limits," and "My Favorite Martian." Two other sixties TV shows with faithful audiences were "The Fugitive" and "The Prisoner," whose heroes dodged danger in their quest to find justice.

All through the sixties, the networks were under great pressure from leaders of the black community to show blacks in TV roles other than those of chauffeur, cook, or maid. Finally Diahann Carroll was starred as a middle-class nurse in "Julia," and the stereotype was broken. Another milestone was "I Spy," which costarred Bill Cosby with Robert Culp. "Amos 'n' Andy," a staple radio program since 1928 and later a TV comedy, was finally booted off the air in 1965 as offensive to blacks.

The era saw a pivotal change in children's programming. In 1960 the bland "Howdy Doody" show went off the air. The stormy decade made young parents demand better, more educational programs for children than the networks' Saturday morning parade of violent cartoons and old Westerns. In 1969 National Educational Television offered "Sesame Street."

Westerns were still favorite adult TV fare in the sixties—"Gunsmoke," "Wagon Train," "Have Gun, Will Travel," "Bonanza," and "Rawhide." These perpetuations of the stereotype of males as tough, gunslinging, macho men was matched by the stereotype of women as too silly to be taken seriously, as in the popular Lucille Ball comedy series, "Lucy." It was hardly surprising that most counterculture youth disdained TV.

Middle America also had a love affair with doctors in the sixties. This was reflected in the TV series "Dr. Kildare," "Ben Casey," and "Marcus Welby, M.D."

The impact of TV in the sixties was so powerful that it took millions of Americans away from reading magazines. Big advertisers spent their money instead on TV commercials. The loss of both circulation and ad revenue was so great that the famous *Saturday Evening Post* was forced to discontinue publication, soon to be followed by the disappearance of two other giant weeklies, *Look* and *Life*, the picture magazines.

At the end of the decade, the National Commission on the Causes and Prevention of Violence, headed by Milton Eisenhower, reported, "Violence on television encourages violent forms of behavior." That report marked the beginning of a constant struggle between parents and the networks over how much violence should be permissible in prime time TV shows.

Broadway plays of the sixties had less impact on the decade than either movies or TV, because of smaller audiences. They were important, nevertheless, for the influence they exerted in establishing patterns. The 1960 musical *Camelot*, starring Richard Burton as King Arthur, recreated the romantic aura that gave its name to the Kennedy years.

The following year, the cynical musical *How to Succeed in Business Without Really Trying*, starring Rudy Vallee, expressed in farce many of the beliefs of the counterculture about the Establishment—that it was a waste of a life to pursue a career in Big Business; that those at the top were foolish knaves; and that cooperation, not competition, was the only humane goal, as expressed in the curtain song, "The Brotherhood of Man."

In 1965 a musical version of the Don Quixote story, *Man of La Mancha*, starring Richard Kiley, stirred Americans with its popular song "The Impossible Dream." The message was highly inspirational to millions, urging the pursuit of ideals at whatever cost.

If any play epitomized the sixties it was the rock musical *Hair*, which opened off-Broadway in 1967, making such a hit that it moved to Broadway a year later. A colorful, exciting theatrical experience, it was filled with great music, brilliant dancing, and irreverent humor. *Hair* dealt with a key conflict of the era—the clash between long-haired, pot-smoking hippies and uptight adults. Its songs—"Aquarius," "Good Morning, Starshine," and "Let the Sunshine In"—expressed the joy and optimism of the flower children.

The musical declared, "The draft is white people sending black people to make war on yellow people to defend the land they stole from the red people," and urged audiences to "make love, not war." *Hair* became a great international hit, as well as a movie, earning over eighty million dollars.

Another popular Broadway play attacking the Vietnam war was *MacBird*, starring Stacy Keach. A takeoff on Shakespeare's *Macbeth*, it satirized mercilessly the Johnson administration.

In 1968, the issue of homosexuality was raised by the play *The Boys in the Band*, which focused more attention on the gay life than any play had ever done before. The issue was a part of the sixties' revolt against conventional life-styles.

The era closed in 1969 with a Broadway revue that also reflected a change in moral code—*Oh! Calcutta!* Featuring songs and sketches with nude performers, the revue played to sold-out houses in New York. Performances outside the city were raided by the police, who also gave a hard time to nightclub entertainer Lenny Bruce. He was sentenced to four months in the workhouse for using profanity in his performances. Bruce had a great influence on other young performers, who began to be freer in their public language, as a way of defying the conventional morality of Middle America. Bruce died at thirty-nine of a drug overdose.

The decade opened with the suicide in 1961 of writer Ernest Hemingway, whose clipped, spare style in novels like *A Farewell to Arms, For Whom the*

Bell Tolls, and *The Sun Also Rises* influenced writers everywhere. The following year, another literary giant, William Faulkner, died, leaving behind such somber chronicles of the deep South as *The Sound and the Fury*, *As I Lay Dying*, and *Sanctuary*. Their deaths aroused new interest in their books during the sixties.

Although the rapid spread of TV cut into the habit of reading books, there was a resurgence of book-buying when publishers began to issue a flood of cheap paperbacks.

Readers turned on by the counterculture were influenced by *Howl*, a long, obscene poem by Allen Ginsberg, which made them tolerant of homosexuals. When *One Flew Over the Cuckoo's Nest* was published in 1962, it made Ken Kesey's reputation as a counterculture novelist. His wild escapades made him a role model to counterculture youth, who felt encouraged to live outside the society.

Poetry, rarely published in book form because of small demand, suddenly blossomed in the sixties as a result of counterculture heroes admired by youth. John Lennon, the lyricist of the Beatles, published books of poetry and stories, including *In His Own Write*, which sold very well.

Another influential young poet was Rod McKuen, whose books included *Stanyan Street and Other Sorrows*, which he described as "love words . . . for music"; *Listen to the Warm*; *Lonesome Cities*; *In Someone's Shadow*; and *Twelve Years of Christmas*.

Although the turbulent events of the sixties made millions iconoclastic, millions of others sought salvation in some kind of spiritual belief. Conservative Americans made a new translation of the New Testament a bestseller. The counterculture explored Eastern religions. Kahlil Gibran's *The Prophet*, originally published in 1923, enjoyed a rebirth of popularity. The religious mysticism of India was extolled by Herman Hesse, whose earlier novels, *Steppenwolf* and *Siddhartha*, were reprinted in the early sixties.

Human potential movements like California's Esalen and est were influenced by the books of Carl Gustav Jung, whose concept of synchronicity taught that no happening is accidental, but is part of some mysterious preordained plan. Jung also held that all of us carry unconcious memories of the human condition that go back to the beginnings of our species, centuries before we were born.

Jung's mysticism, accepted, curiously enough, by many prominent physicists, was capitalized on in the sixties by self-styled mystics, prophets, astrologers, and other apostles of the occult. Millions of Americans, upset by the chaos of the decade, felt a need to pin their faith on something beyond unpleasant realities, but were uncomfortable with the conventional creeds with which they had grown up.

There was relief to be found in such books as *A Gift of Prophecy* by Ruth Montgomery, extolling the predictions of psychic Jeanne Dixon, and in Dixon's own book, *My Life and Prophecies*. Both books conveniently overlooked many prophecies that had failed to materialize. *Edgar Cayce—the Sleeping Prophet*, by Jess Stearns, added to a widespread belief in supernatural powers.

Another form of escapism in the sixties took the form of science fiction novels and films, stimulated by the adventures of real-life astronauts in space. Perhaps the most influential science fiction novelist, who made Americans think about what may lie ahead in the next century, was Kurt Vonnegut. His books *Cat's Cradle*; *God Bless You, Mr. Rosewater*; and *Slaughterhouse Five* made Americans apprehensive about the future.

The yearning of many to escape from their troubled world into some never-never land was gratified by J. R. R. Tolkien's *The Hobbit*, one of a series of adult fairy tales based on an imaginary world called Middle-earth. Fantasy soon to become fact accounted for the success of Michael Crichton's novel *The Andromeda Strain*, which dealt with outer space. It appeared in 1969, in lucky congruence with the American astronauts' moon shots.

John F. Kennedy's book, *Profiles in Courage*, written while he was a senator, first called attention to his presidential ambitions. Theodore H. White wrote about Kennedy's campaign in *The Making of the President*, while Victor Lasky attacked him in *The Man and the Myth*.

In the last year of Kennedy's life, Americans were treated to *The Kennedy Wit*, compiled by Bill Adler. *A Day in the Life of President Kennedy*, by Jim Bishop, appeared one week before JFK was killed. After the assassination, Americans couldn't read enough about the terrible event, and about Kennedy.

A Thousand Days, by Arthur Schlesinger, described events in the Kennedy White House. *Rush to Judgment*, by Mark Lane, suggested that the assassination had resulted from a political conspiracy and was not just the work of one fanatic. William Manchester's *Death of a President*, appearing in 1967, became the definitive analysis of the Kennedy tragedy.

At the end of the decade, Joe McGinniss shocked Americans with a book exposing the shoddy 1968 presidential campaign of Richard M. Nixon, the candidate Kennedy had defeated in 1960. *The Selling of the President* revealed how the public had been cynically manipulated to accept a phony image of the man who was elected president in 1968, increasing the disillusionment of those turned off by mainstream politics of the sixties.

An attack on U.S. foreign policy, and the way the media reported foreign news, was the thrust of William Lederer's book *A Nation of Sheep*. National anxiety about nuclear war was reflected in *Fail Safe*, a 1962 novel by Eugene Burdick that described a presidential crisis resulting from the accidental launching of a missile. One year later President Kennedy offered, and the USSR accepted, a proposal to reduce the risks of accidental nuclear war between the superpowers.

With Vietnam increasingly becoming the national preoccupation, Morris West's novel *The Ambassador* dealt with the problems of an American diplomat in Saigon. Robin Moore's novel *The Green Berets* glorified the military "advisers" Kennedy sent to South Vietnam to help its troops. But in 1967 Norman Mailer's angry book told Americans *Why We Are In Vietnam*.

One of the most important books of the sixties was William Shirer's *The Rise and Fall of the Third Reich*, the definitive study of Adolf Hitler and Nazi Germany. It explained the horrors of Fascism to young Americans who had been small children during World War II, serving as a powerful reminder that Communism was not the only brand of non-democratic government that Americans had to fear. On the other hand, anti-Communist sentiment was intensified by *Cancer Ward*, Soviet refugee Aleksander Solzhenitsyn's exposé of the USSR's treatment of dissidents.

Some books of the sixties reflected the mood of young Americans who found the Establishment unjust. Michael Harrington's *The Other America*, published in 1962, described the trapped lives of the poor. It inspired many students to join Freedom Rides to the South, and it influenced President Kennedy to prepare an antipoverty program that was developed and carried out by President Johnson.

Joseph Heller's 1962 novel, *Catch 22*, lent weight to Vietnam draft resistance by its portrayal of World War II military life as absurd and insane.

Writer Truman Capote (center) and artist Andy Warhol (right) were major influences on writing and art in the sixties. Cornelia Guest, a socialite, stands beside them at a New York disco in 1982.

That year the novel *Seven Days in May* by Fletcher Knebel and Charles W. Bailey II described a military plot to take over the White House and establish a military dictatorship. Few readers knew that their book was actually based on a real but hushed up 1934 plot by some powerful industrialists to overthrow President Franklin D. Roosevelt.*

Another important exposé of the sixties was *The American Way of Death* by Jessica Mitford, which signaled the first attack on funeral directors who exploited the grief of distracted relatives to extract high burial costs. The book was hailed by the consumer movement, which demanded corrective action. Reforms were hastily enacted by the funeral industry.

Right wing books were fewer in the sixties, but no less strident. Russian-born Ayn Rand rallied Middle America against liberals and the counter-culture. Her earlier books, *The Fountainhead* and *Atlas Shrugged*, enjoyed a new vogue among conservatives during the decade because of her praise of Capitalism and her attacks on liberal ideas, Buddhism, and Socialism. Ayn Rand clubs sprang up at some universities. She won an enthusiastic following among the right wing Young Americans for Freedom.

Rand was a favorite of Republican Senator Barry Goldwater, whose own book, *The Conscience of a Conservative*, paved the way for his bid for his party's 1964 presidential nomination.

As the TV and movie spy craze suggested, the cold war intensified public interest in spies, who were constantly making headlines by being caught either by the Russians or the West. Ian Fleming created the James Bond craze with three best-selling spy novels, *On His Majesty's Service*, *You Only Live Twice*, and *The Man with the Golden Arm*. Helen MacInnes wrote *The Venetian Affair*, and John Le Carré's best-sellers were *The Spy Who Came in from the Cold* and *The Looking Glass War*.

The public was also fascinated by headlines about brutal crimes. Truman Capote's *In Cold Blood* dramatized the savage 1959 murder of a Kansas farm family by two vicious killers. The book introduced a new kind of nonfiction that soon spawned many imitators—fact written with the drama of a novel.

One famous book whose advice to parents helped rear most of the young

* This plot was detailed in my nonfiction book *The Plot to Seize the White House* (Hawthorn, 1973).

people in the sixties, *The Common Sense Book of Baby and Child Care* by Dr. Benjamin Spock, had first appeared in 1946 in the midst of the postwar baby boom. It continued to coach millions of young parents in the sixties. However, many conservative older Americans accused Dr. Spock of encouraging the parental permissiveness they blamed for producing the "self-indulgent" youth of the counterculture.

It was true that Dr. Spock's advice contributed to the making of a new generation less subject to regimentation than any earlier generation. For that reason, he was subjected to even more bitter attacks by Middle America when he decided to devote all of his time and energy to campaigning against the Vietnam War.

The sixties also saw the rise of "how-to" books, which some critics derided as "non-books." Do-it-yourself medicine was advocated by *Folk Medicine: A Vermont Doctor's Guide to Good Health* by D. C. Jarvis. Dr. Herman Taller taught weight control in *Calories Don't Count*. The personal growth movement received a strong impetus from *Games People Play: the Psychology of Human Relationships* by Eric Berne, explaining how to escape from miseries created by role-playing. *The Whole Earth Catalog* was directed toward environmentalists and the counterculture.

Sixties books accentuated ethnic awareness. Jewish mothers were satirized in *How to Be a Jewish Mother* by Dan Greenberg and *Portnoy's Complaint* by Philip Roth. Italian family life in Mafia circles was portrayed realistically by Mario Puzo in *The Godfather*, which was made into two powerful films. Black bitterness was expressed in *The Autobiography of Malcolm X* and in *Soul on Ice* by Eldridge Cleaver. Bel Kaufman's novel *Up the Down Staircase* portrayed the difficulties of a white teacher in an inner-city school. William Styron's fact-based novel about a historic black uprising, *The Confessions of Nat Turner*, appeared in 1967 to help explain the black riots exploding in one American city after another.

In the moral upheaval that characterized the countercultural revolution, taboos on frank sexual descriptions were increasingly defied. In 1960 D. H. Lawrence's novel *Lady Chatterly's Lover*, formerly banned by the U.S. Post Office because of obscene language, had its ban overturned in court. Henry Miller's *Tropic of Cancer*, banned for the same reason, also won admission into the United States after twenty-five years.

When Mary McCarthy published her 1963 novel, *The Group*, about Vassar girls ten years later, the *Saturday Review of Literature* called it "too sexy for words." It also broke the taboo against portraying lesbians. In that same year John Rechy presented a picture of big-city male homosexuality in his book *City of the Night*.

The role of drugs in the entertainment world was mirrored in *The Valley of the Dolls*, by Jacqueline Susann, in 1966. She also made the best-seller list subsequently with her novel *The Love Machine*. Other popular sex-saturated novels of the late sixties included *The Inheritors* by Harold Robbins, *The Seven Minutes* by Irving Wallace, and *Myra Breckenridge* by Gore Vidal.

A serious 1966 book on sex that had as powerful an influence on Americans as the *Kinsey Report* of an earlier decade was *Human Sexual Response* by William Masters and Virginia E. Johnson. It held out new hope for people secretly suffering from sexual problems, and it helped to usher in an era of total sexual frankness.

10

THE SEXUAL REVOLUTION

*I*n 1960, a new pill came on the market that touched off a sexual revolution during the decade. Until its appearance, couples having sexual relations who wanted to avoid pregancy had to rely on cumbersome contraceptive measures that for many interfered with spontaneity. Then Dr. John Rock and biochemist Gregory Pincus developed a successful birth control pill, as predicted two years earlier by Aldous Huxley in his novel *Brave New World Revisited*.

Available by prescription, the Pill, swallowed by women for a prescribed cycle of days, was considered one hundred percent reliable in preventing pregnancy. Within two years it was being used by 750,000 women; by 1966 there were six million women on the Pill; and by 1968, eleven million.

Pressure and funding for the experiments that led to the oral contraceptive had originated with two feminists: Margaret Sanger, who had invented the phrase "birth control" in 1914, and Katherine McCormick, who had married into the International Harvester fortune. Dr. Rock explained why he had agreed to work on the Pill despite belonging to the Roman Catholic Church, which opposes birth control: "I wanted to accomplish a pill that would allow my patients free sexual expression without the burden of childbirth."

Although originally prescribed only for married couples, the Pill soon became easily obtainable by single women. It quickly brought about sweeping changes in the sexual attitudes and practices of women, especially of college girls who led the way in defying traditional moral values because they could now do so without worrying about an unwanted pregnancy.

In a 1962 *Esquire* article, feminist Gloria Steinem reported that when twenty-seven college girls were interviewed, sixteen admitted to having affairs. Of the eleven who said they were still virginal, half professed embarrassment at admitting it, believing that premarital sex was now the norm, along with the concept of living together without benefit of marriage.

Millions of girls and women began taking responsibility for contraception, some using diaphragms, but more and more switching to the Pill as less trouble. In a poll of male and female college students, almost all agreed with the statement, "Sexual behavior is something you have to decide for yourself," shocking parents who had been raised conventionally.

TV producers, aware of the growing sexual revolution, began to reflect it in their programming. Advertising agencies made commercials even bolder. Model Gunilla Knutsen sold shaving cream by sexily wooing male viewers with the double entendre, "Take it off—take it *all* off!" And actress Barbara Feldon sold a male after-shave lotion by insinuating, "Sic 'em, tiger!"

The movies also grew more daring in their depiction of sexual subjects. In 1960 *Butterfield 8*, *The Apartment*, and *From the Terrace* all suggested that upper-class adultery was widespread. As the decade progressed, films reflected the society's changing sexual mores. Prostitution was portrayed sympathetically in *The World of Suzie Wong* (1961) and *Irma La Douce* (1963). A bawdy, lighthearted attitude toward sex was encouraged by *Tom Jones* (1963) and *Cat Ballou* (1965). Frank sexual scenes and talk were featured in *Who's Afraid of Virginia Woolf?* (1966). A blend of sex and violence was offered in 1966 by Michelangelo Antonioni in his box-office success *Blow-Up*. Male prostitution was depicted sympathetically in *Midnight Cowboy* (1969). The Swedish films *I Am Curious Yellow* and *I Am Curious Blue* offered pornography as "art" films.

The outcry of Middle America against the increased sexual candor of films led groups to try to censor them, but in 1965 the Supreme Court labeled such attempts unconstitutional.

A controversy also broke out over the right of women's colleges to inhibit the free sexual expression of students. In 1962 Sarah Gibson Blanding, president of Vassar, condemned premarital relations as "offensive and vulgar behavior." She emphasized the importance of chastity for single girls. Students protested her right to concern herself with their morals.

Many young people felt that it was unnatural and hypocritical to deny their sexual urges, especially with the protection of the Pill. They considered that it was not sex itself which was bad, whether in or out of marriage, but how it was used that mattered.

It became almost taken for granted that engaged couples would test their sexual compatability before marrying. Many couples considered that mutual love and desire were sufficient justification for expressing their feelings sexually. Still others considered the Pill their license to indulge in worry-free, recreational sex as the occasion presented itself.

Many women began to claim the right to gratification in sex relations on an equal basis with men, a development that many men found worrisome.

Some deans of women's colleges accepted the sexual revolution as a desirable development. Shortly after her retirement as president of Barnard, Millicent McIntosh declared that she found students "more realistic, more honest, and actually more courageous than we were. Their sex ethics are founded on knowledge instead of ignorance; they are honest rather than hypocritical."

But many adults worried that increased sexual activity would threaten young girls with unwanted pregnancies. Some joined Planned Parenthood, pressing for sex education in the schools and advocating abortion as an option of last resort.

The Pill liberated millions of wives from unwanted pregnancies. It allowed single women to have lovers while pursuing careers, instead of compelling them to marry just to satisfy their erotic urges. Some found their sweethearts pressing for marriage, while they preferred to wait.

With the Pill easily available, some counterculture groups began experimenting with communal living. In a few communes, sex was considered no more than just "the friendliest thing two people can do for each other."

Dr. John Rock developed a successful birth control pill. Many new methods of contraception were developed in the sixties.

In front of Independence Hall in Philadelphia, protesters picket to end discrimination against homosexuals.

"Your place or mine?" became a standard question men asked women at singles' bars. The new relaxed morality changed the concepts of sex for many women from "not until a ring is on your finger" to "not on the first date."

Dr. Andrew Elia, chairman of Boston University's School of Medicine obstetrics and gynecology department, declared in 1965, "The Pill, in time, will usher in the golden age of womanhood. It will set them free as nothing before in history has. It will enable them to plan not just for their pregnancies, but their lives. . . . Women will be able to pursue higher education. . . . They will also be free to spend more time with the few babies they do have. . . . It will usher in the age of the wanted child."

The sexual revolution did not come about without angry opposition from the conventional forces of morality. Roman Catholics were up in arms over the Pill, and many threatened to boycott the products of companies that marketed it. Many women feared that the Pill would almost require them to abandon their traditional roles and exercise their new "freedom" by becoming sexually aggressive. Conventional men, too, were unnerved by realizing that the Pill could free their wives and sweethearts to have affairs with other men without fearing pregnancy.

Millions of women who used less reliable methods than the Pill, or no contraception at all, continued to suffer unwanted pregnancies. Finding it impossible to get abortions legally unless a pregnancy endangered their lives, some women who could afford it sought abortions outside the country. Others resorted to illegal abortionists or tried to abort themselves, sometimes dying in the process.

The growing sexual revolution made it possible in 1967 for Governor John Love of Colorado to sign a bill that made his state the first to legalize abortions for victims of rape or incest, for women who felt that having a child could damage them mentally or physically, or for those whose unborn child was deformed. Intense Roman Catholic and fundamentalist Christian opposition compelled other states to continue prohibiting abortion. Not until 1973 did the Supreme Court overturn all restrictive abortion laws.

By 1968, when sociologist Ira L. Reiss took a survey of 248 unmarried college students, he found that sixty-four percent considered sex relations proper and were having them. Love was the driving force for seventy-eight percent of the females involved. And fully eighty-seven percent declared that they had come to accept sex activities that once had made them feel guilty.

Women who were on the Pill in the sixties were disturbed by a subsequent revelation that the Pill could have fatal side effects in some women, causing blood clots, strokes, heart attacks, gall bladder disease, and malignant tumors. The Food and Drug Administration soon required drug companies to insert warning labels on all packets of the Pill. Millions of fearful women gradually returned to older forms of contraception.

The sexual revolution was even reflected in children's toys. For Christmas in 1965, parents could buy youngsters "The Visible Man" and "The Visible Woman," complete with sex organs. Sexy Barbie and Ken dolls were popular, with wardrobes that cost $150 or more. Role reversal even allowed boys to play with dolls; G.I. Joe became the first such doll to succeed.

The sexual revolution sparked a great deal of interest in questions of male and female hormones. In 1966 Johns Hopkins University Medical School in Baltimore performed the first successful sex-change operation in the U.S., giving female sex organs to a seventeen-year-old male.

Homosexuals began coming "out of the closet" during the decade, asserting their right to reject heterosexuality. In 1967 Columbia University became the first to recognize a gay organization on campus. By 1969 Greenwich Village was full of gay bars where homosexuals picked each other up. That June the New York City vice squad raided a favorite gay hangout, Stonewall Inn. When they tried to arrest some of the two hundred homosexuals present, two hundred more rushed to immobilize the paddy wagon, and some raced through Greenwich Village smashing windows. Thirteen were arrested, and four policemen were hurt.

But nothing could stop the sexual revolution of the sixties. It started couples living together freely. It also gave homosexuals the opportunity to pursue their own life-style openly, no matter what conventional America thought about it.

11

THE FEMINIST REVOLUTION

*I*n 1960, a statistician estimated what it would cost the average American male to have his meals prepared and served, his laundry done, his house cleaned, his children cared for, his shopping done, his sexual needs met, and his social obligations catered. The bill came to something like $40,000 a year before inflation. "Yet," observed the statistician, "all it costs the average man, who couldn't afford all those services otherwise, is a wedding ring."

One exhausted housewife was asked what she wanted more than anything else in the world. "What I need," she sighed, "is a wife."

It has been a man's world for as long as history records, and many women have protested this arrangement down through the centuries. A fifteenth-century writer named Christine de Pisan challenged man-made laws and attitudes that postulated women were men's property to do with as they wished. One medieval version of the Bible even declared that a husband with a balky wife had the right to "beate the feare of God into her heade."

An important early fighter for women's rights was England's Mary Wollstonecraft, who wrote in her 1791 book, *Vindication for the Rights of Women*, "It is time to restore women to their lost dignity and to make them part of the human race." Her book was widely read in Europe and America, strongly influencing feminists who came after her.

The struggle for equal rights originated mostly with middle-class women who had the time and money to write and publish tracts, organize feminist societies, and put pressure on legislators for both the vote and equal rights before the law.

Before the Civil War, free high schools were open only to boys, who alone were allowed to study math and science. But in 1821, educator Emma Willard founded the Troy Female Seminary in Troy, New York, to give girls a free education equal to that of boys. In 1845, literary critic Margaret Fuller argued for the full development of women in her book *Woman in the Nineteenth Century*.

That women today can wear pants if they wish was largely the victory of Amelia Jenks Bloomer, who got women out of hoopskirts that hampered movement by daring to wear publicly pantaloons called "bloomers." When the new style caught on among liberated women of the 1840s, *New York Herald* editor James Gordon Bennett wrote scornfully, "If the women mean to wear the pants, then they must also be ready in case of war to buckle on the sword!"

Another famous American crusader was suffragette Elizabeth Cady Stanton, who issued a call in 1848 for the first Women's Rights Convention. Held in Seneca Falls, New York, it issued a Declaration of Independence for Women that demanded not only the vote for women, but justice for the American wife because "man has made her, if married, civilly dead." Wives, Stanton insisted, should have full equality with their husbands before the law. She was joined in her fight by Susan B. Anthony and Lucy Stone.

Elizabeth Blackwell was denied admittance to twenty-nine medical schools, but she persisted until one finally admitted her. She became the first American woman doctor, only to find that no patients would consult her and no hospital would admit her. So she opened the New York Infirmary in 1857 with an all-woman staff, and she subsequently established medical schools for women. In the 1870s Dr. Bethenia Owens outraged macho Oregon males by becoming the first woman doctor in the West.

The first clinic to provide birth control information and assistance was opened in Brooklyn, New York, in 1916. Its founder, nurse Margaret

Sanger, was distressed by the number of poor women who had more children than they wanted or could feed properly and by those who died or were mutilated at the hands of backstairs abortionists. Arrested and jailed, she was released eleven days later after a hunger strike, only to be convicted later and imprisoned for a month for refusing to close her clinic.

Not until 1919 were women finally given the right to vote, as a result of dramatic suffragette demonstrations led by firebrand Carrie Chapman Catt, who founded the National League of Women Voters.

In 1953, French author Simone de Beauvoir created a stir with a book called *The Second Sex*, accusing the world's patriarchal societies of still treating women as second-class citizens.

By the 1960s American women still suffered unequal treatment in employment, marriage, bank credit, and education. Then a time bomb was set off in 1963 by journalist Betty Friedan with her best-selling book *The Feminine Mystique*.

Friedan was the daughter of a woman journalist who had bitterly regretted giving up her career for marriage. When Friedan married, she kept her job reporting for the labor press until she was let go for becoming pregnant with a second child. Turning to free-lance writing for magazines, Friedan found that she could not sell any article that described what life was really like for most women. The image of happy female domesticity pleased advertisers and presumably kept women readers in a docile mood conducive to buying their products.

In 1961, President Kennedy established a national Commission on the Status of Women, which reported that women were given little or no equality with men and that eighty percent of those forced to subsist on welfare rolls were women and children. But nothing was done to change the situation.

In *The Feminine Mystique*, which created an instant sensation among women readers, Friedan exploded the simplistic myth of women as happy little homemakers or mistresses. Like de Beauvoir, Friedan insisted that women were intensely dissatisfied with their second-class citizenship, their subordination of their own need for growth and development to the needs of husbands, and their lack of equal opportunities with men in the marketplace. But, Friedan said, women unhappy with the lives they were forced to lead were made to feel guilty as "neurotics."

Thousands of women wrote or spoke to Friedan, validating her findings from their own lives. Her speaking engagements at home and abroad brought her before large audiences of women who voiced their own protests. Her book had put into words for millions of housewives and female workers what they had long felt but had been afraid to express.

Friedan suddenly found herself in the eye of the feminist storm she had unleashed. Fired now with the desire to do more than just articulate injustices to women, she made it her lifelong goal to end them. She traveled constantly, lecturing to more and more women, urging them to speak out and break the chains of passivity that bound them.

It did not escape women that Congress had passed the Equal Pay Act of 1963 and the Civil Rights Act of 1964 in response to pressure from the black civil rights movement. When congresswomen sought to make it illegal to discriminate also against women, Congress reluctantly permitted a clause against sexual discrimination to be added. "Who cares?" shrugged one senator. "How is any woman going to prove she was discriminated against in a job just because she is a woman?"

Even in progressive political or protest movements, women were automatically assigned to menial tasks like mailing, filing, stapling, dusting, and serving coffee. "Licking stamps began to taste like licking boots," complained one woman in an environmentalist organization. A black woman, given only lowly jobs in a civil rights organization while black males were given the important assignments, asked acidly, "Power to *what* people?"

Sparked by Friedan's book, however, the women's liberation movement kept growing steadily. Wherever she lectured, women pleaded with her to found a political organization that would fight for women's rights. In 1964, Friedan founded NOW—the National Organization for Women.

NOW charged that our society victimized low-paid and black women especially; that women were deliberately barred from postgraduate education and professional associations; that companies sought to escape feminist fire by hiring a "token" woman executive they could point to when criticized.

NOW became a powerful organization advancing the rights of American women. It was also largely responsible for getting Congress to pass the Equal Rights Amendment, which was fought by conservatives led by Phyllis Schlafly. The ERA failed to become part of the Constitution only because a few states balked at ratifying it.

A 1969 photograph of Gloria Steinem, who helped found *Ms.* magazine. She has played a major role in the development of the feminist movement and the bitter fight to end discrimination against women.

Members of the National Women's Liberation Party protest the Miss America Pageant as exploitive of women. These demonstrators objected to the perception of women as mere sex objects.

"No organized group protest—and in a decade that has produced so many—came so quickly, so powerfully, to impose itself on the American scene," observed editor Midge Decter, "as did the women's liberation movement. Within something like two years of its first official stirrings, women's lib swept to the top of . . . the American cultural mood."

"Women's lib" became a prime topic for TV talk shows and magazine and newspaper articles. NOW members invaded and integrated male-only bars and clubs. Some invaded the editorial offices of *Ladies Home Journal* and won the right to edit a whole issue from a feminist viewpoint.

The movement not only successfully changed the society's patronizing stereotypes of the female role but also won equal rights for many women. The telephone company, for example, was forced to pay several million dollars to women to make up for higher wages paid to men for the same work.

One of women's lib's greatest successes was its campaign to abolish antiabortion laws. Whether a woman chose to terminate a pregnancy or not, NOW insisted, was a private matter between her and her physician, not something for male legislators to decide. The Supreme Court finally agreed in 1973. A counter-resistance was mounted by a Right to Life movement, which sought to have the states continue to outlaw abortions.

The women's lib movement created great consternation among the male population, particularly older men and those brought up in the macho tradition that insisted that women "know their place" and that their primary function was to please men. Some men were dismayed by sudden displays of independence by their wives. Encouraged by the female revolution, many wives began voicing dissatisfaction with the status quo, making demands upon their men that would take their own wishes into account.

Most college-educated younger males acknowledged the justice of these complaints and tried to make their relationships more equitable. They agreed that if a wife shared the economic burden by working, then a husband should share in the burdens of housework and child care. In a few special cases there was role reversal—with "househusbands" staying home to look after the children and cook, while their wives went into the business world to earn the family income.

But even while cataclysmic changes were taking place in the lives of many women, the fashion industry, depending on women to play their traditional roles in the society, kept emphasizing styles that dramatized women's bodies. Some designers were promoting the topless bathing suit, the see-through or peekaboo blouse, and miniskirts, while others were catering to the millions of young girls who sought to imitate the skinny, boyish look of Twiggy, a very influential model.

Yet while these sexist developments made headlines, in 1965 Martha Griffiths, a congresswoman from Michigan, was prevented from raising feminist issues before a government commission hearing on the status of women. She responded angrily by joining Betty Friedan in organizing NOW.

NOW's struggle to unify women in the feminist movement was difficult because many women were fearful of offending husbands, fathers, and bosses. Women were also divided by class, race, religion, and ethnic background, so that it was not easy to unite them in a common struggle to improve their lot as wives, mothers, workers, and career women. NOW's task was made even more difficult by the ridicule of the male-controlled media, which frightened off many women by portraying feminists as strident viragos and man-hating lesbians.

But nothing daunted Friedan, who worked tirelessly night and day to make NOW powerful enough to compel Congress and the White House to take women's issues seriously. Thanks to NOW, employers were no longer able to advertise separately for "Help Wanted—Male" and "Help Wanted—Female." Now all jobs had to be open to both sexes.

NOW went after companies that barred women from applying for jobs previously reserved for men alone—fire fighters, telephone line workers, railroad engineers, airline pilots, truck drivers, bulldozer operators, construction workers, and the like. When heavy industries sought to bar women under the pretext of legislation "protecting" them from having to lift over thirty-five pounds, NOW fought the law as discriminatory. Pressure was also brought to bear against companies that fired older women to save the costs of pensions and promotions by replacing them with low-salaried younger women.

Stewardesses sought NOW's help in fighting airlines that forced them to quit if they married or reached the age of thirty-five, measures intended to make them seem alluring and available to male passengers. NOW waged battles to force employers to reward women employees for their ability, rather than for how well they gratified male fantasies.

Wherever women were segregated or discriminated against, NOW raised its battle standards. When inflation and the high cost of living forced more and more married and divorced women into the work force, NOW lobbied for funds to establish more day-care centers for their children. NOW also helped tear down the barriers that segregated living arrangements on college campuses and pressured schools and colleges to fund athletics for women on an equal basis with male sports.

In 1968, the women's lib movement sent a hundred women to picket the Miss America Pageant in Atlantic City. Attacking "the degrading, mindless, boob-girlie symbol," the demonstrators burned their bras in protest. Their picket signs read: "We shall not be used"; "Miss America is a walking commercial—wind her up and she sells your product"; and "Welcome to the Miss America cattle auction." Their objection to the contest was its judgment of women by how their looks pleased men, rather than on their value as individuals.

If Betty Friedan was the godmother of the women's lib movement, its role model was writer Gloria Steinem. In 1963 she posed as a Playboy Club "bunny" to expose the humiliations that young women hired for those jobs were compelled to endure. Joining Mexican-American field workers' boycott of lettuce and aiding the anti-Vietnam campaign of Senator Eugene McCarthy, Steinem encouraged women to fight for social causes.

In 1969, she attended an abortion hearing and was galvanized to fight antiabortion laws. "How much power would we ever have," she asked women, "if we had no power over the fate of our own bodies?" Helping to raise funds for the struggle, she carried on the fight with her pen three years later when she helped found *Ms.* magazine, which became the bible of the feminist movement. Its frankness created great controversy. Upset parents wanted it banned from high school libraries.

Steinem made women feel that it was all right to remain single. Although extremely attractive, she did not marry, declaring, "I can't mate in captivity." Her example heartened millions of single women who had been suffering guilt feelings for their inability or unwillingness to marry.

In 1970, Friedan, divorced and exhausted from the long feminist struggle she had begun, stepped down as president of NOW, while remaining active in the organization. Her last major act as president was to organize the Women's Strike for Equality, with a march down New York's Fifth Avenue. Mayor John Lindsay denied NOW a march permit, but almost 50,000 women nevertheless left their jobs and homes to join the march. Mounted police tried to stop them, but Friedan told the women to join hands across the street and keep marching. The baffled police on horseback didn't dare rough up the women, and backed out of the way. NOW's march for equality, covered by the media, impressed millions of Americans with woman power.

Having made great strides in the sixties by raising the consciousness of both men and women about women's rights, in 1971 NOW leaders Friedan, Steinem, former congresswoman Bella Abzug, and others formed the National Women's Political Caucus. The NWPC carried on the struggle by supporting political candidates and judges pledged to eliminate sexism, poverty, and racism. The NWPC also pressed for greater female representation in the political life of America.

NOW and the NWPC continued to be powerful forces behind the female revolution all through the seventies and eighties, making it possible for Sally Ride to become the first woman astronaut in space in 1983, and Geraldine Ferraro to become the first female major party candidate for vice president in 1984.

12

New Ways to Salvation

*T*he cult of Transcendental Meditation (TM) was popularized in the late sixties by the Maharishi Mahesh Yogi, who became the personal guru of the Beatles, Mia Farrow, and other theatrical stars. The Maharishi, an enigmatic East Indian mystic, explained their fascination with him: "They know they lack something in their lives, but they cannot pinpoint it. They have millions, cars, fine houses—then what, then what?"

Man was not born to suffer, he said, and would not suffer if he practiced the TM taught by the Maharishi. The Beatles agreed. "TM is good for everyone," Paul McCartney said.

Ringo Starr declared, "Since meeting His Holiness, I feel great."

John Lennon insisted, "This is the biggest thing in our lives."

George Harrison praised his new religious experience as "occupying every minute and every second of life." Their enthusiasm gave the Maharishi a captive audience of Beatles fans when he toured the United States in 1968, charging $35 a ticket to his lectures.

Becoming a celebrity with TV appearances on the "Today Show," Johnny Carson's "Tonight Show," and National Educational Television, he also won important publicity in magazines like *Time, Newsweek, Life,* and *Look.*

He was estimated to have won a quarter of a million followers, who spread his gospel of TM.

According to the Maharishi, Jesus had founded a faulty church because he had let his mind wander, leading to an "absurd" emphasis on faith. "Faith, at best," the Maharishi declared, "can let a man live and die in hope. The churches are driving people away because that is all they have to offer."

TM sessions were staged by disciples with candlelight and incense before small pictures of the Maharishi. Bliss was to be found, he explained, by meditating upon a single word like "Rama," a secret personal *mantra* given them by the teacher. Repeated over and over again for two half-hour periods a day, this *mantra* presumably blurred all external distractions, making the word and the senses one, bringing spiritual peace. The Maharishi promised that TM would also bring tangible rewards in the ability to do a better job, winning promotions and raises that would let adherents afford everything they wanted.

But the Beatles eventually decided that they had "made a mistake" in adopting TM, and the cult began to die out.

The Maharishi simply shrugged. "They come and they go, they come and they go."

Early in the sixties, conventional religion still had a strong following. "Recording gospel songs has become big business," observed gospel singer Mahalia Jackson in 1962. "Every saint and sinner does it now." But there was growing dissatisfaction, particularly among the young, with mainstream churches and synagogues. This led to the rise of a wide variety of new cults, movements, and pseudo-religions appealing to idealistic youth who felt alienated from a society that seemed soulless to them.

The loss of John F. Kennedy, who had seemed their only hope of social reform, and their failure to stop the Vietnam War filled them with despair. They sought new sources of hope and comfort, viewing organized religion as impotent to challenge the wrongs of their society. They saw their parents as hypocritical Sunday Christians, nodding to biblical platitudes in church and spending the rest of the week violating the Golden Rule.

If conventional religion had failed them, so had science, which seemed to the young to be dehumanizing their lives instead of enriching them.

New technology, robotization, nuclear energy, space shots, billions spent on the latest weaponry, chemical pesticides that polluted the land, water, and air at home and abroad—all of these made the disillusioned young turn away to find some personal spiritual solace. The need was especially strong since they were faced with the gloomy prospect that their lives might be snuffed out in one terrible moment by nuclear warfare.

Many youths sought a new religious experience in the use of drugs. The guru of the drug culture, ex-professor Timothy Leary, told them, "The LSD kick is spiritual ecstasy. The LSD trip is a religious pilgrimage." They were urged to "get out of themselves and into the universe" by taking psychedelic drugs. Some 50,000 youths joined Native American churches that practiced an American Indian religious ritual involving the use of peyote. Others joined the New Religion of American Indians, participating in tribal ceremonies.

The hunger for spirituality was intensified by the decline of meaningful family life. Young people felt alone, isolated by parents who spent evenings watching vacuous TV programs, or who dragged them around the country on job transfers, or who upset them by bitter divorces. Some youths reacted by running away from home to join religious communes, seeking a sense of community in an extended family who lived and worked together, sharing a common goal and purpose.

Alienated youths also turned to the occult—spiritualism, astrology, Tarot cards, the I Ching, Edgar Cayce "search for God" sessions, even witchcraft and Satanism. Belief in psychic phenomena was fostered by ESP and by mind research conducted and publicized by psychologists at such prestigious centers as Duke University. The occult offered a belief system that promised supernatural powers to adherents.

Another strong religious influence in the sixties came out of the Far East in cults like TM, Zen Buddhism, Hare Krishna, Yoga, the Baha'is, and the Unification Church. Allen Ginsberg and Jack Kerouac, the Beat poets of the fifties, were early apostles of the Zen and Hare Krishna cults that flowered in the sixties. Almost every college student and counterculture youth was impressed by the East Indian path to religious experience depicted in German-Swiss novelist Herman Hesse's book *Siddhartha*. Eastern influence was also strong in centers for avant garde movements like Esalen and est.

Most of these cults took seed in California, then spread nationwide.

Offering new ways to salvation in the sixties, they incorporated many key aspects of the Asian religions. By nourishing the individual psyche, they sustained adherents through periods of self-doubt, developed their creativity, and turned them away from materialism to seek spiritual growth.

Conventional churches, needless to say, were unhappy about losing millions of young people to the cults. During the sixties, church attendance fell off by eleven percent. In vain preachers quoted the Gospel according to Saint Matthew: "There shall arise false Christs, and false prophets, and shall show great signs and wonders; insomuch that, if it were possible, they shall deceive the very elect."

Many churches were further dismayed when, in 1963, the Supreme Court decreed that it was unconstitutional to read the Lord's Prayer and Bible verses in public schools. Some church leaders saw that ruling as a death knell to the concept of the United States as a Christian nation, serving further to open the door wider to all new cults.

Hoping to hold more young people in the faith, the Roman Catholic Church began to liberalize some of its dogma. In 1963 the Twelfth Ecumenical Council declared that it was wrong to blame Jews for Christ's death. In 1966 the Vatican Council lifted the ban against eating meat on Fridays. In 1969 Pope Paul VI dropped hundreds of saints, including St. Patrick and St. Christopher, from the church calendar, labeling them just myths.

Although most mainstream churches suffered losses of membership and attendance, as well as of new recruits for the clergy, fundamentalist and evangelical churches thrived as new millions proclaimed themselves "born-again" Christians. Many of these adherents were older Americans angered by the youth revolt against traditional values. In 1966 the Reverend Billy Graham declared, "I can tell you that God is alive, because I spoke to Him this morning." The next year he announced that he had saved a total of over one million souls.

The nation's first Zen Buddhist monastery, Tassajara, was founded in 1967 in Big Sur, California, by Berkeley graduate Richard Baker and Zen master Shunryu Suzuki. Women as well as men were invited to seek enlightenment, or *satori*, by meditation leading them to accept life as it is, including evil as well as good, and achieving peace of mind despite external turmoil.

Young searchers for truth also flocked to a revival of the I Ching cult, based on the ancient, mysterious Chinese "Book of Changes." Believers threw three coins to locate a chapter and passage in the sixty-four-chapter book most appropriate to their situation, as a guide to what to expect and what to think or do about it. According to the Chinese, nothing is accidental; everything has a purpose, including the way coins turn up when thrown. Dr. Carl Jung, Freud's associate, agreed and wrote a preface to the first Western translation of the I Ching.

In the late sixties, sales of the book soared when it won high praise from author Tom Wolfe and folksingers Arlo Guthrie and Bob Dylan. The cult developed an estimated 600,000 young followers in the country. There were few youth communes where the I Ching was not regularly thrown.

Another way of salvation that attracted millions of followers in the sixties was astrology. One of the decade's best sellers was Linda Goodman's book *Sun Signs* which promised "How to Really Know Your Husband * Wife * Lover * Child * Boss * Employee * Yourself * Through ASTROLOGY." The rock musical *Hair* emphasized astrology as a cult of the young, labeling the sixties "the Age of Aquarius."

Self-styled witch Sylvia Leek, in her *Astrology Journal,* bragged that over 1,200 of the nation's 1,750 newspapers were carrying a regular astrological column, while most national magazines had their own astrologers. Computers in public places churned out astrological forecasts for $2.50 apiece. Publishers issued a flood of zodiac cookbooks and zodiac coloring books for children. The magazines *American Astrology* and *Horoscope* had half a million readers each, and 100,000 believers bought copies of a book called *Astrology and Horse Racing*. An estimated 175,000 amateur and professional astrologers helped people consult the stars to guide their personal decisions.

Astrology has generally boomed during periods of fear, anxiety, confusion, and dissatisfaction, like the sixties. Disillusioned with materialism, feeling lost in a vast impersonal system, many of the decade's youth searched for some personal, meaningful belief system. Astrology offered them a spiritual connection with the universe, one they could allegedly use to learn what was written for them in the stars.

Some youths were attracted to "search for God" study groups and workshops held by the Association for Research and Enlightenment (A.R.E.), founded by Edgar Cayce. Adherents contemplated extrasensory percep-

These home-grown marijuana plants will be harvested soon. During the sixties
marijuana became increasingly popular.

tion, dream significance, reincarnation, and metaphysical thought. Many of A.R.E.'s concepts derived from early mystery religions in the East and Middle East.

Cayce was a psychic who went into trances and seemed able to diagnose the illness of persons thousands of miles away and to exercise mental telepathy. On the strength of those powers he made prophecies that hundreds of thousands believed. But Cayce predicted that China would become Christian by 1968; that North Carolina and Georgia would be swallowed up by the Atlantic soon after 1960; and that New York and California would slide into the sea in the early 1970s. These flawed predictions hurt his credibility.

Some 150,000 Americans joined 18 different Spiritualist churches to communicate with dead spirits. A surge of interest in Spiritualism occurred in 1967 after Episcopal Bishop James A. Pike, a believer, held a televised séance with medium Arthur Ford, a Disciples of Christ minister, to contact the bishop's dead son, Jim, who had died of an LSD overdose. This dramatic TV session introduced Spiritualism into millions of homes.

In addition to attending séances, Spiritualists attended the cult's regular church services, during which a heavenly spirit guide presumably preached through the mouth of the medium.

The flight from orthodox religion led some few thousands in the sixties into the bizarre cult of witchcraft covens, most of them in California. "There is such a thing as witchcraft; it exists and it works," wrote Dr. John Charles Cooper, chairman of the department of philosophy at Eastern Kentucky University. "And I have seen it work on white, middle-class, well educated people in the heartland of the United States."

Witches, who could be male as well as female, studied the use of drugs, herbs, and ESP and other psychic powers to cast spells. They met at covens during the full moon to perform ceremonies while naked, initiate new members, and celebrate their witchcraft. One high priest, Raymond Buckland, termed witchcraft "a religion of freedom, joy in the sensual appetites and in nature." After seeing the film *Rosemary's Baby*, which portrayed a fanatical witchcraft coven, one group of sixth-grade girls in New York started a coven under the guise of holding pajama parties.

Some forms of witchcraft became the cult known as Satanism. Its high priest was the author of *The Satanic Bible*, Anton La Vey of San Francisco's

First Church of Satan. The numbers "666," said in the Bible to be the sign of the Antichrist, began appearing all over the San Fernando Valley.

Satanism was based on the nineteenth-century cult established by Aleister Crowley. La Vey claimed up to 100,000 adherents, to whom he promised "a blatantly selfish, brutal religion" that would reward them with pleasure if they indulged Satanic impulses. Even though La Vey appeared on Johnny Carson's "Tonight Show" wearing a horned hood and carrying a sword, the Internal Revenue Service recognized his Church of Satan as a legitimate religion.

Some of the fruits of Satanism became evident in August 1969, when ex-con Charles Manson, a Satanist whose "family" recognized him as Satan and God, carried out his "helter-skelter" plan by murdering seven people at random. Manson later explained, "We wanted to do a crime that would shock the world and that the world would have to stand up and take notice." He told reporters, "All my women are witches, and I'm the devil."

In June 1970, another group of Satanist young people killed a gas station attendant and a schoolteacher mother of five. One month later, Satanists murdered a Montana social worker near Yellowstone Park, mutilating his body.

The young people attracted to Satanism were often those who had been rejected by their families as "bad," accepting that image of themselves. They were attracted by a substitute family that welcomed and glorified badness.

Another cult that appealed to disillusioned people in the sixties was Scientology, founded by science fiction writer L. Ron Hubbard. Attracting several hundred thousand members in the United States, the cult practiced "Dianetics," which professed to cure people of problems by probing into their "previous lives" to identify and destroy troublesome "engrams." Opposition from the medical profession compelled Hubbard to change his cult into a religion, the Church of Scientology. Believers paid up to $28,000 each for the Scientology process. The Internal Revenue Service refused to recognize Hubbard's "church" as a legitimate religion.

The slowness of the civil rights movement to effect meaningful change for blacks made many despair and begin listening in the sixties to the message of the Black Muslim church founded by Elijah Muhammad. Its dynamic spokesman, ex-convict Malcolm X, preached that the white man was a devil; that Christianity was the white man's religion; and that only Islam could bring peace, pride, and prosperity to the black community.

By 1961 the Black Muslims had almost seventy mosques and over 100,000 followers, in whom Malcolm X touched a responsive chord by insisting, "You cannot find *one* black man, I do not care who he is, who has not been personally damaged in some way by the devilish acts of the collective white man!"

The Black Muslims continued to thrive all through the sixties. Members opened their own inner-city stores and country farms in several states. Deeply religious, they followed the Islamic rituals of prayer and rehabilitated many black convicts upon their release from prison. Opposed to desegregation, the Black Muslims insisted that only by staying apart from whites could blacks fulfill their destiny. They emphasized African rather than American cultural traditions for blacks.

In the late sixties, a new Jesus movement sprang up among desperate young people, many of them drug addicts seeking a way out of their misery. It began with a young sailmaker converted by the Bible who opened a coffeehouse with friends in the Haight-Ashbury district to spread the gospel. The cult of "Jesus freaks" grew throughout California, then the country, then abroad. Some adherents lived in communes, one of which was the Children of God, later accused of kidnapping and brainwashing young people to alienate them from their parents.

Some youths were attracted by the saffron-robed, head-shaven Hare Krishnas who danced on the streets of New York and Haight-Ashbury, shaking tambourines and endlessly chanting their mantra, "Hare Krishna." This Hindu sect was carried to the Western world by a retired East Indian businessman turned monk, A. C. Bhaktivedanta Swami Prabhupada, on orders from his swami to spread the message of Krishna-worship.

He recruited large numbers of young hippies and other countercultural youths with the promise that they could "stay high all the time and discover eternal bliss." The endorsement of the Hare Krishnas by such rock groups as the Grateful Dead added to their appeal to alienated young people.

The Unification Church, founded by Korean millionaire Sun Myung Moon, was begun early in the decade on the West Coast by his missionaries. But only a few hundred "Moonies," as recruits were called, responded during the sixties because his message, "Repent and prepare for the Second Coming," was too similar to that of religious fundamentalists. It was only after the failure of the sixties' social movement to reshape American society significantly that the Moonies were able to capture thousands of disillusioned youths.

Another cult that thrived in the sixties was the interracial Baha'i movement, which Tolstoy once called "the highest and purest form of religious teaching." The Baha'is preached the "oneness of mankind," emphasizing peace, universal justice, and racial brotherhood. The number of Baha'i centers more than doubled in the decade. Urging unity of Christians, Jews, Muslims, and Buddhists under one God, the Baha'is appealed to many idealistic college students alienated by organized religion.

By the end of the sixties, many bewildered mainstream ministers, priests, and rabbis wondered where they had gone wrong. Why had so many millions of Americans deserted organized religion for new cults that promised a better way to personal salvation? Movements sprang up within clerical ranks to bring back lost flocks by making the churches and synagogues more meaningful to a new generation suffering from cultural shock.

13

THE COLD WAR GETS HOTTER

*F*or a while during the Eisenhower administration, it seemed as though the president had managed to thaw the cold war by establishing negotiations with the Russians on reducing armaments and suspending tests of nuclear weapons. Things were going so well that Eisenhower and Nikita Khrushchev arranged a summit conference in Paris for May 1960 to sign a peaceful coexistence pact.

"The ice of the cold war has not only cracked but begun to melt," Khrushchev assured American newsmen after a trip to the United States. He returned home to advise the Soviet Politburo that the American president was a reasonable, farsighted man opposed to war and to urge cooperation with the United States.

Then a bombshell stunned the world. On May 2 an American U-2 spy plane was shot down over the Soviet Union. Announcing this startling development, Khrushchev sought to offer the president a face-saving way out of the awkward dilemma by implying that the spy flight might have been sent by "Pentagon militarists" without Eisenhower's knowledge.

The State Department hastily announced that an unarmed weather research plane had been missing since May 1 and might "accidentally" have strayed over Russian territory. A spokesman insisted, "There was absolutely no deliberate attempt to violate Soviet airspace . . . and never had been."

But two days later Khrushchev told the USSR Supreme Soviet, "Comrades, I must let you into a secret. When I made my report I deliberately refrained from mentioning that the pilot was alive and healthy." He revealed then that pilot Francis Gary Powers, who had parachuted to earth and been captured, had confessed to being a CIA agent engaged in aerial espionage over Soviet airfields.

Caught in a flat lie, the State Department now acknowledged that the Russians were correct but insisted that the flight had been unauthorized by the White House. Eisenhower himself, however, revealed that this statement, too, was untrue. He accepted personal responsibility for the spy flight.

The president's public admission embarrassed and angered Khrushchev. He had built up Eisenhower to the Russian people as his friend and a man of peace whom they could trust. Soviet critics accused Khrushchev of having been gullible. So when the summit conference opened in Paris on May 16, the furious Soviet leader denounced the American government for its "provocative act" and "treacherous nature." He demanded that Eisenhower apologize, promise to send no more U-2 flights over Soviet territory, and punish those who had organized them. Khrushchev also publicly canceled an invitation to the president to visit the USSR, declaring bitterly, "The Russian people would say I was mad to welcome a man who sends spy planes over here."

Taken aback, Eisenhower refused to apologize or meet the Soviet leader's other demands. Khrushchev stormed out of the summit meeting, wrecking it before it had even begun. James Reston wrote in *The New York Times*, "Mr. Eisenhower was responsible, directly or indirectly, for the greatest series of humiliating blunders suffered by the United States in a decade."

Senator William Fulbright, chairman of the Senate Foreign Relations Committee, agreed with Senator John F. Kennedy that America owed an apology for violating international law. Columnist Walter Lippman, adviser to many presidents, called Eisenhower's failure to accept Khrushchev's offer to let him deny personal responsibility "a fatal error . . . an irreparable mistake."

Eisenhower himself admitted later, "The big error we made was, of course, in the issuance of a premature and erroneous cover story. Allowing myself to be persuaded on this score is my principal personal regret—except for the U-2 failure itself—regarding the whole affair."

The U-2 incident once more plunged the world back into the dangerous atmosphere of the cold war.

The lives of everyone on the planet were dramatically affected during the sixties by the growing rivalry and enmity of the two greatest world powers, who had been allies in World War II—the United States and the Soviet Union. Each feared the other and waged an intensifying cold war that frequently threatened to erupt into a hot shooting war. If that happened, everyone knew it would be a nuclear war—with terrible weapons tens of thousands of times more powerful than the two atomic bombs dropped on Hiroshima and Nagasaki.

When Albert Einstein was asked what weapons might be used in a third world war, he replied, "I don't know, but in the fourth world war it will be the slingshot "—provided any survivor was left to reinvent one. Understandably, hundreds of millions of young people around the world felt hopeless about planning for a future they might never see and disgusted with the cold war leaders who threatened to annihilate each other instead of cooperating for the benefit of humanity.

Under three presidents in the sixties—Eisenhower, Kennedy, and Nixon—the American government was kept on a collision course with the Soviet Union. Military action was undertaken against small nations viewed as Communist or left wing, while support was given to others regarded as anti-Communist or right wing. Washington accused the Soviet Union and the (Communist) People's Republic of China of an international conspiracy to subvert and take over the whole world for Communism.

The Soviet Union, under first Khrushchev, then Leonid Brezhnev, viewed the United States as a Capitalist power determined to crush Communist and left wing regimes wherever they won power. The Kremlin feared another Western invasion of the Soviet Union like that during World War II, which had cost the Russians over twenty million lives. The Russians kept an iron grip on East Europe. They wanted to exploit these countries to help rebuild the Soviet economy shattered by World War II. They also wanted to keep these countries as a buffer zone to make certain the West would never again be able to invade Russia through central Europe as Hitler and Napoleon had. American military moves that surrounded the Soviet Union with U.S. bases were viewed with deep suspicion in Moscow.

The Soviet Union also worried about its eastern border with China. Despite the apprehension of Eisenhower's Secretary of State, John Foster Dulles, about "monolithic Communism"—an alliance between China and the USSR—the truth was that there was no love lost between the two great Communist powers. Each feared the other's nationalistic territorial ambitions. Both sent aid to North Vietnam for its resistance against American attacks, but each maneuvered against the other to become the dominant power in Southeast Asia.

When Kennedy took office in 1961, he was determined to reach a new understanding with Khrushchev. His determination grew after the disastrous failure of his effort to overthrow the Soviet-supported Cuban government of Fidel Castro by the Bay of Pigs invasion. The two leaders met in Vienna in June 1961.

Khrushchev expressed the hope that Kennedy was prepared to accept a coexistence policy. Kennedy asked Khrushchev if he appreciated the American concern that he not encourage Communism in areas of the world vital to Western interests.

Khrushchev countered that mutual trust could not be developed if Americans continued to believe that whenever there was a revolution in a country, the Soviet Union had manufactured it. The United States, he pointed out, was itself actually provoking revolutions by bolstering right wing dictatorships that violated human rights, inciting rebellion.

Kennedy reminded Khrushchev that the Soviet leader had pledged support for all wars of "national liberation." Wasn't *that* interference in other nations' affairs? Khrushchev replied that the Americans, who had waged their own revolution against Great Britain, had no right to deny their example to other oppressed peoples around the world.

Their discussion grew acrimonious when it turned to the problem of East (Communist) and West (Capitalist) Germany. Khrushchev demanded that a final peace settlement of World War II be reached that would give East Germany control of all Western access to East and West Berlin. "West Berlin is a bone that must come out of the Soviet throat," Khrushchev insisted.

He warned that any attempt by the Western powers to violate East Germany's borders by forcing entry into East Berlin would be met by force. "I want peace," Khrushchev told the president sharply, "but if you want war, that is your problem."

A nettled Kennedy replied, "We cannot negotiate with those who say: 'What's mine is mine, and what's yours is negotiable.' It is you, and not I, who wants to force a change."

He added grimly, "It will be a cold winter."

The New York Times correspondent James Reston spoke to the president afterward and found him shaken by Khrushchev's abrasive rhetoric. "I think he [Khrushchev] did it because of the Bay of Pigs," Kennedy mused. "I think he thought that anyone who was so young and inexperienced as to get into that mess could be taken, and anyone who got into it, and didn't see it through, had no guts. So he just beat the hell out of me. So I've got a terrible problem. . . . Until we remove those ideas, we won't get anywhere with him. So we have to act."

That view of the summit conference in Vienna had tremendously important consequences. Kennedy decided to show Khrushchev that he could be tough by sending fifteen thousand American military advisers and Green Berets to Vietnam, to wage counterrevolutionary warfare against the Communist regime of Ho Chi Minh.

On July 25, in a national address on the Berlin crisis, Kennedy proposed an increase in U.S. armed forces by 217,000 men and an increase in defense spending to $3.4 billion, to meet the Soviet "worldwide threat."

In August the East Germans began building the ugly Berlin Wall to stop hundreds of thousands of East Berliners seeking to escape to West Berlin. Nevertheless, in 1963 over three thousand more still managed to flee the Communist side. Kennedy defied Khrushchev by going to West Berlin that year to pledge continued support to West Berliners and to praise them for their courage in resisting Soviet pressures. The city roared its delight when the president cried, "Today in the world of freedom, the proudest boast is: *'Ich bin ein Berliner!'* "

Tension mounted sharply between the U.S. and the USSR.

Khrushchev canceled cuts in the Soviet military budget and resumed testing nuclear weapons. Kennedy responded by ordering a U.S. resumption of underground nuclear tests.

Another major obstacle to cooperation between the two powers lay in the Russian persecution of dissidents like scientist Andrei Sakharov, which was a violation of the human rights covenant Moscow had agreed to earlier. Many Americans felt that it was impossible to reach any real understanding with a government that permitted no freedom of speech or press. But the Kremlin maintained that Russian internal affairs were none of their business.

If Khrushchev viewed West Berlin as a Western bone in the Soviet throat, Washington considered Cuba a Russian bone in the American throat. Castro was regarded as a foothold for Moscow in the Western hemisphere.

After the Cuban leader had succeeded in overthrowing dictator Fulgencio Batista in 1959, he first sought recognition and aid for his revolutionary government from Washington. He was coldly rebuffed by the Eisenhower administration because of his nationalization of all private enterprise on the island. American business owned almost all Cuban mines, four-fifths of Cuban public utilities, almost half the sugar plantations, and a large number of its industries.

Former President Harry S. Truman observed that Castro "seems to want to do the right thing for the Cuban people, and we ought to extend our sympathy and help him." As a senator, John F. Kennedy, too, criticized the Eisenhower administration for failing to give "the fiery young rebel a warmer welcome in his hour of triumph." But Eisenhower was determined to destroy Castro as a dangerous example to the rest of Latin America.

In July 1960, the president boycotted any further American purchases of Cuban sugar, the island's most important export, and embargoed U.S. exports to Cuba. He pressured other Latin American countries to follow his example. Castro, in a speech to the UN, denounced U.S. attempts to destroy his revolution.

When he appealed to the Soviet Union instead for help, the Russians came to his rescue by buying Cuba's sugar.

Eisenhower embarked on a 15,000-mile tour of South America, urging crowds who turned out to hear him to choose the path of social reform with American help, rather than the path of revolutionary Castroism. But on all sides he heard blunt criticism of U.S. foreign policy for turning its back on the poor of Latin America, instead propping up their rich dictators.

Eisenhower sought to respond by setting up a Pan-American conference in Colombia. He promised U.S. financial support for Latin American countries willing to carry out economic and political reforms for their people.

Before leaving office, Eisenhower and his vice president, Richard M. Nixon, set up a secret plan to invade Cuba with an army of Cuban exiles trained, armed, and supported by the CIA. When Castro revealed that he knew of this plot, the White House denounced him for "shrill . . . anti-American propaganda." Castro demanded a reduction of personnel assigned to the U.S. Embassy in Havana. Eisenhower responded by breaking relations.

Many Latin Americans admired Castro, sharing his opposition to *imperialismo yanqui*. In September 1960, pro-Castro mobs in Panama attacked the U.S. embassy for refusing to allow the Panamanian flag to fly alongside the American flag in the Panama Canal Zone.

When Kennedy took over the White House in 1961, the CIA and the Joint Chiefs of Staff pressed him to unleash the invasion of Cuba they had plotted. When he consulted his advisers, only Senator William Fulbright opposed the intervention as dangerous and doomed to fail because it would not have the support of the Cuban people. But Kennedy, unsure of himself, let himself be persuaded by all his other advisers.

After only three days, the invasion of the Bay of Pigs on April 17, 1961, proved a total disaster. World opinion condemned the United States for backing a flagrant act of aggression. The new president groaned, "How could I have agreed to such a stupid mistake?" At a gloomy gathering of his advisers, he admitted to Fulbright, "You are the only person here who has the right to say: 'I told you so!' "

The invasion stirred a furor in Latin America. "You killed women and children in Playa Giron [Bay of Pigs]," Carlos Fuentes, Mexico's famous novelist, accused Kennedy. "You bombed the first decent houses, the first schools, the first hospitals of Cubans who never before, during the long American protectorate over Cuba, had a roof, an alphabet, or their health. And you did it in the name of liberty, democracy, and free enterprise."

The Bay of Pigs blunder not only hurt American prestige in the eyes of the world, but it also drove Castro to turn to the USSR for protection and aid. The installation of Soviet missile bases in Cuba was a direct consequence of the Bay of Pigs.

Taken to task by newsmen for having denied the American role in the Bay of Pigs, Assistant Secretary of Defense for Public Affairs Arthur Sylvester defended the right of government officials to lie to the public "to protect national security." He later told reporters, "Look, if you think any American official is going to tell you the truth, then you're stupid!"

CBS reporter Morley Safer said, "He then went on to the effect that American correspondents had a patriotic duty to disseminate only information that made the United States look good."

Thus the White House had felt no qualms about instructing UN Representative Adlai Stevenson to deny in the UN that the U.S. had been behind the Bay of Pigs invasion. When Stevenson learned the truth, he was furious at having been deceived and used to cloak the CIA's guilt, damaging his own credibility.

Congress, too, was angry that the president had secretly committed an undeclared act of war without its knowledge and consent. His fingers badly burned by his mistake, Kennedy vowed to take control of foreign policy himself and not let his advisers press him into any more misadventures.

Seeking to undo the damage to U.S.–Latin American relations, Kennedy developed the Alliance for Progress, providing a ten-year, twenty billion dollar program of public aid and private investment in Central and South America. The program was aimed at thwarting Communism in those countries through economic help and social reform. All Latin American countries except Cuba signed the charter in August 1961.

Late in October 1962, the world was chilled by a dangerous new crisis in the cold war. A grim-jawed Kennedy took to TV to reveal that Khrushchev had secretly delivered Soviet missiles to Cuba. He angrily ordered a naval blockade of Cuba until the Soviet Union agreed to dismantle and withdraw the weapons.

"It shall be the policy of this nation," the president warned, "to regard any nuclear missile launched from Cuba against any nation in the Western hemisphere as an attack by the Soviet Union on the United States, requiring a full retaliatory response upon the Soviet Union."

The world held its breath as twenty-four Soviet ships steamed toward Havana, while ninety American ships and eight aircraft carriers moved into position to intercept and search them for missiles. Would a naval

Soviet Premier Nikita Khrushchev and President John F. Kennedy meet for talks in Vienna. Kennedy envisioned "a world of diversity" where "every country can solve its own problems according to its own traditions and ideals."

These bricked-up windows in a building along the city's dividing line are an example of East Berlin's attempt to prevent refugees from escaping to the West.

clash between the U.S. and the USSR precipitate the long-dreaded unleashing of nuclear weapons?

Some aides in the Kennedy administration worried about the wisdom of the president's military response. Secretary of Defense Robert McNamara told McGeorge Bundy, Kennedy's National Security Adviser, "I'll be quite frank. I don't think there *is* a military problem here."

Historian Richard J. Walton reported from the UN that representatives there were terrified by the "eyeball-to-eyeball crisis." He observed, "It could have been solved by using diplomacy, and Kennedy didn't use diplomacy at all. He used a nuclear threat."

The first Soviet response to Kennedy's challenge was a furious accusation that the United States was trying to foment a nuclear war. "If indeed war should break out, then it would not be in our power to stop it," Khrushchev warned Kennedy. "You, too, will receive the same that you hurl against us!"

But he offered the president a *quid pro quo*. The Russians would remove the missiles from Cuba if Kennedy would pledge no further aggressive acts against the island. "Only lunatics or suicides . . . want to perish and to destroy the whole world before they die," the Soviet leader told Kennedy. "Mister President, we and you ought not to pull on the ends of the rope in which you have tied the knot of war, because the more the two of us pull, the tighter that knot will be tied. . . . Let us take measures to untie that knot."

After a tense period of suspense for the whole world, Khrushchev took the first conciliatory step. Deciding not to challenge the U.S. naval blockade, he ordered the Soviet ships en route to Cuba to turn back. Relieved, Kennedy pledged not to invade Cuba, and Khrushchev agreed to withdraw the Soviet missiles from the island. In November Kennedy ended the naval blockade.

"Both sides showed that if the desire to avoid war is strong enough," Khrushchev declared, "even the most pressing dispute can be solved by compromise." Kennedy praised the Soviet Premier's contribution to the cause of peace. The near disaster led the two leaders to install a hot line between the Kremlin and the White House in June 1963, providing instant communication in case of any similar future crisis.

Under the Johnson administration, the United States continued its policy of opposing left wing reform in Latin America. In 1964 the CIA supported a military coup in Brazil that toppled the democratically elected reformist president, Joao Goulart, replacing him with a repressive military junta. Johnson sent his "warmest wishes" to the Brazilian generals.

In 1962, the first free elections in the Dominican Republic in 38 years had elected Juan Bosch president. The following year he was overthrown by a three-man military junta. In 1965, a popular uprising of Dominicans sought to restore Bosch to office. President Johnson sent twenty-two thousand marines to the Dominican Republic, insisting that they were there only to protect American lives and "prevent a Communist takeover."

Todd Szulc of *The New York Times* reported from the island that the president's excuse was a fabrication. TV news films showed the marines helping the the junta's troops suppress the uprising. Anti-American demonstrations erupted all over Latin America. The press began to talk about the administration's "credibility gap"—its lack of believability.

College students in the sixties became increasingly disillusioned by the White House's obsession with Communism, seeing every liberal and left wing government as a pawn or ally of the Soviet Union, while supporting every repressive or right wing dictatorship for its anti-Communism. Campus leaders accused the administration of a hypocritical foreign policy.

To bolster public support for that policy, the CIA secretly bankrolled some student groups, a dozen book publishers, some radio stations, over fifty news organizations, and some one hundred journalists working for U.S. newspapers and TV networks. The American public had no way of knowing at the time that many views they were led to believe were propaganda paid for by the CIA.

When a military coup overthrew the elected government of Greece in 1967, the United States at first halted arms aid to the junta, which was hated by the Greek people, but then lifted the ban, explaining that the junta's cooperation was needed as a checkmate to the Soviet Union's expansionism.

Soviet-American relations were worsened by the Vietnam War. Finally, in January 1967 Johnson proposed to Premier Aleksey Kosygin, who with Communist Party Chairman Leonid Brezhnev had succeeded Khrushchev at the helm of the USSR, that they hold a summit conference at Glassboro, New Jersey, to end the arms race between the two superpowers. When

Kosygin and Johnson met, they agreed not to let any crisis in Vietnam or elsewhere push their nations into war with each other.

"Use of the hot line for this purpose, to prevent misunderstanding, was exactly what both parties had envisioned," declared the president. Kosygin said that their agreement had helped them accomplish "more on . . . one day than others could accomplish in three years."

In 1968, there was a popular revolt in Spain against the Fascist dictatorship of Generalissimo Francisco Franco. The Pentagon ordered U.S. Army and Air Force units to join Franco's army in "antiguerrilla" activities in the hills of Spain.

"We have a habit," complained Senator Mike Mansfield, "of trying to get our fingers into every corner of the globe."

One of those fingers was rapped in January 1968 when the USS *Pueblo* and its eighty-three man crew were seized off the coast of Communist North Korea, which accused the *Pueblo* of being a spy ship. Commander Lloyd Bucher confessed to a "criminal act of sheer aggression," but he repudiated his confession when the Americans were released eleven months later.

The cold war in that area heated up further under the Nixon administration. In April 1969, North Korea shot down a U.S. Navy reconnaissance plane for invading its airspace. Angered, Nixon was ready to bomb North Korea in retaliation, until he was dissuaded by Secretary of State William Rogers.

The most dangerous aspect of the cold war was the regional hot war that dominated the sixties and spilled over into the seventies—Vietnam, the war fought by Americans and their proxies against the proxies of the USSR and China. The world was frightened that the losing side would unleash its nuclear arsenal, bringing reprisals and doomsday. Even if there were to be any survivors, the earth would be swept by fire storms and become too radioactive for life anywhere to continue.

In the fall of 1961, the Soviet Union scared Americans by exploding their largest nuclear bomb ever, despite a 1958 test ban treaty signed with the Eisenhower administration. Kennedy ordered a resumption of U.S. underground nuclear tests.

The thunder of H-bombs touched off a new round of bomb shelter hysteria in America. The civil defense coordinator of Riverside County warned California suburbanites to arm themselves against hundreds of thousands from Los Angeles who would flee if their city were bombed. Some ministers insisted it would be morally right to shoot panicky city dwellers who tried to force their way into suburban shelters.

One company reported selling a thousand ready-made shelters a week. "My best salesmen," said its owner, "are Kennedy and Khrushchev." When civil defense drills were ordered, some students at Drew University in New Jersey were arrested for refusing to participate, denouncing the drills for whipping up war hysteria.

Kennedy's experts informed him that the shelters would be largely useless if H-bombs fell. Over one hundred million Americans would be killed instantly, and another fifty million would die from radiation burns. Kennedy persuaded Khrushchev to hold new test ban talks as a first step toward nuclear disarmament. When these began in November, Kennedy ordered a cutback in the procurement of nuclear warheads to prove America's sincerity. Hawks bitterly attacked this move as a blow to national defense.

But John J. McCloy, the president's adviser on disarmament, revealed that the United States was already dangerously overloaded with nuclear weapons. "It is not inconceivable," he said, "that we could blow ourselves up without help from the Russians."

In Moscow on August 5, 1963, the U.S., the USSR, and Great Britain finally signed a treaty banning nuclear tests in the atmosphere, in outer space, and underwater. Limitations were also placed on underground testing.

The following year, China exploded its first atom bomb but declared it would never be the first to use it in a war. The major powers worried about the growing proliferation of nuclear weapons around the world.

In 1965, Americans and Canadians were frightened that nuclear war had begun when a power failure plunged all of Ontario, Buffalo, Rochester, Boston, Albany, New York City, Connecticut, Rhode Island, and Vermont into darkness. Over thirty million people were left without power. The emergency lasted up to thirteen hours, stranding people in subways, skyscraper elevators, and railroad stations. It made millions wonder what they would have done in a blackout caused by nuclear bombs.

Another scare developed the following year when an American B-2 bomber collided with a refueling plane over Spain and crashed, losing four hydrogen bombs. Spaniards worried about the release of radioactivity in their waters.

To add to the war jitters, in March 1968 six thousand sheep in Skull Valley, Utah, suddenly lay down and died. A Congressional investigation found they had been exposed to a nerve gas from an army proving-ground where it had been tested.

On July 1, 1968, to stop the spread of nuclear weapons, President Johnson and representatives of the USSR, Great Britain, and over fifty other nations signed the Treaty on the Nonproliferation of Nuclear Weapons. Nations without a nuclear capability pledged not to try to make or import such weapons. Nuclear nations promised to negotiate arms control and disarmament. The U.S. and the USSR also agreed to put no nuclear weapons into satellites orbiting the earth.

During Nixon's first year in office, Moscow urged further steps leading to disarmament, which resulted in the 1970 Strategic Arms Limitation Treaty (SALT). But the ever-present threat that the cold war would suddenly become a hot nuclear war, by design or by accident, continued to worry the planet.

Sixteen years after writing his cheerful book *The Power of Positive Thinking*, the Reverend Norman Vincent Peale sighed, "This is an awful world, just frightening, and we're stuck with it."

14

SCIENCE LEAPS INTO THE TWENTY-FIRST CENTURY

*T*he Space Age dawned on October 4, 1957, when the Soviet Union electrified the world by shooting *Sputnik I*, the first artificial satellite, into orbit around the earth. A great outcry arose in the American press that American science was lagging behind Soviet science, creating a "missile gap." American education, the media accused, had grown inferior to Russian education, giving the Soviets scientific superiority.

Americans had previously prided themselves that their country was always first and best. As though to humiliate the United States further, in November the Russians shot up *Sputnik II*, a satellite almost ten times larger than its predecessor, with a live dog as its astronaut.

What distinguished the cold war of the sixties was that the conflict took a quantum leap from earth to space. The USSR and the U.S. developed spacecraft and space suits that led them into a race to dominate and control outer space.

The feasibility of rockets capable of great lift and distance had been demonstrated as early as 1926 by Dr. Robert H. Goddard, who had shot a liquid-fueled rocket 184 feet in two and a half seconds at Auburn, Massachusetts. During World War II, Germany's Wernher von Braun had developed the Nazis' V-2 rocket bombs, which had showered terrible devastation on London. After the war, he had been spirited off to America to help the Pentagon develop U.S. rocketry.

Russia's Sputniks served as a spur to American space efforts. Eisenhower created the National Aeronautics and Space Administration (NASA), to develop America's own space program. A new National Science Foundation (NSF) was set up to encourage the nation's brightest science students by providing funds and scholarships. By January 1958, Americans were finally able to put their first earth satellite, *Explorer I*, into orbit.

Through 1959 and 1960, the Russians launched a number of unmanned Sputnik and Lunik cosmic rockets, some going into orbit around the sun and moon. The Soviets released photos of the hidden side of the moon, relayed from their spaceships.

On April 12, 1961, they sent a 27-year-old astronaut, Major Uri Gagarin, into space in *Vostok I* for an orbit of the globe 203 miles above the earth and brought him safely down. From space he reported enthusiastically, "I see the earth in haze . . . it is beautiful." This scientific feat of the first magnitude won the applause of the world for defying gravity, freeing humans for the first time to enter the weightless universe of space.

In the United States, admiration was mixed with chagrin, but President Kennedy sent his congratulations to Khrushchev. Gagarin's historic 108-minute flight at 18,000 miles an hour made him a world hero, but he did not live to see the inevitable follow-up to his mission—the first man on the moon. Seven years later, he was killed in a plane crash while testing a new Soviet aircraft.

Spurred by the Russian feat, the U.S. space program went into high gear. On May 5, 1961, less than a month after Gagarin's accomplishment, American astronaut Alan B. Shepard, Jr., took a suborbital flight 115 miles up, lasting 15 minutes at 5,000 miles per hour, in the one-ton Redstone capsule *Freedom VII*.

"What a beautiful view!" he exulted. Shepard parachuted safely down into the Atlantic and was quickly rescued.

"Do we have a chance of beating the Soviets . . . to the moon and back with a man?" Kennedy asked Vice President Johnson. As chairman of the new U.S. Space Council, Johnson reported a scientific consensus that the Americans did have that chance.

On May 25, 1961, Kennedy gave orders to NASA for a crash program to reach the moon. "I believe that this nation should commit itself to achieving the goal, before this decade is out, of landing a man on the moon and returning him safely to earth," he declared. "No single space project in this period will be more impressive to mankind, or more important for the long-range exploration of space; and none will be so difficult or expensive to accomplish." He proved right on all counts.

Shepard's feat was duplicated on July 21 by Captain Virgil I. Grissom in *Liberty Bell VII*. On August 6, Russia's Gherman S. Titov made the first spaceflight of more than a day in *Vostok II*. During 17 orbits of the earth, Titov admitted that he was occasionally spacesick, but he reported that men could flourish for an indefinite time in a weightless state.

When the Seattle World's Fair opened in 1962, its theme was "Man in the Space Age." The U.S. exhibit featured a "spacearium," offering a simulated spaceship ride that gave visitors film views of outer space. A plastic globe "Bubbleator" lifted them to exhibits demonstrating what life would be like in 2000 A.D. The Russians refused to exhibit their space accomplishments, declaring tersely that they were too busy achieving them.

Americans finally found their own astronaut hero in Marine Lieutenant John Glenn, the first American in outer space. He orbited the earth three times in the *Friendship VII*, traveling 81,000 miles at 17,500 miles per hour. His 5-hour space trip brought a roar of delight from his fellow Americans, who gave him a ticker tape parade in New York City, with Vice President Johnson at his side.

The rocket that launched Glenn into outer space also subsequently launched him into a seat in the U.S. Senate and a bid for the presidential nomination in 1984.

The Russians were impressed enough with America's rapid progress in space for Khrushchev to accept Kennedy's proposal that the U.S. and the USSR cooperate in outer space exploration and research.

On May 24, 1962, Navy Lieutenant M. Scott Carpenter duplicated Glenn's feat in *Aurora VII*. In returning to earth, he overshot his landing site in the Caribbean and was lost to radar for an hour. Although a navy search plane picked up his life raft signal after half an hour, it took another half hour to determine that Carpenter was in it and alive. He had to bob around in the sea for two more hours before a helicopter rescue.

Seven *Mercury* astronauts. Left to right: M. Scott Carpenter, L. Gordon Cooper, Jr., John Glenn, Jr., Virgil Grissom, Walter Schirra, Jr., Alan Shepard, Jr., Donald K. Slayton.

Astronaut Edward White II, pilot for the *Gemini-Titan IV* space flight, floats in space. He is tied to the spacecraft by a twenty-five foot umbilical line and a twenty-three-foot tether line. The visor of White's helmet is gold-plated to protect him from the unfiltered rays of the sun.

Astronaut Edwin E. Aldrin, Jr., walks on the surface of the moon during *Apollo XI* extravehicular activities.

In August, two Soviet cosmonauts, Major Andrian Nikolayev and Lieutenant Colonel Pavel Popovich, made simultaneous space flights in *Vostok III* and *IV*, one with 64 orbits, the other with 48 orbits. Making radar and visual contact with each other, they landed back in the Soviet Union six minutes apart.

The closest splashdown to target was achieved in October after Navy Commander Wally Schirra, Jr., made six orbits lasting nine hours in *Sigma VII*. Returning to earth, he almost landed his spacecraft right on the recovery carrier's deck.

In May 1963, Major L. Gordon Cooper, Jr., made 22 orbits in the Mercury capsule *Faith VII*. His experiments in flight enabled American space scientists to make their first evaluation of the effects of one day in space on a human.

The Russians made history again the following month by sending the world's first woman into space—cotton-mill worker Valentina Tereshkova, 25, who had married Soviet cosmonaut Andrian Nikolayev the year before. She made 48 orbits in *Vostok V*, accompanied by Lieutenant Colonel Valery Bykovsky in *Vostok VI*. Their twin flight included a trial rendezvous and docking maneuver.

In 1963, a U.S. space probe to the planet Venus, launched a year earlier, sent back radio signals that revealed Venus's 800-degree heat—too dry to sustain life. Another scientific breakthrough came with the development of Telstar, Relay, and Syncom satellites. These made it possible for TV networks to exchange live programs with the rest of the world. The U.S. had 52 satellites in orbit, compared to only 15 for the Russians. But former president Eisenhower was not impressed with Kennedy's space aspirations. "Anybody who would spend [so much money] in a race to the moon for national prestige is nuts," he scoffed.

Kennedy prepared a speech to answer him: "This effort is expensive—but it pays its own way, for freedom and for America." But he did not deliver the speech, because Congress took note of Eisenhower's views and sliced NASA's budget.

In October 1964, the Russians established a new record by sending up the first spaceship with three cosmonauts. They worked and lived in the *Voskhod I* without space suits, staying up a day and making 16 orbits. That year, meanwhile, the U.S. sent unmanned *Ranger VII* to take close-up pictures of the moon and search for suitable landing sites. It ended by crashing onto the moon's surface, the first physical contact between earth and its natural satellite.

In March 1965, the Russians thrilled the world again when Colonel Aleksei Leonov made the first walk in space from the *Voskhod II*, floating over the USSR for 10 minutes.

Five days later, the U.S. scored its own first, when Virgil Grissom and John Young, in *Gemini III*, became the first astronauts to steer a spacecraft onto a new orbital path. This historic flight freed astronauts from imprisonment in fixed orbits, giving spacecraft nearly the maneuverability of airplanes.

Less than three months after the Soviet walk in space, the U.S. duplicated the feat with *Gemini IV*, which made 62 orbits in three and a half days. Air Force Colonel Edward H. White, Jr., walked in space over California. When a worried Ground Control tried to get him to return to the spacecraft, the exhilarated White protested, "This is fun—I'm not coming in!"

He set a new space walk record of 20 minutes.

On August 21, 1965, astronauts L. Gordon Cooper, Jr., and Charles Conrad, Jr., set a new space record in *Gemini V* by staying up for 120 orbits lasting almost 8 days. Even that record was bettered in December by *Gemini VII*, when astronauts Frank Borman and James A. Lovell, Jr., flew 206 orbits lasting over 13.5 days. *Gemini VI*, commanded by Wally Schirra and Thomas Stafford, was sent up while *Gemini VII* was still in orbit. The two spaceships flew in formation for 4 hours, coming as close as one foot from each other.

In February 1966, the Russians achieved the first soft landing on the moon by steering a 200-pound sphere to it from a *Lunar IX* spacecraft.

In March 1966, the U.S. became the first nation to complete a docking maneuver. The *Gemini IX*, manned by Commander Neil Armstrong, the first American civilian astronaut, and Major David R. Scott, linked with the satellite Agena, opening up the possibility of linkage between a space station and supply spaceships.

But after seven hours, their spaceship began to shake violently and roll. Ground control ordered them to unlink and come down. When *Gemini* parachuted into the Pacific, not all Americans watching on TV were fascinated. Hundreds of thousands protested angrily to NBC and CBS for canceling their favorite TV shows in order to cover the splashdown and rescue effort.

Four months later, Navy Commander John W. Young and Major Michael Collins flew *Gemini X* for 43 orbits, docking again with the Agena target. Collins made a 50-minute space walk, the longest to that date. A similar flight followed in September by Charles Conrad, Jr., and Richard Gordon, Jr., who set an altitude record of 739.2 miles above the earth. In November, Jim Lovell and Major Edwin E. (Buzz) Aldrin took *Gemini XII* on a 4-day flight. Working on the outside of the spaceship, they took photos of a solar eclipse from space.

The first physical contact with another planet was made in 1966 by the Russians, after a 106-day trip to Venus. Their unmanned *Probe III* crashed on the planet's surface.

In December, the U.S. and the USSR negotiated a "Treaty on Principles Governing the Activities of States in the Exploration and Use of Outer Space, Including the Moon and Other Celestial Bodies." The treaty foreshadowed joint flight in space less than a decade later by Soviet and American astronauts. It was agreed that no matter who reached the moon or any planet first, these bodies would be considered the property of all humanity. The treaty also banned using nuclear or other destructive weapons in outer space.

Tragedy struck the U.S. space program on January 27, 1967. Fire broke out aboard the spacecraft *Apollo I* while on the ground at Cape Kennedy, Florida. Three astronauts—Navy Lieutenant Commander Roger B. Chaffee, Grissom, and White, the first American to walk in space—were killed as they sat in the command module during a preflight exercise. Grissom had once acknowledged, "The conquest of space is worth the risk of life." The deaths of the three astronauts put a damper on the American space program.

Not until October 11 of the following year were astronauts Schirra, Air Force Major Donn Eisele, and civilian Walter Cunningham allowed to fly *Apollo VII*. Their pre-moon, 11-day flight involved separating from and rejoining a second-stage rocket. In TV broadcasts from space, they joked about "the one and only original Apollo road show, starring the great acrobats of outer space," referring to the weird gymnastics they could perform while weightless.

Then in December, *Apollo VIII* rocketed off with astronauts Borman,

Lovell, and Major William A. Anders, the first humans to fly around the moon. Views of the lunar surface were televised to fascinated viewers on earth. When their orbit took them to the far side of the moon on Christmas Eve, leaving them out of radio contact for 36 minutes, there were fears that they might be pulled down by the moon's gravity. Americans breathed easier when the *Apollo VIII* reappeared on schedule, then made 10 orbits 70 miles above the moon, surveying possible sites for a future landing. Lowell described the moon's surface as "a sort of grayish beach sand."

The Russians were able to get a *Soyuz III* flight to circle the moon that year, but it was only an unmanned flight. Americans were jubilant that they had overtaken and passed the USSR in the space race. In January 1969, however, the Russians did succeed in docking *Soyuz IV* and *Soyuz V*, with a spectacular interchange of astronauts between the two spacecraft.

The old love song "Fly Me to the Moon" proved prophetic in 1969, the target date set by John F. Kennedy. In May, astronauts Thomas P. Stafford, Eugene A. Cerman, and John W. Young, launched from the *Apollo X*, made the first lunar module orbit of the moon. They photographed the best landing sites from just 47,000 feet above the moon.

Then on July 16, Neil Armstrong, Buzz Aldrin, and Michael Collins took off in the *Apollo XI* for an 8-day lunar trip. Collins kept the spaceship in orbit 65 miles above the moon. During its 13th orbit on July 20, Armstrong and Aldrin crawled into the *Eagle*, *Apollo's* 16-ton piggyback module. Rocketing toward the moon's surface, they skimmed along, looking for one of the recommended landing zones.

But they were forced to land quickly when they had only 15 seconds' worth of fuel to spare, if they were to conserve enough to raise off the moon for a later rendezvous with the *Apollo XI*. At 4:17 P.M. Cape Kennedy time, they landed on a rocky, boulder-strewn site. The extended legs of the *Eagle* made it look like some science fiction monster crab.

Aldrin had been selected as the first to step out on the moon, but Armstrong, as flight commander, designated himself to be first. At 10:56 P.M., with the whole world watching and listening on TV, Armstrong climbed down the ladder of the *Eagle* and set foot on the moon. "That's one small step for man," he told the world, "one giant leap for mankind." He bounced around the surface for 19 minutes in an appearance of slow motion, raising little clouds of moon dust. When Aldrin joined him, they reported that the moon's surface was fine and powdery, adhering to their space boots.

Earthlings watched the spacemen make comical, floating jumps while conducting scientific experiments and collecting 50 pounds of moon rocks and soil. Although temperatures ranged from 243 degrees in sunlight to 279 degrees below zero in shade, they were comfortable in their space suits. Aldrin described the moon as "beautiful, beautiful—magnificent desolation."

The astronauts planted the U.S. flag and a plaque reading: "Here men from planet earth first set foot on the moon, July 1969 AD. We came in peace for all mankind." Aldrin left cans with messages from 76 other nations. Speaking to them on the moon, President Nixon declared, "This certainly has to be the most historic telephone call ever made."

After 2 hours and 14 minutes of their historic moon walk, the astronauts climbed back into the *Eagle* and rocketed off to rendezvous with *Apollo XI* on its 31st orbit of the moon.

After a successful splashdown back on earth, the lunar explorers were accorded a tremendous welcome home by New York City, which had celebrated their adventure with a simultaneous "moon bash" in Central Park. Millions had danced to "moon music" as they had watched the televised lunar landing on huge outdoor screens. The thrilled city gave the astronauts a heroes' ticker tape parade. Americans felt proud that the U.S. had come from behind to win the space race.

In October, the first triple spaceship orbit of the earth was made by the Russians' *Soyuz VI, VII,* and *VIII.* They made space lab construction tests and welded metals in space for the first time, opening up commercial possibilities for producing new alloys impossible to achieve on earth.

The remarkable space decade closed in November when Charles Conrad, Jr., Richard F. Gordon, and Alan L. Bean made a second trip to the moon. Conrad and Bean became the third and fourth men to walk on the lunar surface as they collected almost 75 more pounds of rock and soil samples for over 3 hours.

Despite the thrill of watching the first men on the moon, a Harris poll in July found that 56 percent of Americans opposed further spending of $4 billion a year for space programs. They felt that since the moon had been conquered, such huge sums could better be used solving problems at home.

The Reverend Jesse Jackson, a leading spokesman for black Americans and later a presidential candidate, declared, "While we can send men to the moon, we can't get foodstuffs across town to starving folks in the teeming ghettos." Other skeptics charged that costly spaceflights were primarily a form of national showboating to score prestige points against the Russians.

But space technology had important ramifications in the form of new scientific techniques and equipment quickly adopted by industry as advanced technology, known as "high tech." The advances made in copy machines, color TV, videotape, computers, video games, push-button phones, weather satellites, freeze-dried foods, calculators, plastic and paper clothes, and other modern products owed much to the development and release of space-age technology.

Science in the sixties opened up the possibilities of future space travel and living in space. It also brought about a remarkable quantum leap in medicine. In 1967, Dr. Christiaan Barnard of South Africa accomplished the first successful heart transplant. This was followed in the U.S. by a second transplant by Dr. Adrian Kantrowitz. These operations opened up the possibility of extending human life indefinitely through replacing diseased organs with healthy ones from deceased donors.

Before the sixties, travel to the planets and stars and the replacement of worn-out vital organs of the body were only the stuff of science fiction. After the sixties, the question was no longer *if*, but *when*.

15

Defenders of Consumers and the Environment

A nonprofit youth organization, Environmental Action, Inc., staged "Earth Day" on April 20, 1970, to dramatize the pollution problem. It was a climax of the struggle to stop pollution of the American environment during the sixties. Over twenty-two U.S. senators took part, along with many governors. Over 2,000 college campuses, 2,000 community groups, and 10,000 schools joined in nationwide demonstrations.

Volunteers helped clean up littered ghettos. Car engines were buried as polluters in mock funerals. Students wore gas masks to protest air pollution. Young people collected trash and returned it to the companies that had produced it.

Former senator Gaylord Nelson warned, "Progress—American style— adds up each year to 200 million tons of smoke and fumes, 7 million junked cars, 20 million tons of paper, 48 million cans, and 28 billion bottles."

Pollution rose sharply in the wake of the material prosperity of the sixties. Americans were spending freely to provide themselves with an affluent life-style. As more and more people moved to the suburbs, shopping malls began to proliferate all over the country, offering stores, restaurants, movies, and fountains with benches where teenagers hung out. Middle-class youths in the sixties were raised with far more comforts than youngsters of any previous generation.

The middle-class American home provided its family with hair dryers, washer-dryer combinations, electric carving knives and toothbrushes, frozen foods, patio barbecues, pocket radios, disposable diapers, electric can openers, disposable milk cartons, kitchen wall phones, and two, and sometimes three, color TV sets per home.

Modern technology also made changes in the way people in the sixties ate and drank. Food and drinks could be bought from vending machines. Millions of women bought liquid diets, like Metrecal and Sego, and low-calorie diet sodas. Foods could be sprayed onto bread from aerosol cans. Freeze-drying allowed coffee, cheese, and other products to be condensed in small containers, with water added to restore the product to its original form. To cut down on food preparation time, potatoes, cream, soft drinks, and whole breakfasts could be bought in instant form.

A California health food craze spread to the rest of the country, glorifying alfalfa sprouts, yeast, wheat germ, bran, yogurt, and organically grown vegetables. At the same time, inexpensive fast-food drive-ins like McDonald's flourished, offering what health food addicts contemptuously called "junk food"—low-cost hamburgers, french fries, and milk shakes.

Alert to the public embrace of this cornucopia of material blessings, some manufacturers and business interests pursued a "fast buck" by offering unsafe or defective products and using deceptive advertising. American consumers were often vexed by the failure of the government to stop these practices.

With the arrival of John F. Kennedy in the White House, consumers found a sympathetic ear in Washington. In a special message to Congress, the president delineated four basic consumer rights—to be safe, to be informed, to choose, to be heard.

During the Kennedy and Johnson administrations, consumers found these acknowledged rights to be more than lip service. For example, a Truth-in-Lending Act compelled finance companies and stores to state clearly, in big print, exactly how much consumers were being charged for borrowing money or for buying merchandise on time.

A growing consumer movement was spearheaded by Ralph Nader, an

Earth Day brought a new awareness of environmental issues to the public. Here a student wears a gas mask to dramatize pollution dangers.

Students make their opinions known during an antipollution project called Earth Week.

incorruptible crusader who organized a band of idealistic young lawyers and investigators to expose shoddy products, deceptive ads, and products or practices hazardous to the public health. They were primarily responsible for the passage in Congress of the Wholesome Poultry Product Act and the Consumer Product Safety Act.

Nader exposed mismanagement of the Federal Trade Commission (FTC). This agency was supposed to prevent deceptive business practices, but instead it often covered up offenses of the industries it was supposed to regulate. Nader's pressure compelled the FTC to issue new regulations requiring advertisers to prove the truthfulness of their advertising claims. Many advertisers were forced to cancel deceptive ads.

The consumer movement also caused the Food and Drug Administration (FDA) to crack down hard on unsafe drugs. In 1961, Dr. Frances Oldham Kelsey, an FDA pharmacologist, refused to allow a drug company to market sleeping pills called thalidomide in the United States, insisting that there were not enough data to support claims that they were safe and effective.

Her wisdom was proved in 1962, when ten thousand deformed babies, with dwarfed arms and legs and damaged organs, were born to European mothers who had taken thalidomide. Congress immediately broadened the FDA's inspection powers to make certain U.S. drugs were safe as well as effective. Kennedy gave Dr. Kelsey the Presidential Award for Distinguished Service. In 1963, the FDA declared the alleged "miracle cure" for cancer, Krebiozen, to be worthless and refused to allow it to be marketed here.

In 1964, the Public Health Service (PHS) branded cigarettes a leading cause of cancer, heart disease, emphysema, and bronchitis. Eventually tobacco companies were forced to stop advertising on TV, and they had to label cigarette packs and cartons with the warning, also carried in newspaper ads, "Caution: Cigarette smoking may be hazardous to your health."

The consumer movement compelled Congress to set up committees investigating fraudulent products. In 1965, a Senate committee found that useless food fads and quack cures were costing Americans over a billion dollars a year. Many victimized the elderly, who resorted to them because they could not afford the crushing burden of doctor and hospital bills.

The Social Security Law was amended in 1965 to provide Medicare—health insurance for Americans 65 or over, giving them access to legitimate medical service.

The public was shocked and aroused in 1962 by disclosures in Rachel Carson's book, *Silent Spring*. She reported that DDT, the pesticide farmers used to spray fruits and vegetables, was passed from mother to embryo, so that babies were being born with poison in their systems. She also warned that pesticides were putting the balance of our ecology in serious peril. Public agitation brought about a ban on the use of DDT in American farming and forced the chemical companies to develop less dangerous substitutes.

These substitutes also came under attack by conservationists and environmentalists, who charged that their massive use still constituted an ecological threat. The Sierra Club made Americans more conscious of the need to protect our environment not only for ourselves today, but also for our children tomorrow.

In 1962, Congress passed an agricultural act that provided subsidies for farmers who agreed to take land out of production, either putting it in a soil bank—holding it in reserve for future planting—or using it for water, forest, wildlife, or recreational resources.

Pressure for a stronger federal role in water purification came in 1963 with the U.S. Surgeon General's report that over thirty million Americans lived in 1,500 communities that permitted either sewage or factory wastes to be discharged into the streams from which they drew their drinking water. State water laws were highly ineffectual. In one-third of the states, not a single polluter had been brought to court before the sixties, because states feared to drive away industries guilty of polluting streams. In 1961, Congress amended the Water Pollution Control Act to strengthen its enforcement provisions.

Many states were also reluctant to enforce air pollution control programs because of the expense involved. In 1963, Congress passed the first Clean Air Act, increasing federal financial and technical assistance to state and local pollution control agencies. Three years later, on Thanksgiving Day, air polluted by industry smokestacks was trapped by a weather inversion above New York City, killing 168 people with respiratory problems. The tragedy emphasized the still urgent need to purify the air over America's cities. In 1967, Congress passed a second Clean Air Act establishing new smokestack standards for industry.

Proposing his "Great Society" in May 1964, President Johnson declared, "The water we drink, the food we eat, the very air that we breathe, are threatened with pollution. Our parks are overcrowded, our seashores over-burdened. Green fields and dense forests are disappearing." He promised federal programs that would tackle all of these problems.

One result was the Wilderness Act of 1964, placing over nine million acres of government land into a wilderness conservation system, with car travel and commercial establishments banned. But conservationists fought the administration's plans to divert water from Northwest rivers to irrigate the dry Southwest. Additional dams and waterworks, they charged, would impair the natural beauty of the canyons.

Through the active support of the First Lady, Lady Bird Johnson, Congress was induced in 1965 to pass a highway beautification bill to end the spoiling of landscaping on federal highways by outdoor billboards and junkyards.

That year Nader's "Raiders" brought about the Water Quality Act to improve the safety of the nation's drinking water.

The whole issue of pollution so aroused Americans in the sixties that Congress heard from them in no uncertain terms. No less than thirteen congressional committees were set up to study environmental problems and try to solve them.

Second only to the impact of *Silent Spring* was Nader's own book, *Unsafe at Any Speed*, published in 1965. In it he exposed all the dangerous features of cars produced by the major motor companies. The book infuriated the Detroit carmakers, who claimed that customers didn't care anything about safety features. But Nader's pressure led to the 1966 Vehicle Safety Act, setting up a federal agency to enforce such design changes as padded dashboards, headrests to prevent whiplash, safety belts, and safety glass. They also compelled the recall of cars that were found to have defective features.

Infuriated executives of General Motors hired a private detective to "get something on this guy . . . get him out of our hair . . . shut him up." But their investigation could not discover a single unsavory thing about the valiant David who was attacking the Goliath auto industry. Even worse for them, their spying was exposed, and Nader sued General Motors for invasion of privacy. The case was settled with a public apology by GM, accompanied by half a million dollars that Ralph Nader promptly used to expand his crusades on behalf of the public.

The book, the lawsuit, and Nader's successful fights against shoddy corporation practices won him instant access to members of Congress, who invited him to testify at committee hearings. Nader left his impact on all kinds of consumer legislation.

In 1968, his exposé of dangers to workers on gas pipelines and in coal mines led to the Natural Gas Pipeline Safety Act. That same year his revelations about the risks of exposure to nuclear radiation brought about the Radiation Control for Health and Safety Act.

"All my life in politics," said former senator Gaylord Nelson, "I've heard that there ought to be someone to represent the general interest of the public. Ralph is the first one to come along and show us the impact that a single informed voice can have. His contribution has been greater than that of anyone else in contemporary times."

In February 1969, an oil rig near Santa Barbara blew out and began spilling oil that fouled forty miles of southern California beaches, destroying sea life, killing seabirds, and soiling thousands of small boats. Outraged Sierra Club conservationists and environmentalists forced the Department of the Interior to order offshore oil rigs to stop drilling operations. They also went to court to fight the oil companies that held drilling leases on coastal waters. That issue continues to be fought, with coastal states insisting on the right to protect their environment against the federal leasing of offshore oil fields.

The sixties marked the beginning of a vigorous consumer movement fighting for the rights of the American public to be considered before corporation profits.

"Consumers have begun to make themselves heard in legislative hearings, before regulatory agencies, and in the courts," observed Philip J. Dodge, an official of the Cooperative League of the USA. "They have gained a grudging respect from lawmakers . . . who earlier had hardly recognized their existence, and from business itself."

16

Revolution Now— the New Left

*T*he sixties revolt on many U.S. campuses paralleled the example of college students around the world, who had long been active in revolutionary movements against their governments. Scott Buchanan, late dean of St. John's College, Annapolis, observed, "In Asia, Africa, and probably in South America . . . you haven't quite got your credentials unless you have a jail record. You are not quite decent. You're not certified as honest unless you have been to jail." Historically, revolutionary movements in France, Germany, and other European countries had also been sparked and fought by college students.

Many American students were radicalized by the stormy events of the sixties. Some were influenced by the Old Left—the Communist Party and other Marxist groups—which persuaded them that it was a waste of time trying to reform the system. But most belonged to what became known as the New Left—an unorganized radical movement with no specific program of its own except a dedication to bringing down the Old Order as corrupt, immoral, and obsolete.

New Leftists led the assault on the university system. They challenged the way the universities were run—the irrelevance of many courses; the neglect of undergraduates by professors who concentrated on research, much of it for big business and the military; the depersonalization of education by big "multiversities" that numbered as many as thirty thousand students on a single campus; the indifference of universities to the civil rights and Vietnam crises; and university regulations that treated students as children instead of as responsible young adults.

Some New Leftists sacrificed their own comfort, time, college degrees, and future to work full-time at changing both the universities and the larger society. Neglecting classes or dropping out of college, they sought defiant confrontations designed to radicalize popular sentiment behind them.

The most militant New Leftists used deliberately provocative tactics to compel a university administration to call police onto campus. That would also bring in press and TV photographers to record scenes of police charging student demonstrators. Public indignation would be aroused, on and off campus, at the sight of boys and girls brutally clubbed and bloodied.

When a college president fell into the militants' trap, they would then organize a strike to shut down the campus. Students and faculty members who had not been part of the original demonstration, but who were outraged by the use of police on campus, would support the strike. The uproar sometimes compelled the president to resign, and his successor would grant concessions to the strikers in order to reopen the university.

Off campus, violent black militants organized the Revolutionary Action Movement of the Black Liberation Front of the U.S.A. Begun in 1963, RAM was based on the teachings of Robert Williams, a black ex-marine. Williams had been so embittered by the treatment of blacks in America that he had once written to President Eisenhower expressing his desire to renounce his citizenship.

As head of the Monroe, North Carolina, NAACP, Williams began to arm its members, insisting, "Negroes . . . must henceforth meet violence with violence." Suspended by the NAACP and wanted by police on a kidnapping charge, he fled to Cuba in 1961, where he was given asylum as a political refugee. From Radio Havana he told American blacks, "Not only does freedom require the will to die, but it also requires the will to kill."

Dedicated to the overthrow of American Capitalism and its replacement by a Communist system like China's, RAM recruited black militants and sent them to Williams in Cuba for training in guerrilla warfare and sabotage. Two were subsequently arrested in New York for conspiring to murder moderate black leaders Roy Wilkins and Whitney Young. Fifteen other RAM members were arrested in Philadelphia and New York City for planning to assassinate government officials and murder police officers.

Rising discontent among blacks during the sixties led police departments to target many black individuals and organizations for surveillance by infiltration and wiretapping. In the summer of 1964, when black militant Robert Collier formed a revolutionary group in Harlem, the New York City Red Squad assigned black officer Raymond Wood to infiltrate it. Wood tipped off a plan by Collier to blow up the Statue of Liberty, Washington Monument, and Liberty Bell to dramatize Collier's accusation that America no longer deserved these symbols of liberty. Wood accompanied Collier to Quebec to secure the dynamite, after which police and FBI agents arrested Collier and his confederates.

In the South, another black militant group was active—the Deacons of Defense and Justice. Their heavily armed members guarded black homes, opening fire on harassing Ku Klux Klansmen. The Deacons, said their vice president, Ernest Thomas, intended to use pistols and rifles to dispel a southern belief that attacked blacks feared to fight back.

The student New Left began in June 1962 with Students for a Democratic Society, which became a highly effective, militant faction in the forefront of organizing confrontations with the government.

"We wanted action, not discussions," Carl Oglesby, SDS president in 1965-66, explained. SDS was pressed to become more and more radical by members who were Maoists, Socialists, Trotskyites, anarchists, and Castroites, while moderate members sought to limit SDS to peaceful protest demonstrations.

A similar struggle was going on in civil rights organizations. In 1966, SNCC's black leader, John Lewis, who sought to keep the organization nonviolent, was replaced with black militant Stokely Carmichael, who urged Black Power violence.

Beginning in 1966, the CIA Office of Security secretly trained city police at Ft. McClellan, Alabama, to spy on dissident groups. Trainees were told, "The individual or organization that threatens to destroy our society must be identified." They were taught how to break into buildings, crack safes, pick locks, and use telephotography and other surveillance methods.

The New Left, angered at being targeted for surveillance and police brutality, turned increasingly to revolutionary-type actions in despair of accomplishing their goals peacefully. They began cooperating with black militant groups.

In 1966, Huey Newton, Bobby Seale, and Eldridge Cleaver were leaders of the Black Panther Party, which was demanding complete black control of the ghettos, including businesses, police, and the courts; freedom for all blacks in prison, who were considered victims of a racist society; and draft exemption for all blacks from the "racist war" in Vietnam. They espoused frankly revolutionary tactics and sought to win support in the ghettos by feeding free breakfasts to underprivileged black children. Black Panther coloring books for children glorified the killing of white police.

In Los Angeles, three Panthers were killed in a gun battle with police who had stopped and searched them for weapons. A grim feud broke out between police and Panthers all over the country. Shoot-outs caused deaths on both sides. Cleaver, Newton, and Seale were all charged with murder.

White police were convinced that the Panthers were arming to gun them down as front-line forces of the white Establishment. The Panthers accused the police of seeking to exterminate them under any pretext. They armed their followers to defend themselves, and they sandbagged their head-quarters against police attacks.

In May 1967, while the California State Assembly was debating gun control, twenty-six Black Panthers invaded the legislature with shotguns, pistols, and rifles, none of the weapons concealed. Security guards dis-armed them.

Armed Panthers clashed with police in city after city. Although the Justice Department denied it, police raids on Panther headquarters to seize stockpiles of weapons seemed synchronized to wipe out the Panthers as a force.

Many Panthers were shot and killed. A split developed in Panther ranks between leaders who considered violent tactics suicidal and those who felt that only armed resistance could protect the ghettos. Alarmed, Congress viewed these chaotic developments as signs of a widespread revolutionary conspiracy.

"We have the leaders of SNCC and similar organizations going around from state to state preaching Black Power and inciting riots," complained Mississippi Congressman William Colmer. "Here we are with one Stokely Carmichael and one Rap Brown . . . traveling from state to state and from

A Cornell University building was occupied by militant students who emerged thirty-six hours later.

The clenched fist held meaning for many organizations and a great number of people in the sixties. Among other things, it symbolized revolution, student strikes, black power, women's rights, and the antiwar movement.

city to city, and in their wake comes conflagration, blood-spilling, whole-sale pilfering, and the loss of life and property."

Although Congress had passed what was known as the Rap Brown Act (which made crossing state lines to "stir up trouble and cause riots" punishable by a ten-year jail sentence and twenty thousand dollar fine), Attorney General Ramsey Clark objected, stating that riot control was a local problem. He argued that Washington should not prosecute demonstrators but should instead protect their First Amendment rights of free speech and assembly against arbitrary punishment as "rioters" by local officials.

"Let's forget the First Amendment!" snapped Louisiana Congressman F. Edward Hébert. The Rap Brown Act was used by the Nixon administration to prosecute the Black Panthers and other dissenters.

"There is a constitutional right to be an 'outside agitator,' " protested the ACLU. It pointed out that a Rap Brown law in the 1850s could have sent abolitionists to jail for ten years for crossing state lines to agitate against slavery. Most prosecutions under the Rap Brown Act were subsequently overturned on appeal to higher courts.

Eldridge Cleaver was the voice of the black revolutionary movement. "There was a great big gap in my soul that had to be filled," he wrote. "I filled it with the Black Revolution."

He led the Black Panthers into a working relationship with white militants. After white antiwar demonstrators had been brutalized by Chicago police at the 1968 Democratic Convention, Eldridge wrote, "They've been beaten, maced, teargassed. They themselves have now experienced what's been happening to black people for so long. . . . They never thought it could be done to them. They are turning into a revolutionary force, and that's why we believe the Black Panthers can enter into coalitions with them as equal partners."

Collaboration had already begun in the spring of 1968 when Mark Rudd, heading SDS, had led the student seizure of five buildings of Columbia University. Carmichael and Rap Brown had joined the revolt. Brown urged that if the gym barred Harlemites, "the people in Harlem should blow it up." SDS distributed over two million leaflets attacking Columbia for racism and for cooperating with military research. The university was forced to shut down, and Mark Rudd vanished into the revolutionary underground.

More and more white SDS militants saw cooperation with Black Power revolutionaries as the best way to force significant change in America. They were impressed by the considerable media attention the Black Power movement received, as evidenced during the Summer Olympics in Mexico in 1968, when black runners Tommy Smith and John Carlos won gold and bronze medals in the 200-meter race. At the victory ceremony, while the U.S. flag rose and "The Star Spangled Banner" was played, the two athletes raised their arms in the clenched-fist Black Power salute. Sensational photos of the incident made front pages and magazine covers. The two black athletes were thrown off the Olympic team.

Black Power made headlines again in April 1969 when armed black students at Cornell seized Willard Straight Hall to protest racism and demand an African Studies college.

More and more, moderate SDS members grew discouraged by the failure of peaceful tactics to create any significant change after almost a decade of resistance. "In 1969 I wrote a book about it," declared SDS activist Dotson Rader, "and tried to face up to the fact that only extreme measures would bring change here."

That summer, Brown University valedictorian Charles Magaziner gave a commencement address he called "The Necessity for the Cultural Revolution in the United States." He listed a long list of lies about the Vietnam War that he charged the government with telling, leading to his disillusionment.

That same summer, SDS broke up in a struggle between moderates, who still wanted to continue resistance tactics, and radicals, who felt that only open revolution could effect change. The militants had lost interest in trying to win effective support from liberal students. They demanded that SDS form alliances with black revolutionaries and white working-class radicals.

By the end of August, SDS had split into three groups—the Worker Student Alliance (WSA), the Revolutionary Youth Movement (RYM), and a number of unaffiliated chapters. The WSA became the principal SDS organization, affiliated with the Chinese Communist-oriented Progressive Labor Party.

A rump group of about 1,500 split off from the RYM to form the Weathermen. They vowed to practice revolutionary tactics as an underground paramilitary group, fighting the Establishment with guerrilla tactics. Their leaders, some of them women, soon appeared on the FBI's list of Ten Most Wanted Criminals. Chief among them were Mark Rudd and Bernadine Dohrn.

The Weathermen identified strongly with the Black Power militants. "The most important task for us toward making the revolution," they declared, ". . . is the creation of a mass revolutionary movement . . . with a full willingness to participate in the violent and illegal struggle." They proclaimed themselves unafraid to die while carrying on activities to destroy the American Capitalist system.

The Weathermen took credit for a number of bombing attacks against the New York City Police Department, the Long Island City Courthouse, and the Bank of America offices in New York City. Most of their bombs were homemade Molotov cocktails made with apple juice bottles. The FBI infiltrated the Weathermen with two undercover agents.

Early in October 1969, the Weathermen's underground newspaper announced they were sponsoring four "Days of Rage" in Chicago. The paper declared, "We're going to Chicago to fight anyone who plays pig," meaning police. But the WSA warned the event would prove a police trap: "No one should go to it."

The four-day "Rage" brought to Chicago four hundred youths wearing crash helmets and carrying long nightsticks. Rampaging through the streets, they broke car windshields and store windows. Three were wounded by police gunfire, and 150 were arrested. Next month twelve Weathermen leaders were indicted for complicity in the violence.

Meanwhile the police escalated clashes with the Black Panthers, ninety-five of whom had been arrested by the end of May 1969. The leader of the Illinois Panthers, Fred Hampton, held a joint press conference with representatives of the Blackstone Rangers and the Black Disciples, rival Chicago gangs, to announce a truce.

"Now we are all one army," they declared.

The police began raiding Panther offices and residences; gun battles erupted frequently. In New York, twenty-one Panthers were indicted for conspiring to bomb department stores, police stations, and the Statue of Liberty. In Los Angeles, four shoot-outs resulted in the wounding of three Panthers and three police. Eight other Panthers were shot dead in Los

Angeles and San Diego. Chicago Panthers, constant targets of police raids, accused the police of destroying their office, stealing money, setting a fire, and ruining food and medical supplies.

The Chicago police denied the charges. Their war with the Panthers came to a climax at dawn on December 4, 1969, when fourteen heavily armed Chicago police raided the apartment of Fred Hampton, where seven other Panther members were also sleeping. In the blazing gun battle that ensued, Hampton was killed in his bed and four others were wounded. Police claimed the raid had been intended to seize weapons stashed in the apartment, and officers had fired only in self-defense. But an investigation showed that up to one hundred police bullets had been fired, with a return fire of only one shot.

"They came in shooting," wounded Panther Brenda Harris testified. "They shot me, they shot Mark Clark, and this other pig, he came in with a machine gun and he started shooting toward the back, he sprayed the wall, he was shooting toward the back and they were yelling to each other, 'There is some over there in the back, get them,' and he would shoot over toward that direction and he was just shooting with the machine gun, just going crazy."

Thirteen of the fourteen police raiders were subsequently indicted, but none were convicted. Public feeling ran high against the Panthers, whom Attorney General John Mitchell had branded a threat to national security.

From jail in San Francisco, Huey Newton accused the police of genocide against the Black Panther Party. By the end of the sixties, the leadership of the Panthers had been effectively crippled. Hampton was dead, Newton was in jail, Cleaver had fled to Cuba to escape a prison sentence, and Carmichael was in Africa.

With the Weathermen's leaders indicted or running for cover in the underground, the "revolution now" movement seemed to have run its course.

"The sixties, like they came so fast," reflected Yippie Abbie Hoffman later. "Bang! Wham! Zowie! We don't even know what hit us. We're still spinning! We got to figure out what the hell we are and what the future is. . . . The movement's finished. It's *weirds*ville! It's over."

The main reason it was over was that the New Right had routed the New Left with the presidential choice of the Moral Majority. At the end of 1968 Richard M. Nixon was elected by a public weary of demonstrations, riots, and confrontations.

17

"AMERICA: LOVE IT OR LEAVE IT!"—THE NEW RIGHT

*E*arly in the sixties, extremist right wing propaganda created a Red scare that alarmed many Americans. In 1963, the U.S. Army began a field training exercise in Georgia called Water Moccasin III. Some troops were assigned the role of simulated enemy forces in war games. The exercise included 124 foreign officers attending a U.S. combat school, as well as civilians.

Right-wingers spread a nationwide rumor that Water Moccasin III was a UN plot to plant foreign troops on U.S. soil under the control of a Russian general. Congress, local papers, and radio stations were deluged with hysterical protests. The Americans United Council in Long Beach, California, warned: "Your Country, your Native Land—the United States of America—has just been invaded by military troops of foreign lands!"

Senator Thomas H. Kuchel observed, "Clutching at half-truths and downright falsehoods, the fright peddlers fabricate hoaxes, as we have seen, which frighten Americans. . . . They sow suspicion and hatred. . . . They degrade America and Americans, and do it as well as—or better than—the Communists do."

The right's paranoia about Communist subversion had also been the excuse for cracking down on liberal Americans who opposed right wing causes.

Americans who had relied on the Bill of Rights to protect their free speech, free thought, and free association had been badly shaken by the assault on civil liberties during the late 1940s and 1950s by Senator Joseph McCarthy and the House Un-American Activities Committee (HUAC).

With the cooperation of the FBI under J. Edgar Hoover and of right wing organizations, many liberals had been smeared with a Red label and targeted for harassment and persecution.

By 1960, the FBI had collected approximately 423,000 dossiers on individuals and groups considered "subversive." The list included educators, labor union organizers and leaders, writers, lecturers, news reporters, lawyers, doctors, scientists, and "other potentially influential persons on a local or national level."

Extreme right-wingers joined businessman Robert Welch's John Birch Society, which he founded in 1959. It spread so rapidly that in two years it had chapters in thirty-four states, with a hundred chapters in California alone. Welch accused President Eisenhower of being a Communist Party member and "a dedicated, conscious agent of the Communist conspiracy." Other Americans he named as Red agents included the president's brother, Milton Eisenhower; Secretary of State John Foster Dulles; his brother Allen Dulles, head of the CIA; and five-star General George Marshall.

In September 1960, Welch instructed Birch members to "join your local PTA at the beginning of the school year, get your conservative friends to do likewise, and go to work to take it over." PTAs, he ordered, should be turned into forums for right wing ideas. The Birchers also led campaigns to disrupt school boards, harass city councils and librarians, and furtively paste Communist labels on any Polish hams seen on store shelves.

In *The Blue Book* of the John Birch Society, Welch warned that unless right-wingers joined the Society and donated all the time and money they could to its purposes, in a few years they would be forced to donate "*all* to the maintenance of a Communist slave state." Democracy, Welch explained, "leads to the dangerous path of Socialism and Communism."

When Kennedy became president, Welch labeled him an "immoral man who can do a tremendous amount of ball-carrying on behalf of Communism here in the United States." In June 1962, Welch said, "I categorically predict that the United States will be occupied by Chinese Communist troops by summer 1972. This is the Kennedy plan."

Some southern fundamentalist preachers attacked many American churches as Communistic. The Reverend Billy James Hargis of Tulsa, Oklahoma, broadcast his Christian Crusade over two hundred radio stations and a dozen TV outlets. He told his listeners, "Eighty-two hundred Protestant ministers have joined Communist fronts since the 1930s."

Major General Edwin A. Walker, commanding the 24th Infantry Division in Germany, indoctrinated his troops with Birch Society propaganda. "For twenty years," he declared, "the United States government has acted as if it were the agent of the Soviet Union." Senator William Fulbright protested. "If the military is infected with this virus of right wing radicalism," he told President Kennedy, "the danger is worthy of attention." Kennedy forced Walker's resignation from the army, and Secretary of Defense Robert McNamara forbade military officers to express politically partisan views in public.

Senators Strom Thurmond and Barry Goldwater, both major generals in the Reserves, furiously denounced Fulbright for "an insidious attack upon our military leaders." The radical right raised a huge campaign fund to defeat Fulbright in the next election, but Arkansas voters reelected him with a huge majority.

FBI Chief J. Edgar Hoover approved of right wing organizations and was hostile to those on the left. In October 1961, he secretly began Operation COINTELPRO, which permitted the FBI to spy on and harass the Socialist Workers Party (SWP) and its affiliated Young Socialist Alliance (YSA), because of their support for "such causes as Castro's Cuba and integration problems . . . in the South."

The growth of the student protest movement led to a small right wing backlash on America's campuses. In opposition to SDS was the Young Americans for Freedom (YAF), most of its members from prosperous, conservative homes. They were enthusiastic devotees of novelist Ayn Rand, Senator Barry Goldwater, and William F. Buckley, the polysyllabic editor of the conservative *National Review*.

In 1964, Senator Goldwater sought the Republican nomination for president to oppose Johnson's election. He urged greater military defiance of the Soviet Union "with appropriate nuclear weapons if the ultimatum is rejected." He was enthusiastically endorsed by the far right, which wanted to use atomic weapons against North Vietnam and wage "preventive war" on China.

House Speaker Joseph Martin resigned from the Republican National

Committee in protest at the Republican Party "becoming a branch of the John Birch Society." He pointed out that Goldwater was the only Republican candidate "vigorously supported by the Birchers and the rightist lunatic fringe." When New York Governor Nelson Rockefeller tried to denounce the Birchers at the 1964 Republican Convention, he was drowned out by boos.

Roars of approval greeted Goldwater's acceptance speech with its famous line, "I would remind you that extremism in the defense of liberty is no vice."

Goldwater went down to overwhelming defeat in the 1964 elections. But exactly twenty years later, a similar ultra-conservative platform was approved by the Republican Party National Convention that renominated President Ronald Reagan.

The anti-Vietnam opposition that grew in intensity as Johnson expanded the war brought a governmental backlash. In 1964, the CIA created a secret Domestic Operations Division (DOD) with offices in twenty cities to spy on anti-Vietnam groups. Dissident organizations were also infiltrated by the Minutemen, who secretly trained in guerrilla warfare.

Following Goldwater's defeat, Minutemen leader Robert B. DePugh wrote in a newsletter to his secret army of self-styled "patriots": "The hopes of millions of Americans that the Communist tide could be stopped with ballots instead of bullets have been turned to dust. . . . You are now living in a Communist-occupied territory. . . . If you are EVER going to buy a gun, BUY IT NOW! . . . Form a secret Minuteman team."

In June 1965, Senator Thomas Dodd warned that the Minutemen aimed at developing a "vast underground army." The following year their plan to assassinate Senator Fulbright was discovered, and one Minuteman was arrested. Several private Minutemen arsenals were located and confiscated.

Another army of "patriots" was the American Nazi Party led by George Lincoln Rockwell, a former Navy commander dismissed from the Naval Reserve in 1960 for his Nazi activity. Three months after the assassination of President Kennedy, their publication carried a picture of President Johnson with a gun sight pattern across his head. Above it was the word "Next?"

Rockwell and his Nazis went into the deep South to stir up white violence against civil rights marchers. "The nigger revolution," he warned,

A member of the Minutemen, a militant anti-Communist group, aims a rocket launcher during guerrilla-style maneuvers.

Yippies with painted faces march at the 1968 Democratic Convention in Chicago. Hundreds of antiwar demonstrators were clubbed by local police.

"will openly threaten to plunge its final dagger into the beating heart of our Republic." After black riots erupted in Chicago, the Nazis organized white gangs that attacked and beat up blacks.

Although the Birch Society, the Minutemen, and the American Nazis represented only the more extreme right-wingers who viewed Democrats as Communists, there were Americans in high places whose outlook was similar. During Senator Strom Thurmond's 1966 campaign for reelection, he called President Johnson "a traitor to the nation as well as to the South," because of Johnson's civil rights program.

The right wing was deeply upset by Supreme Court decisions during the sixties. Chief Justice Earl Warren, although appointed by conservative President Eisenhower, presided over the Court during its period of greatest liberal influence for social change. The Warren Court compelled school integration through busing; banned school prayers; enforced black voting rights; upheld the right of free speech; and strengthened the rights of persons accused of crimes.

In 1963, the Court set aside the conviction of penniless Clarence Gideon for burglary because he had been denied the right of counsel at public expense. (In a later trial Gideon was found not guilty.) In 1966, the Court overturned the conviction of Ohio osteopath Sam Sheppard for killing his wife, because of excessive pretrial publicity. That same year, the Court forced dismissal of a rape-murder charge against Ernesto Miranda because arresting police had failed to read him his Fifth Amendment rights.

Most Americans were deeply disturbed by a steadily increasing wave of violent crime in the cities. In March 1964, a twenty-eight-year-old Queens, New York, woman, Kitty Genovese, was attacked on the street by a man who kept stabbing her. Her screams woke thirty-eight apartment-dwellers, who watched from their windows for half an hour, with no one going to her aid or phoning the police, for fear of "getting involved." The news story shocked the nation.

In 1966, crime statistics reported one car theft every minute, one assault every three minutes, one robbery every five minutes, one rape every twenty-six minutes, one burglary every twenty-eight minutes. Public indignation led President Johnson to call for a war on crime. The right wing accused the Warren Court of releasing criminals to continue their violence against society, instead of sending them to prison for long terms.

During 1967, the CIA and the National Security Agency (NSA) stepped up spying activities on the antiwar movement. Yet a CIA study of all U.S. intelligence-gathering activities found that they were collecting "too much information," much of it duplicated or useless. CIA Director Richard Helms suppressed this report.

FBI agent Robert Wall revealed that the FBI, in its efforts to disrupt the antiwar movement and the political New Left, had resorted to forgery, break-ins, tapping phones, and many other illegal acts. "In trying to suppress and discourage a broad-based national political movement," Wall declared, "it acted as a national political police."

Local law enforcement agencies cooperated with the CIA, FBI, and army intelligence in surveillance of the New Left. Sometimes even rulings by the Supreme Court were not enough to stop illegal spying activities. In August 1967, the Court ruled that New York's laws permitting bugging were unconstitutional, yet Brooklyn District Attorney Aaron Koota declared defiantly that he would still continue to wiretap.

In 1968, FBI Chief Hoover testified before the National Commission on the Causes and Prevention of Violence chaired by Milton Eisenhower. Hoover said that Communists were in the forefront of civil rights, antiwar, and student demonstrations. The commission rejected his views as wrong. Yet in May 1968, Congress passed an Omnibus Crime Control and Safe Streets Act that allowed the government to use electronic surveillance to "protect national security."

That summer, the anti-Vietnam demonstrations outside the Chicago Democratic Convention were infiltrated by army spies who wore concealed radio transmitters. They reported to nearby army trucks disguised as delivery vans. One spy, Ronald Weber, admitted later, "If the media ever got hold of the fact that there was an army intelligence unit . . . operating in Chicago . . . a lot of people would have had to answer a lot of questions."

Conservative Americans watching the demonstrations on TV considered them unpatriotic. When Mayor Daley's police began to crack heads indiscriminately, millions of viewers were less outraged by what was later officially judged a "police riot" than by seeing demonstrators there.

Bewildered and angered by the stormy events of the sixties, conservatives demanded an end to the disruption of their peace of mind. Blue-collar workers joined hands with lower middle-class whites to form the New Right, shouting the slogan: "America—love it or leave it!"

Praising them as the "silent majority," Republican candidate Richard

Nixon promised to restore "law and order." The New Right understood these code words for cracking down hard on the black ghettos, both to wipe out street crime and to suppress racial rioters, and on student militants. Nixon also appealed to the New Right by attacking Supreme Court decisions upholding the rights of those accused of crimes. He wooed southern conservatives by vowing to curb integration of the nation's schools.

Third party candidate George Wallace competed for New Right votes by campaigning under a banner that read: STAND UP FOR AMERICA! He voiced conservative frustration over demonstrations, riots, crime, and integration. A Washington bureaucracy, Wallace cried, was ignoring the ordinary American's problems while pampering the lazy and undeserving, the criminal and unpatriotic.

He also demanded Bible reading in the schools, and he opposed gun control laws as subversive. "We ought to register Communists, not guns!" he cried, adding, "We're gonna show 'em in November that the average American is sick and tired of all these over-educated ivory-tower folks with pointy heads lookin' down their noses at you and me!"

Wallace's appeal to the New Right garnered almost ten million followers. But the split in Democratic ranks over the Vietnam War let Nixon beat him to the White House with the votes of conservative Southerners, "hard hats," and "middle Americans," although Nixon captured only 43.4 percent of the popular vote.

At the outset of the Nixon administration, Attorney General John Mitchell signaled its intention to turn America to the far right. "Watch what we do," he suggested, "not what we say."

One of Nixon's first significant acts was to appoint conservative Warren Burger the new Chief Justice of the Supreme Court. Nixon followed that with three other appointments of conservative new justices, changing the Court's orientation from liberal to conservative. Ironically, even after Nixon was forced to resign the presidency, his handpicked Supreme Court majority continued to impose his influence on the nation.

The polarization of Americans intensified when Nixon refused to end the war, despite his campaign pledge that he had a plan to do so within six months. The split was deepened by his alienation from the student world and by his favoring his white "silent majority" at the expense of the black community. When demonstrations against his policies grew thunderous, Nixon appealed to the New Right for support.

In 1969, a Gallup poll found that the man most admired by Americans was Richard M. Nixon, who, only five years later, became the first president compelled to resign to escape impeachment. The third most admired American was his vice president, Spiro Agnew, also compelled to resign his office, for accepting bribes as a governor.

"We Americans are an essentially decent people," sighed one news reporter, "but we sure are lousy judges of character!"

Encouraged by the Nixon administration, the New Right stepped up attacks on all liberal programs initiated by the Democrats. In January 1969, the John Birch Society led its members in "organized, nationwide, intensive, *angry*, and determined opposition to the now mushrooming program of so-called sex education in the public schools."

In April, Nixon ordered his aide John Ehrlichman to have the government's spy agencies probe for evidence that protest demonstrations were Communist-inspired from abroad. Nixon also ordered him to sabotage dissident groups. With these orders, the government aligned itself with the New Right's attacks on both liberals and the New Left.

Senator Adlai Stevenson III, Congressman Abner Mikva, folksingers Arlo Guthrie and Joan Baez, child authority Dr. Benjamin Spock, and civil rights leader Julian Bond subsequently discovered that they all had one thing in common—a dossier in the files of army intelligence. They, among one hundred thousand other civilians opposed to the Vietnam War, were spied on by 1,500 army secret agents. Reports on their private and public activities were fed into data banks all over the country. One young woman member of SDS was fired as a substitute postal clerk when the FBI reported her participation in a protest demonstration.

Nixon tripled the budget of Attorney General Mitchell, who increased the number of bugging operations by six hundred percent. The FBI infiltrated the ranks of antiwar, New Left, and black militant organizations with informers and *agents provocateurs* who provoked violence to discredit these groups.

At the same time, Mitchell did little to enforce desegregation, in spite of Supreme Court decisions and the Civil Rights Acts of 1964 and 1965. This was the reward to southern leaders for their election support.

Mitchell testified in Congress against renewal of the Voting Rights Act to enfranchise blacks. He also proposed a "no knock" bill allowing police to break into homes without showing a search warrant, despite the Fourth

Amendment protecting citizens against unreasonable search and seizure. He won passage of the bill in Congress.

"In the '60s," observed political satirist Mort Sahl, "we saw the pernicious effect of accepting the big crimes—the assassinations, the war—and classifying the small crimes as violations of law and order."

The right wing backlash against civil disorders encouraged police to get tougher with demonstrators. In 1967, civilian law enforcement agencies spent one million dollars on tear gas and other riot control weapons. In 1968, that sum increased to twenty-two million dollars. In 1969, the army also spent eleven million dollars for that purpose.

The right wing was delighted in 1969 when the biggest threat to a second term for Richard Nixon, Senator Edward Kennedy, became involved in a controversial incident that made his future candidacy questionable. On July 19, Kennedy drove his car off a bridge in Chappaquidick, Massachusetts. His passenger, Mary Jo Kopechne, a former staff aide to his brother Robert, drowned in the accident. Kennedy swam to safety. Many questions were raised about the propriety of his behavior during the tragedy. He told his side of the story on national TV, offering to resign if the people of Massachusetts requested it. Chappaquidick crippled the hope of the Democrats to nominate Kennedy to recapture the White House from the Republicans in 1972.

When the New Left mounted huge demonstrations in 1969 to protest Nixon's expansion of the Vietnam War into Cambodia, the president, angered by media coverage of these events, told his aides, "The press is the enemy." He was particularly enraged at critical evaluations by TV network commentators immediately after his TV speeches.

Vice President Agnew was assigned the task of delivering stinging speeches against the media's "effete corps of impudent snobs," charging TV newspeople with anti-Nixon bias. The president's chief aide, H. R. Haldeman, organized a campaign by Nixon's right wing supporters to "pound the magazines and networks" with letters and wires protesting as unpatriotic any criticism of the president. Over CBS-TV, Nixon speechwriter Pat Buchanan urged viewers to demand that "every legal and constitutional means" be taken "to break the power of the networks."

The TV networks grew alarmed. Station licenses depended on government approval; they could be revoked if TV broadcasts were judged to be "not in the public interest." The networks began blacking out reports of protest demonstrations. Some militant demonstrators, denied public attention, turned to violent tactics to compel media coverage. This, in turn, only intensified the New Right backlash.

Haldeman also orchestrated a campaign of blistering telegrams, letters, and phone calls from New Right supporters all over the country to senators opposed to Nixon's programs. "The president," observed *The New Yorker* writer Jonathan Schell, "had set in motion an elaborate hidden machine for manufacturing the appearance of public enthusiasm for himself."

In September 1969, the Nixon administration was applauded by the New Right for prosecuting the leaders of the alleged conspiracy to create the riots at the 1968 Chicago Democratic Convention. The trial was intended to intimidate the antiwar movement from mounting new demonstrations against Nixon.

So the sixties, which changed the political climate of America to one of fierce New Left protest demonstrations, ended with a New Right backlash that threatened to make the nation more conservative than it had ever been.

"This country is going so far right," declared Attorney General Mitchell in July 1970, "you are not even going to recognize it!"

18

Aftermath—Consequences of the Sixties

*T*he stormy sixties were followed by the disillusioning seventies. Popular resistance to the Vietnam War soared in May 1970 when President Nixon expanded the war into Cambodia. Over two hundred thousand protesters staged a huge, orderly March for Peace in Washington, resulting in thirteen thousand mass arrests, a record high for any civil demonstration in American history.

Four days after the killings at Kent State, construction workers in New York City broke up a student antiwar demonstration on Wall Street, injuring nearly seventy with fists and clubs as they attacked any long-haired youths within reach. When Mayor John Lindsay lowered the flag at City Hall to half-mast in honor of the dead Kent State students, the hard hats invaded City Hall to raise it back.

One worker expressed hard hat resentment of student demonstrators: "We put our sweat and blood into building this city. Now these punks want to bring it all down with bombs and riots. They ain't American. Send 'em to Russia. This is our city and our country. We built it."

Over the four years of Nixon's first term, troop withdrawals from Vietnam took place slowly, and in small numbers. As troops were replaced by ARVN forces, the war went on.

194

New vindication for the resistance was provided in June 1971 by Daniel Ellsberg, a former Pentagon official, who turned over classified Pentagon documents to *The New York Times*. The paper defied the Nixon administration's attempt to prevent publication. The Pentagon Papers revealed that the government had lied about, and misrepresented, the Vietnam War to the American people.

American involvement in Vietnam finally wound to a dismal end on January 27, 1973, a week after Nixon's second inauguration, as peace terms were hammered out in Paris. All American forces were to withdraw from South Vietnam, and Hanoi was to return all U.S. prisoners of war. North Vietnamese forces would remain in areas of South Vietnam they occupied. These were the same terms Hanoi had offered Nixon four years earlier, which he had then rejected.

So ended a disastrous war that had cost the lives of at least 58,655 U.S. servicemen and caused the wounding of another 155,419. Over a million Vietnamese civilians had also been killed. The war had cost Americans tens of billions of dollars, and the billions spent on armaments contributed to soaring inflation.

On April 30, 1975, South Vietnam surrendered to North Vietnamese forces, and the whole country fell under Communist rule.

The Vietnam disaster shook the American conviction that U.S. power was so great it could win any war. Many Americans were angry and incredulous that American might had not prevailed against a tiny Communist nation. Right-wingers believed that the U.S. had fought "with one hand tied behind its back," refusing to understand the difficulties of defeating a people patriotically united in guerrilla warfare against a superior foreign power.

The Vietnam War made Americans wary of getting involved in another prolonged guerrilla war on foreign soil. When President Reagan sent troops to invade the Caribbean island of Grenada in 1984, charging that its Marxist government was a proxy for Moscow, he was careful to withdraw almost all U.S. forces quickly after overthrowing the regime in power.

Although Reagan used the CIA against both the Socialist government of Nicaragua and left wing rebels in El Salvador, he avoided direct military intervention in those Central American countries for fear of getting bogged down in another Vietnam and facing voter outrage. Thus the sixties' anti-

Vietnam movement exercised an important and significant brake on American foreign policy, which would probably hold for the indefinite future. Congress in the sixties had adopted the Tonkin Gulf Resolution that had permitted President Johnson to wage undeclared war in Vietnam. Congress in the eighties was extremely wary of giving another president similar war powers.

The seventies and eighties created some changes in public perception of the Vietnam veterans. Upon their return home, they had received a chilly reception, as though the unpopular war had been their fault. Many who had been forced by the draft to fight in Vietnam or go to prison felt unjustly treated.

Amends were made when many Americans, including those who had most bitterly opposed the war, realized the unfairness of blaming those who had been compelled to fight it. A special memorial to the Vietnam War dead was raised in Washington, D.C. The public also insisted on a genuine effort by the Veterans Administration to offer rehabilitation to veterans crippled physically or mentally by the war. Veterans were compensated with a $180 million fund for injuries caused by the dangerous defoliant Agent Orange. This had been sprayed on the Vietnam countryside to remove concealment of Viet Cong and North Vietnam troops, but had also injured the lungs of American troops fighting there.

Public support rallied as well to the side of army veterans of the sixties who had been exposed to nuclear bomb tests in Nevada, which the government had insisted were harmless. When many developed cancer, a federal judge blamed the government for offering both soldiers and civilians false assurances. Towns around the bomb sites showed up to eight times the normal incidence of cancer. Thus atomic tests of the sixties taught the public to distrust government claims that such tests do not cause cancer, miscarriages, liver damage, nerve injury, and birth defects to people exposed to them.

This distrust was extended to government assurances about the safety of dumps for dangerous chemicals and radioactive nuclear wastes, which often proved a public health hazard.

The resistance movement, powerful during the sixties, dwindled with the signing of the Vietnam peace treaty and the end of the military draft. Nevertheless its impact lingered on, with no administration in the seventies or eighties daring to reintroduce the draft, each relying only on voluntary enlistments.

The Vietnam War hit the headlines again in 1984 when General William Westmoreland sued CBS and Mike Wallace for libeling him in a 1982 "60 Minutes" program. It had declared that he had deceived President Johnson and the Joint Chiefs of Staff in 1967, just before the Tet offensive, by misrepresenting the enemy's strength, to make it appear that the U.S. was winning the war. In 1985, the suit was settled out of court.

As though the Vietnam fiasco weren't enough to cause millions of Americans to lose faith in their government, they were shocked further by the Watergate scandal. This resulted from Nixon's attempt to cover up an illegal break-in at Democratic headquarters by a Republican burglary team seeking political ammunition for the 1972 reelection campaign. White House prestige had never sunk lower than when Nixon became the first president in American history forced to resign to escape impeachment proceedings, which the House had already voted to begin.

Thus when Jimmy Carter and Ronald Reagan subsequently became presidential candidates, they both appealed to the electorate with campaigns emphasizing that they were *not* identified with the discredited Washington Establishment.

Republican President Gerald Ford, finishing Nixon's term, sought to restore public confidence by promising an open administration. His successor, Democratic President Jimmy Carter, tried to revive America's international prestige by emphasizing his administration's concern for human rights around the world. But Americans saw him as a weak leader when he failed to free fifty-two U.S. hostages held by the hostile government of Iran.

In 1980, Republican candidate Ronald Reagan projected himself as a strong leader who would restore American prestige to its pre-Vietnam level and stop inflation by "getting government off our backs." His administration reversed the sixties domestic policy of enlarging social programs, but ironically it echoed Lyndon Johnson in fighting Communism by involving American power in the civil wars of little countries. It also echoed Jimmy Carter in making blunders in the Middle East. Reagan stationed U.S. Marines in strife-torn Lebanon until Shiite Moslems killed 241 with a truck bomb in 1983.

Moving the nation to the right again, President Reagan escalated the military budget and enacted legislation favorable to big business. Personally popular, he was reelected by a landslide in 1984, when employment was high and inflation low.

In a survey of its 1984 graduating class, Bucknell University compared the results with a similar survey of its 1968 graduates. Eighties collegians were found to be much less absorbed in politics—only forty-two percent compared to fifty-three percent in the stormy decade. Liberal arts had been the program of choice of the sixties. In the eighties, economics majors tripled in number. There would be fourteen times fewer high school teachers among the eighties graduates. Only thirty-three percent of sixties students had wanted to work for a large corporation, compared to forty-five percent in the eighties. Clearly, the anti-Establishment feeling of sixties students had diminished considerably by the eighties, the years of the business-oriented Reagan administrations.

Eighties students were also found to feel a stronger sense of allegiance to their parents than the rebellious students of the sixties. They tended to study harder instead of spending time in political demonstrations.

Some changes wrought by the sixties in our social structure have now faded into mere memories. Other changes are still with us, part of the fabric of today's world. Transient or enduring, they shaped the values of the youths of the sixties, many of whom are the parents of today's young people.

The tragedy of Kent State, traumatic in its time, has almost been forgotten today. But not entirely. When the university sought to erase its memory by erecting a building on the grounds where the four students were killed by National Guardsmen, angry protests by the student body forced them to abandon the plan. Instead a memorial to the dead students was erected at the site where they died.

The lesson of Kent State still influences university policy today, as a result of the President's Commission on Campus Unrest, which found in October 1970 that the National Guard at Kent should never have been sent onto campus with loaded weapons. They reached the same conclusion about the police who killed two black students and wounded ten others at Jackson State College later that year. Today college students feel free to mount protests on campus without fear of being shot down for doing so.

In 1984, the Free Speech movement that began at Berkeley in 1964 was commemorated by a week-long celebration. Some five thousand Berkeley students listened to its leader, Mario Savio, recall the excitement and significance of those earlier days. "The Free Speech movement," he declared, "was a brilliant moment when we were both moral and successful." Now, he told his listeners, the American government was "preparing a bloodbath" in Central America. "It will destroy their society and tear ours absolutely apart," he warned. This time he wasn't arrested.

The Age of Camelot, as the Kennedy years were known, died with the assassination of the youngest elected president in American history. Today he is still remembered sadly by many adults who were young in 1963, but who now often tend to be cynical about whoever occupies the White House. The Kennedy style, however, influences some younger presidential candidates who hope to inspire the same kind of enthusiasm he engendered. In the 1984 Democratic race for the presidential nomination, one of the front-runners, Senator Gary Hart, was seen by the media as striking Kennedy poses and sounding very much like the late president.

Hart won the support of the "Yuppies"—young, upwardly mobile professionals—but he narrowly lost the nomination to Walter Mondale, who was swamped in the election by Ronald Reagan.

During the storm-tossed sixties, it often seemed as though black Americans had given up on the hope of social justice in America and had resolved on a course of violent Black Power confrontation as the only way to compel meaningful change.

But despite the traumatic assassination of black leader Martin Luther King, Jr.—and possibly in part because of it—the civil rights movement made enough progress in the seventies and eighties to sweep black mayors and legislators into elective office in greater numbers than ever before. In 1984, the Reverend Jesse Jackson became a serious candidate for the presidency.

This was the result of the sixties civil rights movement, which registered millions of new black voters who exerted their numerical power at the polls. Most black leaders also succeeded in convincing followers that violence only destroyed their own neighborhoods and killed their own people, while change by ballot gave them control over their own lives. By the eighties, Black Power violence had become a dead issue, with many former advocates like Eldridge Cleaver preaching instead a new adherence to born-again Christianity.

White America also learned a lesson from the Black Power violence of the sixties. The racists who had sought to suppress the Freedom Riders with clubs, guns, police dogs, and fire hoses, lost popular support. Most Americans realized that if social justice were denied to blacks, they could reap the whirlwind in fire storms and cries of "Burn, baby, burn!" It made more sense to Americans of the seventies and eighties to keep the peace by letting blacks participate fairly in the electoral process, winning wherever they had the votes and assuming responsibility for the direction of their own lives.

The intense countercultural movement of the sixties faded during the seventies and eighties with the ending of the Vietnam War and of opposition to civil rights. Significantly, Yippie Jerry Rubin took a job in Wall Street. SDS leader Tom Hayden married actress Jane Fonda, who helped him win election to the California legislature. Flower children who had put daisies in troops' gun barrels became suburban housewives.

There were, however, pockets of Establishment opposition that refused to disband. Fifteen years after the tumult over the People's Park in Berkeley, when police battles with demonstrators had left one dead and 128 wounded, the university finally yielded and made the site a park.

"This place means we've done something to the entrenched institutions—the Reagans, the corporations, the damn war machine," proudly declared George Kaufman, who had been on the staff of the *Berkeley Barb* when it had originally urged seizure of the park. "No matter how they build, no matter how many skyscrapers, there's one place where the sun's gonna shine. And it's *our* sunshine."

Although the hippie movement faded rapidly during the seventies and eighties, some twenty-five thousand members of the counterculture joined a "Rainbow Family" reunion in the Moduc National Forest of California in 1984. Many hippies camping in tents, yurts, and tepees openly used marijuana and LSD. Over five thousand joined in an hour of silent prayer on a mountaintop. Many brought children who marched in a parade with painted faces, banners, and balloons.

U.S. Forest Rangers and sheriff's deputies from six California counties expressed bewilderment at the mix of drugs and religion, but they made no arrests. Many hippies expressed confidence that during the nineties the counterculture would once more come into its own.

"I think the sixties will have an effect as long as we're alive," declared folksinger Bob Reid. "It's dormant in a lot of us. Deep inside we have this feeling for what is right, for what we want the world to be."

But when another counterculture reunion took place in Grossinger, New York, in 1984 to celebrate Woodstock, the thousand or so who attended, including Abbie Hoffman, had come a long way from the muddy festival of the sixties. "Now," said observer Dawn Colwell, "they want to reminisce about the sixties during the day, and stay in a nice hotel room and eat rye bread and roast beef at night."

Most eighties youths renounced the symbols of the sixties. Long hair was out; so were hippie clothes. A nationwide 1984 poll taken by the *Daily News Record* found that while most youths of the sixties had never pressed their clothes, fully seventy-four percent of eighties' youths eighteen to twenty-four frequently or always did so.

While rock music endured, it underwent variations like hard rock, punk rock, and heavy metal. Rock festivals continued to attract large audiences, but nothing since ever approached the size, joy, and ambience of the famous Woodstock festival, not even the heavily hyped Victory Tour of superstar Michael Jackson and his brothers in 1984.

Since Woodstock, said critic Albert Goldman in *Life*, "the rock festival has degenerated into a grotesque tragicomedy peopled by swindling promoters, gate-crashing kids, club-wielding cops and money-mad stars. The world that once adored those innocent boys, the Beatles, which decked itself with flowers, practiced transcendental meditation, came together in the joyous Woodstock festival, danced wildly and spoke gently of love and peace—that beguiling world now lies broken."

Shades of Woodstock were seen in 1985 when an international chain of televised simultaneous rock concerts attracted hundreds of thousands of enthusiastic fans and raised sixty million dollars to feed starving Africans.

The Beatles, to the great distress of their fans, split as a group. Each group that sought to take their place seemed faded copies of the original. Fans were further grieved when John Lennon, who had written the anthem of the peace movement, "Give Peace a Chance," was murdered in 1980.

The music world also mourned the death of the Beach Boys' drummer, Dennis Wilson, who drowned in a diving accident in 1984. The Beach Boys' sixties hits had won a fan in First Lady Nancy Reagan. This came to light in the eighties when Reagan's Secretary of the Interior, James Watt, ruled the Beach Boys unsuited to play at a Fourth of July celebration in Washington. Watt subsequently apologized and soon resigned when his pro-business decisions outraged environmentalists.

The artistic innovations of the sixties faded with their adoption by the advertising world and the decline of the counterculture. What did persist were fantasy comics and their extension into TV and movies. These appealed to an audience intent on vicariously escaping humdrum reality through fantasy and science fiction. In the conservative climate of the eighties, TV or movies dealing with nuclear disaster or other unpleasant possibilities attracted increasingly smaller audiences. Two exceptions were the 1984 TV special "The Day After," which revived widespread fears of nuclear war, and "Testament," a dramatization of the dreaded event starring Jane Alexander and William Devane.

In 1984, the Reagan administration sponsored a revival of old-fashioned, religion-flavored patriotism, seeking to erase the last vestiges of national guilt and inferiority feelings over the U.S. disaster in Vietnam. At the Los Angeles Olympics that year, ABC-TV commentators as well as spectators displayed open pride over U.S. athletic victories.

ABC-TV offered a new program, "Call to Glory," glorifying the military. Hollywood produced *Red Dawn*, a film portraying patriotic resistance to a fictional Soviet invasion.

Films dealing with youth no longer represented youth persecuted by redneck America, as in *Easy Rider*, but youth with traditional adolescent problems as they had been depicted in the fifties.

The eighties saw a decided intellectual decline in the fare offered TV viewers, leading many to switch to pay-TV. Soap operas jumped from the afternoon TV "ghettos" to prime time TV, where evening audiences were offered "Dynasty," "Dallas," and other serial soaps as the networks' major efforts. The only consolation for intellectuals was that the Western fad had died. In its place, viewers were offered police dramas, glorifying the pursuit of crime, and medical dramas, glorifying doctors.

On Broadway in the eighties, musical comedies were the main fare. Audiences were not eager to pay high ticket prices to see dramas that questioned the status quo. On the best-seller lists of the eighties, cookbooks, diet books, and self-improvement books increasingly usurped top place, while born-again Christian tomes attracted a large readership.

The sexual revolution of the sixties had lasting effects. Many millions of couples decided to live together without marriage, for as long as they loved each other. But both promiscuity and homosexuality suffered a reverse when it was revealed that an epidemic of incurable genital herpes was sweeping the country, affecting heterosexual couples, while an incurable, fatal disease called AIDS (Acquired Immune Deficiency Syndrome) was affecting homosexuals and others. More and more Americans became sexually prudent out of fear.

Women who went off the Pill out of anxiety over possible dangerous side effects, reverting to less dependable methods of birth control, became more cautious about their sex lives.

The permissive climate of the sixties gave many homosexuals the courage to "come out of the closet" and live openly as homosexuals. Banding together for voting power through the seventies and eighties, they strongly influenced the political structure of some cities and states and had to be reckoned with as a pressure group by candidates. In San Francisco, it was estimated that fifty percent of the population was homosexual.

The feminist revolution of the sixties persisted and thrived, primarily due to the increasing number of women choosing or compelled to enter the labor market. Working women saw no reason why, as breadwinners, they should be paid less than men for similar jobs. Nor when married to or living with a man, why they should be expected to do most of the home chores. Many of their younger, less rigid mates were willing to respect women's equal rights and tried to do their share in the home.

The women's movement grew so powerful that in 1984, for the first time in American history, a major political party, the Democrats, nominated a woman, Geraldine Ferraro, as their candidate for vice president. Most political observers felt that from then on, American politics would no longer be able to ignore qualified women candidates.

During the eighties, with a president who went out of his way to court the born-again Christian vote, the nation saw a vast revival of evangelism. Right wing preachers like Jerry Falwell, Jimmy Swaggart, and Kenneth Copeland attacked conventional churches and organizations like the National Council of Churches for being liberal instead of espousing right wing ideology and Bible dogma.

Some Eastern-inspired religions, like the sect of Bhagwan Shree Rajneesh, ran into trouble with the communities where they sought to take root. Some were forced to move to other states, which also fought them as alien cultures trying to "take over."

At the same time, avant-garde sixties movements like Esalen and others teaching yoga, sensitivity training, est, body awareness, and the like continued to thrive in states like California, where millions preferred the sounds of a different drummer.

The sixties as an era of assassinations had strong overtones that outlasted the decade, with international reverberations. Leaders all over the world became aware of the dangers of assassination, forcing them to be careful in public. Political assassinations became so commonplace during the seventies and eighties, in a world increasingly torn by political strife and warfare, that public officials everywhere came to accept death by terrorists as an occupational risk.

The menace of terrorism intensified with suicide missions by Islamic fanatics who smashed trucks full of explosives into American army posts and embassies. Concrete blocks were built around the White House to prevent such suicidal raids. Even so, in 1981 President Reagan and three of his entourage were shot and seriously wounded in Washington. Six years earlier President Gerald Ford had survived two assassination attempts.

The cold war of the sixties grew steadily worse in the decades that followed. After the Russians shot down a Korean civilian airliner that had strayed over sensitive Soviet military bases, calling it a U.S. spy plane, President Reagan denounced the USSR as an "evil empire." The Russians were infuriated further when he stationed new Soviet-targeted missiles in Europe.

Relations became even chillier in 1984 when, in a supposedly off-the-record microphone test, the president joked about having "outlawed" the

Aerial photograph of the 1982 dedication ceremonies for the Vietnam memorial in Washington, D.C.

On August 8, 1974, President Richard Nixon announces his resignation over nationwide television.

Democratic vice-presidential candidate Geraldine Ferraro holds up a shirt proclaiming "A woman's place is in the White House."

Soviet Union, then announced that he would drop a nuclear bomb on them in five minutes. Millions of Americans and Russians were shocked by this grim jest. The Moscow press pointed to it as symptomatic of the kind of thoughts ever present in the back of the president's mind.

But when it became apparent to the Russians that Reagan would be elected to a second term, they grudgingly allowed Soviet Foreign Minister Andrei Gromyko to meet with the president during a visit to the UN to discuss a resumption of arms control talks between the two nations. These occurred in 1985, when Reagan met in a November summit conference in Geneva with the new Soviet leader, Mikhail Gorbachev.

The Space Age introduced in the sixties continued through the seventies and eighties, with both the Russians and Americans steadily expanding extraterrestrial knowledge through new space flights. In 1975, President Carter scored a breakthrough in Soviet-American relations when the U.S. and the USSR took a joint flight, linking their spaceships, exchanging crews, sharing meals, conducting joint experiments, and holding a joint news conference afterward. The worsening of the cold war, however, dampened further space collaboration.

Nevertheless, humanity's venture into space during the sixties had several important consequences for the decades that followed—some good, some bad. The high tech fallout of the space program brought consumers remarkable new products that improved the quality of daily living. And the world was fascinated by the astonishing pictures and information sent back by unmanned space probes visiting other planets in the solar system.

One of the unfortunate results of the space program was the possibility that future world wars might be fought in space—"Star Wars." President Reagan asked Congress for funds to develop this military capability.

The impact of the sixties space program made an indelible impression on the American public. When people in Florida were polled in 1984, fully eighty percent could not recall who Vice President Spiro Agnew was. But ninety-eight percent recognized the name of Neil Armstrong and knew the astronaut's accomplishment.

In 1984, American space flights set new records. The shuttle *Challenger* went into orbit with the largest crew ever—five men and two women, Sally Ride and Kathy Sullivan—who studied the earth and the oceans. Sullivan made the first space walk by an American woman. The crew accomplished the first refueling of a satellite in space. The Russian *Soyuz*

T-11, with three astronauts aboard, established an endurance record for space flight of almost two-thirds of a year.

The revolutionary New Left dwindled in importance after the Vietnam War and the draft ended, with black voter registration in the South achieved. Many revolutionaries sought by the FBI for violent acts committed during the sixties changed their identities and disappeared to lead quiet lives. Others, like Jerry Rubin and Eldridge Cleaver, left the movement and joined the Establishment they had once fought so hard to overturn.

On the other hand, the New Right grew increasingly strong as Americans turned more conservative. With Reagan in the White House, they saw many of their cherished convictions—the need for prayer in the schools, for outlawing abortion, for sterner punishment for criminals—voiced and supported by the president. When the Republican Party Convention met in 1984 to renominate Reagan, the New Right won every battle to include their planks in the party platform. His reelection victory encouraged them to feel their objectives would soon be achieved.

Environmentalists whose causes flourished in the sixties suffered severe setbacks during the Reagan administrations. The president's first Secretary of the Interior, James Watt, sold off public lands and offshore drilling rights to big corporations before he was forced to resign. Anne Burford, Reagan's head of the Environmental Protection Agency (EPA), was charged with laxity in cleaning up dangerously polluted sites and dumps. When she, too, was compelled to resign, Reagan reappointed her as an adviser, but another uproar again forced her resignation.

Folksinger Joan Baez summed up the views of those who had delighted in the sixties: "People are wanting to get wonderful again, after the disgrace of Vietnam. There's a desire not to think. . . . If you can't laugh in 1984, you might as well drop dead—it's so bloody awful."

To understand the incredible sixties is to understand why millions who were young in those years think as they do today, and why they feel nostalgic for those spirited times.

In some respects, we still live with the liberationist heritage of the sixties. In other respects, we live with the conservative backlash against it.

For better or worse, the incredible sixties will go down in our history as the stormy years that changed America.

Bibliography and Suggested Further Reading

(Suggested further reading indicated by *)

Appel, Willa. *Cults in America.* New York: Holt, Rinehart and Winston, 1983.

Archer, Jules. *Hawks, Doves, and the Eagle.* New York: Hawthorn Books, Inc., Publishers, 1970.

*———. *1968: Year of Crisis.* New York: Julian Messner, 1971.

*———. *Revolution in Our Time.* New York: Julian Messner, 1971.

*———. *RIOT!* New York: Hawthorn Books, Inc., Publishers, 1974.

Astor, Gerald. *The New York Cops.* New York: Charles Scribner's Sons, 1971.

Bayer, William. *The Great Movies.* New York: Grosset & Dunlap, Inc., Publishers, 1973.

*Becker, Howard S., ed. *Campus Power Struggle.* Hawthorne, N.Y.: Aldine Publishing Company, 1970.

Black, Algernon D. *The People and the Police.* New York, Toronto, London, Sydney: McGraw-Hill Book Company, 1968.

Bromley, David G. and Anson D. Shupe, Jr. *Strange Gods.* Boston: Beacon Press, 1981.

*Clavir, Judy and John Spitzer, eds. *The Conspiracy Trial.* Indianapolis, New York: The Bobbs-Merrill Company, 1970.

Conant, Ralph W. *The Prospects for Revolution.* New York, Evanston, and London: Harper's Magazine Press, 1971.

Dorman, Michael. *Under 21.* New York: Dell Publishing Co., Inc., 1970.

Eisenberg, Dennis. *The Re-emergence of Fascism.* New York: A.S. Barnes and Company, 1967.

Forster, Arnold & Benjamin R. Epstein. *Danger on the Right.* New York: Random House, 1964.

Gagnon, John H. & William Simon. *The Sexual Scene.* Hawthorne, N.Y.: Aldine Publishing Company, 1970.

*Garabedian, John H. and Orde Coombs. *Eastern Religions in the Electric Age.* New York: Grosset & Dunlap, 1969.

*Gold, Robert S., ed. *The Rebel Culture.* New York: Dell Publishing Co., Inc., 1970.

Hackett, Alice. *70 Years of Best Sellers: 1895–1975.* New York, London: R.R. Bowker Company, 1977.

*Hope, Marjorie. *Youth Against the World.* Boston, Toronto: Little, Brown and Company, 1970.

*Javna, John and Gordon. *'60s!* New York: St. Martin's Press, 1983.

*Johnson, Mary Anne & James Olsen. *Exiles from the American Dream.* New York: Walker and Company, 1975.

*Kelner, Joseph and James Munves. *The Kent State Coverup.* New York: Harper & Row, Publishers, 1980.

*Keogh, James. *President Nixon and the Press.* New York: Funk & Wagnalls, 1972.

Langer, William L., ed. *An Encyclopedia of World History.* Boston: Houghton Mifflin Company, 1968.

Lens, Sidney. *Poverty Yesterday and Today.* New York: Thomas Y. Crowell Company, 1973.

Long, David F. *The Outward View.* Chicago, New York, San Francisco: Rand McNally & Company, 1963.

Lucas, George, Gloria Katz, and Willard Hyck. *American Graffiti.* New York: Ballantine Books, 1974.

*Mars, Florence. *Witness in Philadelphia.* Baton Rouge and London: Louisiana State University Press, 1977.

Marty, Martin E. *A Nation of Behavers.* Chicago and London: University of Chicago Press, 1976.

McGinniss, Joe. *Heroes.* New York: The Viking Press, 1976.

*Michener, James A. *Kent State: What Happened and Why.* New York: Random House, Inc. and the Reader's Digest Association, 1971.

*Minor, Dale. *The Information War.* New York: Hawthorne Books, Inc., Publishers, 1970.

Mitau, G. Theodore. *Decade of Decision.* New York: Charles Scribner's Sons, 1967.

Morris, Richard B. *Encyclopedia of American History.* New York: Harper & Row, Publishers, 1965.

Pearl, Arthur. *Landslide.* Secaucus, N.J.: The Citadel Press, 1973.

*Peterson, William J. *Those Curious New Cults.* New Canaan, Conn.: Keats Publishing, Inc., 1975.

Platt, Anthony and Lynn Cooper, eds. *Policing America.* Englewood Cliffs, N.J.: Prentice Hall, Inc., 1974.

Quigley, Charles N., Executive Director. *On Authority.* Santa Monica: Law in a Free Society Project, 1973.

Sahl, Mort. *Heartland.* New York and London: Harcourt Brace Jovanovich, 1976.

*Sandman, Peter M. *Students and the Law.* New York: Collier Books, 1971.

*Sann, Paul. *The Angry Decade: The Sixties.* New York: Crown Publishers, Inc., 1979.

*Sayre, Nora. *Sixties Going on Seventies.* New York: Arbor House, 1973.

*Schell, Jonathan. *The Time of Illusion.* New York: Alfred A. Knopf, 1976.

*Sherill, Robert. *Gothic Politics in the Deep South.* New York: Grossman Publishers, 1968.

Simon, James F. *In His Own Image.* New York: David McKay Company, Inc., 1973.

Sixtomania: The 1960's Nostalgia Game. Falls Church, Va.: Kino Press, 1984.

Stearn, Gerald Emanuel, ed. *Broken Image.* New York: Random House, 1972.

*Stephenson, June. *Women's Roots.* Napa, Calif.: Diemer, Smith Publishing Company, Inc., 1981.

*Thorp, Roderick and Robert Blake. *The Music of Their Laughter.* New York, Evanston, and London: Harper & Row, Publishers, 1970.

Unger, Irwin, David Brody and Paul Goodman, eds. *The Course of American History.* Waltham, Mass., Toronto: Xerox College Publishing, 1971.

Van Laan, Thomas F. and Robert B. Lyons, eds. *Language and the Newsstand.* New York: Charles Scribner's Sons, 1972.

Wakefield, Dan. *Home Free.* New York: Delacorte Press, 1977.

Wallerstein, Immanuel and Paul Starr. *The University Crisis Reader.* New York: Random House, 1971.

West, Jr., Elmer, ed. *Extremism Left and Right.* Grand Rapids, Mich.: William B. Eerdmans Publishing Company, 1972.

Wilkins, Roy and Ramsey Clark, Chairmen. *Search and Destroy.* New York: Metropolitan Applied Research Center, Inc., 1973.

Wolfe, Tom. *The Electric Kool-Aid Acid Test.* New York, Toronto, London: Bantam Books, 1969.

Also consulted were articles in issues of *City On a Hill* (UCSC); *Esquire; LIFE; The Nation; Santa Cruz, California, Sentinel; Newsweek; The New York Times; Reader's Digest; The San Diego Union; U.S. News and World Report;* and *Variety.*

INDEX

Index

216

Index

Index

Superman, 102
Supreme Court, 119, 128, 135, 188–91
Sweden, 55, 74, 118

T'ai chi chuan, 86
Talmadge, Herman, 25
Tassajara, 135
Taylor, Maxwell, 55
Teach-ins, 53–54, 62
Teenyboppers, 104
Terrorism, 204
Test Ban Treaty, 153–54
Thalidomide scandal, 170
Thomas, Dylan, 97
Thurmond, Strom, 28, 52, 185, 188
Tiny Tim, 90
Tolkien, J. R. R., 111
Townshend, Peter, 93–94
Toynbee, Arnold, 48, 56
Transcendental Meditation (TM), 132–34
Trudeau, Garry, 103
Truman, Harry S., xii, 147
Truth-in-Lending Act, 168
TV in the sixties, 100, 102, 106–8, 162–65,
    189, 192–93, 202
Twiggy, 129
Twist, the, 88

Underground press, 100–101
Unemployment, xii, 36, 37–38
Unification Church, 134, 140–41
United Nations, 15, 147, 149, 151, 183
University of Alabama, 21
University of California, xi–xii, 50–51, 69,
    75, 78, 200
University of Colorado, 70
University of Michigan, 50, 53, 55
University of Mississippi, 17–18, 22, 26
University of Pennsylvania, 53
Unsafe at Any Speed, 172
U.S. Civil Rights Commission, 29
U.S. State Department, 142–43

USSR (see Soviet Union)
U-2 spy plane, 142–44

Vassar, 115–16, 119
Vidal, Gore, 116
Vienna Conference, 145–46, 150
Vietnam
    Army deserters, 63, 74
    Army of the Republic of Vietnam
        (ARVN), 41–42, 45, 47, 194
    Ben Tre, 47
    Bien Hoa, 49
    Buddhists, 40–42, 54
    Calley, William, 73
    CBS-Westmoreland lawsuit, 197
    Diem, Ngo Dinh, 40–42
    Dien Bien Phu, 40
    Draft for (see Draft resistance)
    French, the 39–40
    Geneva Peace Accords, 40
    Green Berets, 57, 112, 146
    Gulf of Tonkin Resolution, 44, 196
    Ho Chi Minh, 40–42, 45, 61, 146
    Mylai, 73
    National Liberation Front (NLF), 41
    National Mobilization Committee to End
        the War in Vietnam, 65, 67
    Nguyen Van Thieu, 42, 45
    North Vietnam, 41–42, 44–47, 55–56, 61,
        64, 145, 185, 195–96
    October 15 Vietnam Moratorium, 72
    Peace mobilizations, 57–58, 65, 67–68, 96
    Peace treaty, 195–96
    Prisoners of war, 195
    Protests and resistance, xiii, 1–9, 49–74,
        93, 98, 103, 112, 115, 130, 133, 175,
        177–78, 180, 186, 189–95
    Songmy, 73
    South Vietnam, 40–42, 45–47, 56, 60,
        112, 146, 195
    Tet offensive, 46–47, 60, 65, 197
    Veterans, 196
    Viet Cong, 39, 41, 45–47, 55, 57, 196
    Vietminh, 40

222